T0306198

GLOBALIZATION AND THE TRANSFORMATION OF FOREIGN ECONOMIC POLICY

Globalization and the Transformation of Foreign Economic Policy

PAWEŁ BOŻYK
*University of Economics and Computer Science
and Warsaw School of Economics*

Routledge
Taylor & Francis Group

LONDON AND NEW YORK

First published 2006 by Ashgate Publishing

Reissued 2018 by Routledge
2 Park Square, Milton Park, Abingdon, Oxon, OX14 4RN
605 Third Avenue, New York, NY 10017

First issued in paperback 2021

Routledge is an imprint of the Taylor & Francis Group, an informa business

© Paweł Bożyk 2006

Paweł Bożyk has asserted his moral right under the Copyright, Designs and Patents Act, 1988, to be identified as the author of this work.

All rights reserved. No part of this book may be reprinted or reproduced or utilised in any form or by any electronic, mechanical, or other means, now known or hereafter invented, including photocopying and recording, or in any information storage or retrieval system, without permission in writing from the publishers.

A Library of Congress record exists under LC control number: 2005035230

Notice:
Product or corporate names may be trademarks or registered trademarks, and are used only for identification and explanation without intent to infringe.

Publisher's Note
The publisher has gone to great lengths to ensure the quality of this reprint but points out that some imperfections in the original copies may be apparent.

Disclaimer
The publisher has made every effort to trace copyright holders and welcomes correspondence from those they have been unable to contact.

ISBN 13: 978-0-815-38930-9 (hbk)
ISBN 13: 978-1-351-15712-4 (ebk)
ISBN 13: 978-1-138-35701-3 (pbk)

DOI: 10.4324/9781351157124

Contents

List of Figures and Tables

Preface

This book is an attempt to display the principles which determine foreign, international and global economic policy, to what extent these are the laws and regularities governing international economic relations and to what extent these are other factors, including those which depend solely on country, enterprise or private persons.

Foreign economic policy is a new concept covering the influence of the state not only on the flow of goods but also factors of production. It is a descendant of the foreign trade policy formulating the principles of the country's influence on entities participating in international commodity turnover. In the second half of the 20th century, however, the flow of services, capital, technology and labour force between different countries and groups of countries also became another important component of international economic relations next to international commodity turnover. It thereby became necessary to supplement foreign trade policy with service, capital, technology, immigration, and other policies.

This book consists of ten chapters and two basic parts: the first – comprising chapters 1–6 and formulating basic principles of foreign, international and global economic policy (and thus the goals, means and instruments of this policy) and the second – comprising chapters 7–9, which verifies these principles on the basis of the practices pursued by economically developed countries, newly industrialized countries, less developed countries and countries undergoing economic transformation.

The book has no equivalent in Polish and also in foreign literature. It can, therefore, be a valuable source of information on this interesting and new subject area to a wide circle of economists, politicians, lawyers, and also those who are involved in international economic relations on an on-going basis.

It can also serve as a textbook in universities of a wide curricula spectrum.

Chapter 1

Globalization and Economic Policy

1.1. The Concept of Globalization of the World Economy

Globalization of the world economy denotes a process based on the formation of a single market for goods, services and factors of production, including capital, labour, technology and natural resources, covering all countries and economic regions.[1] In the process, national and international markets are combined into a single complex whole. From a theoretical point of view, globalization means an unlimited access to these markets for all interested businesses regardless of country of origin and economic region. It also means increased feedback between these markets.

Uniform economic mechanisms governing the functioning of national and international markets are a condition, as well as consequence, of globalization. Without similar mechanisms, globalization would have been impossible. At the same time, a globally uniform mechanism in the world economy would be unfeasible without globalization. Today the free market and free trade constitute such a mechanism. That is why globalization is defined as a process rooted in the creation of a liberalized market of goods, services and factors of production in the world as a whole.

Contemporary globalization was preceded by the liberalization of commodity markets, a process limited to specific sectors or regions. Efforts soon began to remove barriers to a free movement of goods, initially on select international markets and subsequently on a global scale. Understood in this way, globalization should be treated as a long-term process initiated when businesses (including both corporate bodies and self-employed individuals) began to transgress national borders in search of more favourable sources of supply and better possibilities for selling goods. Global trends continued marginal and sporadic, as long as the international division of labour grew slowly and without impact on individual countries. These processes were invisible in daily practice, though they intensified with time.

Globalization gained momentum in the second half of the 20th century as a result of several simultaneous trends that intensified in the world. This primarily was true of technological progress witnessed by production automation and computerization, accompanied by universal access to information. The international division of labour deepened, leading to a rapid growth of commodity trade. Trade in finished products began to be accompanied by growth in production and investment cooperation

---

1 See P. Bożyk, J. Misala, M. Puławski, *Międzynarodowe stosunki ekonomiczne*, 2nd edn (PWE, Warsaw, 2002), p. 395.

and also the emergence of international and transnational corporations. The last quarter of the 20th century witnessed a rapid international movement of production factors, including capital, labour and technology. Finally, as the century came to close, the movement of speculative capital reached unprecedented proportions. All this combined explains why the world economy as a whole rather than individual countries and regions became the point of reference for decision-making by national and multinational companies.

One sign of globalization is regional integration, a transitional form between doing business within a single country and global operations. Understood in this way, integration and globalization can be treated as complementary trends. To a large extent regional integration is programmed by a group of countries and expressed by institutional solutions that determine its development. In other words, integration is a territorially restricted form of globalization 'commissioned by' interested countries. Globalization, on the other hand, is a spontaneous process that has not been programmed institutionally by countries subject to mechanisms regulating the functioning of the world economy.

Both integration and globalization are the result of liberalization of the economy. In the case of integration, liberalization exclusively applies to the movement of goods, services and factors of production within a specific group. Relations with 'third' countries remain limited. In the case of globalization, liberalization applies to the movement of goods, services and factors of production in the world as a whole, so by definition it rules out all and any limitations whatsoever. From a formal perspective, integration and globalization create equal chances for participating countries and enterprises. Integration offers such opportunities to members of regional groups, while globalization does so to all countries and enterprises, subject to the principles governing the 'opening' of the world economy. In practice, these chances vary. In the case of integration, they are equal only when partners represent similar competitive capabilities, which requires an identical or similar level of economic development, especially technological and industrial. That is why regional integration is treated as merging economic capacities equal in terms of development and with similar economic and institutional (particularly legal) infrastructures.

Globalization, which creates conditions for free movements of goods, services and factors of production in the world as a whole, by definition offers greater opportunities to economically stronger entities to secure a competitive advantage. This applies to both countries and national and multinational enterprises. In this context, regional integration is seen as a form of protecting smaller and weaker countries from the dangers inherent in globalization, by merging their economic capacities. Separately, they would lose in global competition, together they can cope with the requirements of this competition. Understood in this way, integration can represent a stage on the road to globalization.

Globalization in the world economy is accompanied by increased economic dependence in the world as a whole. This involves the sensitivity of individual economies, groups of countries and regions to changes taking place on a global scale, and at the same time the global economy's dependence on changes in different geographic regions, groups of countries and individual countries. Global dependence can be either unilateral (involving the dependence of a specific country on the global economy) or bilateral (the dependence of a country on the global economy and of the global economy on the country). In the second case, interdependence is the motive force at work.[2] At the same time, global dependence can be quantitative or qualitative. The former is exemplified by a relationship between the growth of an individual country and the development of global trade. Qualitative dependence is exemplified by the influence of changes in global prices on prices secured and paid on international markets by an individual country, as well as on internal prices within this country.

The same group includes technological and structural relationships making countries mutually dependent (when they all contribute to technological progress) or unilaterally dependent (when technological progress is driven by only some countries). In structural dependence, differences in natural resources possessed by individual countries as well as other factors of production (such as capital and labour) play a key role. When natural resources are spread equally among countries, one can speak of interdependence, but when some countries are awash with resources, while others suffer from shortages, the situation is indicative of dependence rather than interdependence.

The scope of interdependence and dependence is dynamic, changing in step with the growth of the world economy. If the world economy grows at a faster rate than a given country, and world technological progress, for example, is faster than in the country in question, then the scope of economic dependence increases. Vice versa, increased interdependence is feasible between a given country and the world economy.

1.2. The Advantages and Dangers of Globalization

From an economic point of view, globalization is seen as a positive process, since it contributes to increased average global prosperity. This creates conditions for the dissemination of modern technology and methods adapted to the requirements of modern enterprise management, economic growth financing and so on. In this way, globalization increases labour productivity and contributes to the more efficient employment of factors of production.

In this generally positive assessment, globalization exerts a multiform influence on the participants of this process, giving preference to the economically strong while eliminating the weak. This results from the essence of the free market, on which globalization is based, in which the most competitive enterprises, equipped with the most modern technologies and efficient financial and management systems, reap the greatest benefits. They are capable of offering buyers top-quality and relatively

---

2   A. Lindbeck, *Economic Dependence and Interdependence in the Industrialized World*, Seminar Paper No. 83 (Institute for International Economic Studies, University of Stockholm, Stockholm, 1977).

cheap products. Technologically uncompetitive entities with outdated management systems are ranked at the opposite end, without access to cheap sources of finance and incapable of competing in quality or price in the production of goods and services. In a free market, such enterprises are crowded out by stronger entities.

Consumers benefit from this process, gaining access to better quality and more modern products at prices lower than those previously available. In this manner, globalization positively influences consumption and quality, thereby contributing to technological advancement, primarily in such finished manufactured goods as computers, cars and household appliances.

At the same time, globalization accelerates the international movement of factors of production, especially capital and technology, followed by know-how, modern production management methods, marketing and advertising. The expansion of modern financial and banking services also plays an important role. Taken as a whole, globalization leads to improved technological, financial and managerial knowledge around the world (including less developed countries), contributing to modern methods for managing the economy and increased management effectiveness.

The division of benefits from globalization does give rise to controversy, mainly as regards the disproportionately high benefits derived by the key actors of globalization and the incomparably smaller gains of the remaining entities.[3] The share of the former in globalization is many times greater than that of the latter.

The chief cause is the concentration of physical capital, accompanied by the concentration of production and trade. The most important entities are transnational corporations, which control 75% of the global commodity market.[4] Ties among the 500 largest corporations account for as much as 40% of global trade. At the same time, the rules determining these ties are a far cry from the laws of a free market and free trade.

The division of globalization benefits has no less influence on the unusually rapid growth of financial, especially speculative, capital. In the late 1970s, speculative capital accounted for some 10% of financial transactions. The proportions have now reversed, the share of speculative capital exceeding 90%.[5] In 2004, the value of speculative transactions was 22 times higher than the value of global GDP. The key entities shaping the world speculative capital market are active in highly industrialized countries, so it is no wonder that profits from speculative transactions are invested there as well.

A third factor influencing the division of globalization benefits is the privatization of production assets. Foreign capital participates in this process on an equal footing with domestic capital. The absence of private domestic capital is why in

---

3   See J.E. Stiglitz, *Globalization and its Discontents*, Polish edn (Wydawnictwo Naukowe PWN, Warsaw, 2004), p. 22.

4   T.G. Grosse, 'Dylematy państwa w obliczu globalizacji', *Wokół współczesności*, vol. 2, no. 4, 2002, p. 174.

5   See N. Chomsky, *Zysk ponad ludzi. Neoliberalizm i ład globalny* (Wydawnictwo Dolnośląskie, Wrocław, 2000), p. 18.

less developed countries, including Central and Eastern Europe, privatization boils down to the takeover of production and commercial enterprises as well as banks and insurance institutions by foreign capital, mainly held by transnational corporations.

A fourth factor influencing the division of globalization benefits is deregulation, based on the withdrawal of the state from the economy, including the protection of domestic enterprises from stronger foreign competitors, especially transnational corporations. The opening of borders to unrestricted imports of goods and services leads to the bankruptcy of domestic enterprises unable to compete with them. At the same time, weaker domestic enterprises oriented toward exports find it impossible to sell their products abroad when deprived of state assistance.

These factors lead to a division of the global economy into a centre and peripheries. The centre belongs to transport corporations and economically developed countries in which these corporations are based. The directions of technological progress are determined by the centre, where the main financial, scientific, cultural and educational units are located. Peripheries are treated as areas subordinated to the centre and representing markets where finished products manufactured according to technologies created in the centre are to be sold. Peripheries are also a reservoir of cheap labour.

Qualified technical and research personnel, computer scientists, doctors and engineers tend to emigrate from peripheries to the centre in search for jobs meeting their qualifications and professional ambitions. They want access to modern equipment, know-how and technology and can also count on higher incomes in the centre than in the peripheries. Low-qualified and unskilled labour emigrates to the centre to seek employment in sectors treated as inferior; many of them do find work since their financial demands are more modest.

Despite this, unemployment in peripheral countries is much higher than in those of the centre. This primarily results from the elimination of a substantial portion of domestic production from the market due to competition from goods imported from the centre. The outflow of capital from the peripheries to the centre in search of stable investment conditions, especially in terms of ownership and taxes, also plays an important part. Labour-saving technology introduced by transnational corporations through direct capital investments is responsible for job losses in the peripheries.

The high mobility of speculative capital is a painful problem facing the periphery. In particular, countries where banks are held by foreign capital (subsidiaries of parent organizations based in the centre) report an increased share of speculative investments and a reduced share of physical investments undertaken on loans provided by these banks. This generates greater benefits for these countries and protects them from losses linked with misdirected physical investments by local entrepreneurs. At the same time, the growth of speculative investments in peripheral countries undermines the grown of these economies. Speculative capital may pose such a threat if it suddenly decides to move abroad. Massive outflows of capital have occurred in Argentina, Russia, Southeast Asia and a few other countries. To keep foreign investors interested in buying securities and to prevent a sudden flight of capital, peripheral countries – especially those troubled by a permanent budget deficit – are forced to maintain interest rates higher than those in the centre. This negatively affects investment rates and limits their endogenous economic growth, but has a positive influence on inflation and increases speculative capital profits transferred to the centre.

1.3. Economic Policy under Globalization

Highly divisive opinions exist regarding which economic policy individual countries should follow under globalization. Some economists argue that the role of the state should be restricted to three functions: making laws, enforcing them, and preventing violation of free market and trade rules.[6] Moreover, individual countries should perform these three functions in a uniform manner, which means creating similar laws, exerting a similar influence on businesses so that they respect the law, and act in a similar manner when counteracting violations of free market and free trade rules.

The 'Washington consensus' reflects this point of view.[7] Under its terms, the basic condition of equal participation in globalization of countries with an equal level of economic growth is deregulation, which means the state has to renounce interventionism. The state's role should be limited to responsibility for the parameters of macroeconomic policy in the form of the exchange rate, interest rate, fiscal policy, financial policy, credit policy, pricing policy and budgetary policy. As a result of deregulation, countries should resign from microeconomic policies, including industrial, agricultural, investment, educational and foreign trade policies.

According to this point of view, macroeconomic policy should be oriented toward balancing the national budget and keeping inflation as low as possible. Under the 'Washington consensus', this is the basic condition for speedy economic growth. A wide opening of the economy to free movement of goods, services and factors of production is indispensable to guarantee high labour and capital productivity. Deregulation and privatization of ownership in industry, agriculture and services should be universal and permanent; private ownership takes pride of place over public ownership in all respects, especially management effectiveness.

The International Monetary Fund (IMF) and the World Bank have adopted these principles, requiring indebted countries to implement them as an indispensable condition for obtaining credit assistance from these institutions. The IMF and the World Bank thus became the chief proponents of an economic policy pursued under globalization in line with the 'Washington consensus'.

However, some economists promote a different point of view. In their opinion, a uniform policy that calls for complete deregulation and privatization of the economy cannot be pursued in the globalization process. The specific features of poorly

---

6   See M. Friedman, *Capitalism and Freedom* (University of Chicago Press, Chicago, 1962).

7   The term 'Washington consensus' was introduced to public use by John Williamson of the Institute for International Economics in 1989. See J.J. Teurissen and A. Akkerman (eds), *Diversity in Development: Reconsidering the Washington Consensus* (2004).

developed countries must be considered. Competition under globalization is far from perfect, while only perfect competition can be a basis for activities compatible with the 'Washington consensus'.

J.E. Stiglitz argues that only in theoretical solutions may the existence of a completely private and liberalized economy be assumed. In practice, one deals with mixed economies, exemplified by the United States.[8] In a mixed economy, certain types of business activity are pursued directly by the state. Furthermore, the state – through various legal regulations and economic policy instruments –influences the behaviour of the private sector. In Stiglitz's opinion, the state's active participation in the economy is beyond dispute. The only question is the actual proportions into which the roles of the state and the market are divided. This debate is not free from political undertones. In the United States, for example, economists tied to the Republican Party advocate that the role of the state should be limited, while those linked with the Democratic Party call for greater state involvement.[9]

The state should not replace the market in areas where the latter works perfectly, yet state intervention seems indispensable when the market fails or is counterproductive. One example of market failure is unemployment. A free market is an imperfect tool in combating unemployment. Similarly, without active state participation, it is impossible either to remove or to limit the poverty zone. Nor is a free market capable of preventing the emergence of peripheries. Just the reverse, its logic is headed in the opposite direction. A clash of the economically strong and weak, rich and poor, always guarantees success for the former and spells defeat for the latter. Only state interventionism can prevent this. In other words, the following rule should be followed in globalization: as much free market as possible, as much state intervention as necessary.

Overall, economic policy in the process of globalization cannot be limited to legislation, overseeing respect for the law and preventing free market and free trade violations, even though these functions should be obligatory for all countries participating in this process. In many cases, it would be enough to limit this policy to macroeconomic instruments. Microeconomic policy instruments, whether endogenous or exogenous, should only be permitted as an exception. The former primarily include industrial, agricultural, investment and educational policies. Among the latter, foreign economic policy is the main instrument.

Of course, under globalization, this policy cannot be autonomous but must be contractual – regulated by agreements with international institutions supervising the process of globalization, primarily the World Trade Organization, the IMF and the World Bank. These institutions should change their character: from free market missionaries to defenders of the interests of weaker states threatened by globalization.[10]

---

8 See J.E. Stiglitz, *Economics of the Public Sector*, 3rd edn, Polish edn (Wydawnictwo Naukowe PWN, Warsaw, 2004), pp. 4–5.

9 See ibid., p. 13.

10 See J.E. Stiglitz, *Globalization and its Discontents*, op.cit., pp. 28–9.

Chapter 2

The Concept of Foreign Economic Policy

2.1. Definition and Features of Foreign Economic Policy

The concept of foreign economic policy will be used in this book to signify the influence of the state on economic relations with foreign countries, in particular on commodity and service turnover as well as flow of factors of production (the process of the flow of capital, natural resources and technology).[1]

The concept of foreign economic policy is, thus, connected with the state's competence to make decisions on foreign economic relations. These powers can be more or less extensive due to internal as well as external reasons. In the case of the former it is the economic model that determines the powers of the state; under liberal economy conditions where individual economic entities play the principal role in economic relations, the scope of the state's powers is narrower, limitation of liberalism being accompanied by growth of the powers of the state.

In the case of the latter, where the scope of the state's powers is determined by external reasons, an autonomic policy and an agreement policy can be distinguished.[2] The autonomic policy gives the state unlimited opportunities to influence economic relations with foreign countries. It is simple and easy to conduct, stemming solely from internal reasons specific to a given country. Its drawback, however, is the fact that it can generate retorts, that is retaliatory actions by foreign partners.

The agreement policy means that decisions made by the state are agreed with foreign partners. While being more difficult to conduct, it is, however, free from retaliatory actions.

Foreign economic policy should be, first of all, active, which means that it cannot be the result of the behaviour of economic entities. The active character of foreign economic policy consists, on the one hand, of initiating actions that are not taken by economic entities on their own and, on the other hand, in restricting activities unfavourable from the point of view of the country as a whole. Foreign economic policy has an important role to perform, especially at a time when discrepancies

---

1 Comp. P. Bożyk, 'Zagraniczna polityka ekonomiczna', in P. Bożyk, J. Misala, M. Puławski, *Międzynarodowe stosunki ekonomiczne*, op. cit., p. 293; T. Łychowski, *Międzynarodowe umowy gospodarcze* (PWE, Warsaw, 1968), p. 9.

2 Comp. J. Sołdaczuk, 'Zagraniczna polityka handlowa', in J. Sołdaczuk, *Międzynarodowe stosunki ekonomiczne*, (Fundacja Innowacja, Warsaw, 2001), p. 268; G. Haberler, *The Theory of International Trade with its Applications to Commercial Policy* (London, 1968), p. 337.

emerge between the preferences of the state as a whole and the preferences of individual economic entities.

Foreign economic policy should, simultaneously, be conscious, which means that it should have, at its foundation, the balance of resultant profits and losses. By opting for a given policy, the state can increase profits in one segment, while resigning from profits or even openly accepting losses in another. In consequence, the situation of some economic entities may improve, whereas the situation of others deteriorates.

Foreign economic policy can, therefore, lead to changes in social and political sentiment. The conscious character of this policy thus signifies that it should be based on a balance of not only economic but also social and political benefits, both in the short and in the long term.

Moreover, foreign economic policy should be comprehensive, which means it should cover both economic relations with foreign countries and the internal economic relations of a given country. It should be constructed to make the effects of the foreign economic policy felt far beyond the scope of activity of the entities directly involved in economic relations with foreign countries, affecting all economic entities and sectors, with only the scale of this influence being varying. Foreign economic policy should, therefore, stem from a comprehensive balance of its effects.

2.2. Subjects of Foreign Economic Policy

The state pursues foreign economic policy through two types of institutions and organizations: systemic and special, established for the needs of foreign economic policy. The first group includes the president, parliament, government and other economic entities while the second is made up of customs offices, institutions insuring foreign economic activity, export-financing banks, and the like.

The president performs different functions in individual countries, being the decision-making centre with powers superior to parliament and government in some countries (the USA, Russia) or having purely representative functions and not participating directly in the decision-making process, in others. In both cases, the role of the president in shaping foreign economic policy differs completely. Nevertheless, the president always performs the function of foreign economic policy promoter. By paying visits abroad and receiving foreign politicians, the president creates a climate favouring the pursuit of an effective foreign economic policy by the country. He or she does it by explaining the principles of the policy pursued by the country, convincing foreign partners to the propriety of this policy, preventing negative reactions when this policy is of an autonomic character and collides with partners' interests.

The parliament is a legislative body, adopting resolutions obligatory for government and entities conducting foreign economic activity. These resolutions are a result of a large number of factors, both objective and subjective, depending solely on a given country or also on its external environment. In the first group, a decisive role is played by the distribution of political powers in parliament; when one political orientation dominates, it determines the directions of the foreign economic policy in a way most desirable for it. When power is held by a coalition, the positions of all the coalition parties must be taken into account.

The influence of the external environment on foreign economic policy finds its reflection in political alliances and foreign economic dependence, the significance of the latter growing in the course of time.

The government performs a double role in shaping foreign economic policy: executive and decision-making.

The executive function is performed within the scope subordinated in terms of decision-making to the president or parliament. The role of government consists of implementing resolutions and recommendations formulated by superior levels. To give an example, the government cannot make direct amendments and supplements to a parliament-approved customs tariff; it is parliament that is the sole institution authorized to make such amendments.

The second function of government – the decision-making – concerns the scope of the foreign economic policy that is beyond the scope of power of the president, parliament or any other institutions authorized by law (in Poland, for instance, the Monetary Policy Council is such an institution outside the scope of power of government). This refers, inter alia, to shaping para- and non-tariff instruments of foreign economic policy, held by government.

Enterprises can affect foreign economic policy within the scope specified for them by parliament or government; this scope differs under the conditions of a liberal policy from that under the conditions of a protectionist policy. In the former it is much wider than in the latter. For instance, with power to contract credits abroad, enterprises can influence the policy of maintaining equilibrium in the balance of payments and, indirectly, the exchange rate policy and the interest rate policy.

2.3. Sectors of Foreign Economic Policy

Foreign economic policy can be mentioned as a whole only in an aggregate approach, determining the influence of the state on the basic directions of economic cooperation with foreign countries. In practice, foreign economic policy is disaggregated into a number of sector policies depending on the form of foreign economic relations, into trade, capital, immigration, technological, service policies, and the like.

The term foreign trade policy refers to the shaping by the state of foreign commodity relations and, thus, foreign trade turnover. It includes export policy and import policy.

The scope of export policy comprises the influence of the state on the size of exports, their structure and profitability. The aims of export policy can, consequently, have a short, medium or long horizon. In the short term, the state can stimulate or stifle the size of exports, intervening when the need arises, with export-oriented production growth possibilities or sales possibilities abroad. In the medium term, the state can influence the export of goods by shaping the commodity and geographical structure of foreign trade. Finally, in the long term the state can affect exports by changes to the structure of domestic production, technological progress and economic growth rate.

The scope of import policy covers the influence of the state on the size, structure and profitability of imported articles. Like export policy, import policy can implement targets of short-, medium- or long-term horizon. In the short term, the state can restrict imports (introducing all sorts of barriers) or stimulate imports (eliminating or reducing all sorts of earlier imposed barriers). In the medium term, the state can indirectly affect imports through the wages and income policy; a restrictive policy here lowers the demand for imported goods while a policy of wages and income growth increases the market for imported goods. In the long term, the state can affect imports by a much wider range of methods, notably, through an economic growth policy. An acceleration of the growth rate increases the demand for both raw materials and materials for production as well as for new techniques and technologies (machinery and equipment). Simultaneously, a growth of income associated with increased employment stimulates the demand for imported consumer goods. In the long term, the state can also influence imports through structural changes in the economy, promoting domestic, import-competitive production, contributing to improving quality and upgrading domestic production technologically. Finally, in the long term, the state can influence imports by initiating and promoting technological progress in the country, encouraging enterprises in different ways to implement it.

Foreign trade policy is the ancestor of foreign economic policy. In the past when commodity turnover used to be the only form of economic link with abroad, the influence of the state focused exclusively on this turnover. As time passed and the flow of capital, labour, technology and services came to be the object of international economic relations, trade policy was extended to cover additional ways of exerting state influence to cover all economic links with foreign countries.

The term foreign capital policy as used in this book refers to the shaping by the state of the capital movement from and into the country. This policy embraces credit policy, the policy concerning foreign direct investments and that concerning portfolio investments.

Credit policy comprises the policy of contracting credits abroad and the policy of extending credits abroad. From the point of view of the time horizon, these can be short-, medium- and long-term credits. The interest rate is an important instrument used by the state in its credit policy; an interest rate relatively higher in the country than outside encourages enterprises to contract credits in foreign currencies, while a reduction of the interest rate in a given country makes enterprises tend to contract credits in their own currency.

The policy concerning foreign direct investments consists, notably, of the state luring these investments to a given country. Simultaneously, the scope of this policy also includes the influence of the state on investments abroad made by domestic enterprises. In the first case, the scope of capital policy involves the creation of adequate systemic and political as well as legal, financial and currency conditions that would encourage foreign investors to invest capital within a given country.

The primary aim is to guarantee the stability of the introduced solutions as well as independence in using property. In the second case, which concerns direct capital investments abroad, the policy of the state consists not only of enforcing legal regulations that allow for such investments but also influencing economic growth and the level of the interest rate. A policy of accelerating economic growth hampers the outflow of direct capital investments abroad, a policy of a high interest rate having a very similar effect on these investments.

The policy concerning portfolio investments consists of a large number of elements, including influence on the flow of short-term capital between the country and other countries, the level of the interest rate and the exchange rate, the size of the budget deficit and the issuance of treasury notes connected with it, privatization of the economy, and the like. Among other elements of this policy mention should be made of how excessive inflow of portfolio investments can be countered by limiting budget deficit or imposing barriers to a free outflow of portfolio capital.

The term migration policy is used to denote the influence of the state on the flow of people between the country and other countries. When this concerns the outflow of people, we speak of the emigration policy and when the policy shapes the flow of people into a given country, we speak of the immigration policy.

From the point of view of the time horizon, the migration policy can be divided into short term and long term. The short-term policy focuses on cross-border and seasonal migration of workers. When the cross-border movement is small, the issue is to balance surpluses and deficits of labour between neighbouring countries, achieved through a regular, often long-lasting flow of people to work in border regions, returning home daily or weekly. Seasonal migration of workers occurs every year, during increased demand for additional labour (e.g. picking grapes, strawberries, berries, and the like). In both cases the migration policy consists, first of all, in creating conditions for repeated crossing of the state border, for the repatriating incomes by virtue of this work, for administrative procedures necessary when immigrants break the law, and so on.

The long-term migration policy concentrates on the flow of people for periods of stay longer than one year or for permanent stay. The emigration policy of this time-horizon counteracts the outflow of outstanding, well-educated specialists from a country, especially young people, by initiating development programmes, financing scientific and technical research and activating cooperation with other countries, facilitating access to leading centres of scientific and economic knowledge in highly industrialized countries. The immigration policy focuses on limiting access for foreigners with low professional qualifications, elderly people, potential beneficiaries of social institutions.

The migration policy varies in time, depending on market conditions. When market conditions are good the interest of the state in counteracting both emigration and immigration decreases. In the first case, opportunities of finding a job in the country of permanent residence increase while in the second interest grows in the inflow of additional skilled and cheaper labour. When market conditions are poor, the state lowers emigration barriers but increases barriers to immigration because, under conditions of unemployment, immigrants pose a threat to the employment of the country's own citizens.

The migration policy varies, simultaneously, between less developed and highly developed countries. In the former, it encourages emigration of surplus labour, in particular, low-skilled labour, while in the latter it poses barriers to the flow of such immigrants, regulating this flow closely depending on the needs of the economy.

The term foreign technological policy denotes the influence of the state on the transfer of intellectual knowledge gained in basic and applied research as well as experience gained during production processes between a given country and other countries. This is a *sensu largo* term. Alternatively, a notion may be formulated of the technological policy *sensu stricto*, understood as the influence of the state on the transfer of technical knowledge and its application in the production of specific goods between a given country and other countries.

The transfer of technical knowledge can be gratuitous or non-gratuitous. The foreign technological policy *sensu largo* concerns, as a rule, gratuitous transfer of general knowledge. On the other hand, foreign technological policy *sensu stricto* involves non-gratuitous, payable transfer of technical knowledge.

In this sense, foreign technological policy *sensu largo* covers the influence of the state on the transfer of knowledge through scientific conferences and seminars as well as books, professional press and the Internet. Representatives of a country can participate directly in these forms of knowledge transfer or they can shape them. Foreign technological policy *sensu stricto* is, primarily, of a commercial nature, when the state shapes exports and imports of goods containing advanced technical knowledge (consumer goods involving electronics, cars, and the like) as well as capital goods – machinery, robots, automated production lines - or the flow of specialists possessing specific technical knowledge (through contracts, scholarships, training). It can be expressed in the sphere of production when the state influences the flow of technical knowledge in its relations with other countries through the development of cooperation in production, joint investments or foreign direct capital investments. In all these cases, access to modern and advanced technical knowledge is the principal aim of the development of international cooperation. This cooperation involves access to technical documentation, direct contacts between specialists jointly constructing production objects, and the like. Foreign technological cooperation *sensu stricto* can, in addition, take the form of the influence of the state on the flow of licences playing a dominant role in transfers of specific technical knowledge. The state can introduce restrictions concerning the export of licences (within the scope covered by military classified information), it can support importers of licences or import them on its own for the needs of scientific and technical research or production modernization.

The term foreign service policy refers to the state's influence on trade in services between a given country and foreign countries. This can be direct or indirect influence. Part of the trade in services belongs exclusively to the competence of the state (leasing testing grounds for other countries' military units, peace missions by its own troops abroad, and so on), while the state can influence the remaining part solely indirectly, adopting legal regulations governing this trade, contributing to the development of technical communication (fax, telephone, computer, television, satellite) or establishing branches by foreign producers or consumers of services, and the like. The policy of direct influence on trade in services between the country and foreign countries can favour the opening of the domestic services market to imports but it can also restrain access to services originating abroad. The reasons for protecting the domestic market vary widely, ranging from care for an adequate level of rendered services, hedging against risk, protection of the state's economic sovereignty, national security, protection of cultural integrity, to protection of the position of domestic producers and the resultant profit. As a result, the policy of the export and import of services is highly diversified on the international scale. Highly industrialized countries promoting the export of their own services seek the abolition of barriers to their imports, while less developed countries place the stress on securing the domestic market for their own service renderers.

2.4. Types of Foreign Economic Policy

Broadly speaking, foreign economic policy can be divided into a free trade policy and a protectionist policy. Between these two extreme approaches a number of intermediate solutions can exist, with a larger or smaller dose of liberalism and protectionism.

2.4.1. Free Trade Policy

A free trade foreign policy has its roots in the doctrine of economic liberalism. It goes back to the classical theory of a free market and free trade, according to which market forces automatically ensure full utilization of all factors of production and economic equilibrium.[3] Moreover, this is performed not only on the scale of an individual country but also with respect to all countries as unrestrained international exchange and specialization of production enable the most rational utilization of production factors. As a result, economic growth is possible with the relatively lowest outlays of labour ensuring maximum benefits to all participants in the international division of labour.

At the beginning of the 20th century when the classics of economics formulated their theory, the existing reality (especially in Britain) justified the adoption of such assumptions, since opportunities for the development of production and the growth of employment were then almost unlimited in that country.[4]

Consistent with the theory of free trade, the role of the state should be limited to legislating, ensuring observance of the law by market participants and preventing

---

3 Comp. J. Sołdaczuk, 'Aneks. Ewolucja polityki handlowej w procesie rozwoju gospodarki kapitalistycznej', in J. Sołdaczuk, *Międzynarodowe stosunki gospodarcze*, op. cit., p. 292.

4 A. Smith, *Bogactwo narodów*, vol. 1 (PWN, Warsaw, 1954), p. 27; D. Ricardo, *Zasady ekonomii politycznej i opodatkowania*, (PWN, Warsaw, 1957), p. 150.

any violation of free market and free trade principles, including combating the monopolization of production and trade, forbidding conspiracies of producers restricting freedom in development of market prices, and the like.

The modern theory of free trade upholds the arguments employed by the classics almost in its entirety. It claims that free trade allows losses to be avoided through the effectiveness of economic management connected with protectionism.[5] In this sense, international trade should be not only free of restraints of any kind applied in such trade but should not be restricted by instruments of macroeconomic policy. Instruments applied by this policy should develop on a free market.

Argumentation in favour of the superiority of free trade over protectionism is illustrated in Figure 2.1, displaying losses incurred by a country after the introduction of import duties.

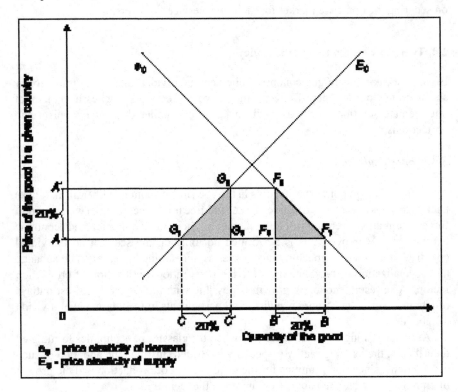

Figure 2.1. Losses in Production and Consumption in Virtue of the Introduction of Import Duties

Source: Author's own analysis on the basis of the work by P.R. Krugman, M. Obstfeld, Międzynarodowe stosunki gospodarcze, vol. 1, op. cit., p. 146.

---

5   P.R. Krugman, M. Obstfeld, *Międzynarodowe stosunki gospodarcze*, vol. 1, trans. and adapted by S. Ładyka (PWN, Warsaw, 1993), p. 145.

According to the figure, before the introduction of an import duty, the country imported $0B$ of good x the price $0A$. Simultaneously, domestic producers found it profitable to manufacture $0C$ of good x. Thus, in total, consumers had access to good x in the quantity $0B+0C$. The introduction of a 20% duty made the imported good x 20% more expensive so, according to Figure 2.1., its price increased by AA' to $0A'$. As a result the demand fell, followed by the import of good x, to $0B'$. A higher price of good x led, however, to an increase of domestic production of CC'.

The area of the triangle F1 F2 F3 means distortion of consumption while the area of the triangle G1 G2 G3 – distortion of production, since without the 20% duty the domestic demand for imported good x would not drop by 20% and production of good x (more expensive than the imported good) would not increase. The size of these distortions depends on the difference in the price flexibility of demand (ep) and supply (Ep). If these flexibilities are the same (see Figure 2.1), then consumers lose as much as producers, who found the production unprofitable before the introduction of the duty and now find it bringing profit.

Consumers' losses stem from the fact that they must buy goods at the higher price $0A'$. Losses in production are expressed in the involvement of manufacturing factors (labour, capital, technology and natural resources) to manufacture goods relatively more expensive in relation to foreign goods, with artificially increased profitability, by introduction of duties on cheaper imports.

Free market and free trade prevent losses of this kind, preventing the introduction of the duty. Consumers gain by paying a lower price, producers also gain by engaging available production factors in the most effective manner.

2.4.2. Protectionist Policy

A protectionist policy in international economic relations consists of the utilization by the state of means and instruments applied by foreign economic policy, including macroeconomic policy, to achieve the goals of this policy. Protectionism in foreign trade is a derivative of the policy of state interventionism in economy.

Advocates of state interventionism believe that the assumptions of the classical free market and free trade theory (including, in particular, the existence of ideal competition on the domestic as well as international scale, ideal distribution and transferability of factors of production from one branch to others in a given country, in the absence of such a transferability on the international scale, and the like) are far from reality. Economic subjects are highly diversified in terms of size, competitiveness and technical level. A large number of markets are monopolized, the number of producers being limited to one or several, which diminishes or even excludes competition among them. Under such conditions, a free market gives rise to the growth of pathological phenomena such as unjustified price rises, lack of interest in improving quality and modernity of output, also rising unemployment and inflation.

Proponents of protectionism have been criticizing liberalism throughout the long history of the development of international trade.[6] In the period of mercantilism, they justified the need to protect the domestic market against competition of imported goods. Simultaneously, they called on the state to support exports through tax relief, surcharges, and the like.

At the turn of the 18th and 19th centuries, when a policy based on the classic free market and free trade policy was gaining popularity in Britain, Germany and the United States witnessed a surge of arguments in favour of protectionism. It was industry in particular which was weak in these countries and had to be protected against competition on the part of better British products. H.C. Carey, an American economist living in that period, tried to reconcile the adherents of the theory of laissez-faire and the adherents of protectionism. According to him, the rules of free trade should determine the behaviour of economic subjects inside the American economy, while protectionism should protect the American economy against external competition. This approach found its practical reflection. In 1816, the United States introduced a restrictive customs tariff towards foreign suppliers, protecting both the American industry and American agriculture against foreign competition.[7] The United States has remained faithful to this approach till this day. On the one hand, it demands free access to foreign markets for its goods and capital and, on the other, it consistently protects access to its market for foreign goods.[8] The policy of state interventionism is, thus, indispensable for the efficient functioning of a market economy. In the opinion of Keynes, the contention of the classics of economics about benefits drawn by every country from rational international specialization under conditions of free trade is true only when factors of production are fully utilized. Failure to satisfy this condition imposes on the state the duty to support exports and reduce imports until a state of full economic equilibrium has been reached (full employment, full utilization of production capacities, and the like).

The arguments of J.M. Keynes were confirmed by the great economic crisis of 1929–33 when the free market mechanism proved completely useless and the state took over the principal role in directing the development of the economy. The policy of state protectionism based on J.M. Keynes's theory constituted the leading trend in world economic policy till the end of the 1970s.

In the 1980s a significant sector of economists returned to the theorems of classical economics justifying the ability of a free market and free trade policy to ensure crisis-free economic development. This direction of thought was based on the thinking of an American economist, M. Friedman, who, in the 1960s, undermined

---

6   Comp. J. Sołdaczuk, J. Misala, *Historia handlu międzynarodowego* (PWE, Warsaw, 2001), p. 55 and following.

7   Comp. statement by President G.W. Bush concerning restrictions on the import of steel to the USA (*Gazeta Wyborcza*, no. 162, of 13–14 July 2002, *Czekam na Aleksandra*).

8   Comp. J.M. Keynes, 'The End of Laissesfaire', in J.M. Keynes, *Essays in Persuasion* (New York, 1932); J.M. Keynes, *Ogólna teoria zatrudnienia, procentu i pieniądza* (PWN, Warsaw, 1956), pp. 174 and 200.

the Keynesian foundations of the protectionist policy.[9] The almost 50 years of crisis-free market economy development after the Second World War allowed Friedman to reach the conclusion that it would develop even more efficiently and rapidly without state interventionism. According to him, interventionism makes the operation of market forces more difficult and distorts the automatic process of eliminating economic disequilibrium in individual countries and in the world as a whole. This is so because state administration often suffers from incompetence and red tape, being late and wrong in making decisions, designating resources for the development of enterprises without prospects, which should have long gone bankrupt. Moreover, social considerations are a significant criterion in state policy (e.g. prevention of a rise of unemployment), while social considerations stand, as a rule, in contradiction to a growth of economic management efficiency. The protective functions of the state in the form of financing social purposes, in turn, give rise to a need to impose high taxes, which restrains the growth opportunities of an economy.

The conclusions formulated by Friedman stipulated a radical limitation of interventionism in the economy and protectionism in foreign trade. According to Friedman, the state should focus on pursuing macroeconomic policy, with basic parameters of this policy also being determined by the free market. In foreign relations, the principles of free trade should be observed, allowing for unrestrained imports of goods, services and factors of production as well as excluding any possible support of domestic exports.

Adherents of this (liberal-monetarist) approach to economic policy allow, however, for some exceptions, which are tantamount to protectionism. They include, notably, prevention of imperfections of the free market and free trade mechanism resulting from failure to adjust conditions existing on the market of a given country to the requirements of this mechanism.[10] For example, a shortage of homes can make difficult or even eliminate a flow of labour from labour-rich regions to regions suffering from its shortage. Restraints distorting the operation of the free market and free trade mechanism can also occur in the flow of capital and technology. This forces the state to apply a protectionist policy that performs in such cases helpful functions, despite being a solution worse than a free market policy, since absence of a protectionist policy would expose the country to losses.

In English literature on the subject, an approach of this type is referred to as 'second best' and the whole theory dealing with this subject is called the second best theory.[11] In accordance with this theory, enabling the attainment of a target difficult to be attained under laissez-faire conditions, protectionism has advantages

9 M. Friedman, *Capitalism and Freedom*, op. cit..

10 Comp. P.U. Krugman, M. Obstfeld, *Międzynarodowe stosunki gospodarcze*, op. cit., vol. 1, pp. 150–52; A. Budnikowski and E. Kawecka-Wyrzykowska (eds), *Międzynarodowe stosunki gospodarcze* (PWE, Warsaw, 1999), p. 257; A. Budnikowski, *Międzynarodowe stosunki gospodarcze*, 2nd edn (PWE, Warsaw, 2001), p. 220; D. Begg, S. Fischer, R. Dornbusch, *Ekonomia. Makroekonomia*, 3rd revised edn (PWE, Warsaw, 2003), pp. 399–405.

11 Comp. ibid., p. 404.

and disadvantages, distorting the implementation of other free market goals. Thus, protectionism is not the best solution but the second best. The free market and free trade mechanism would be the best solution if it could function without restraints.

Advocates of economic liberalism allow also for an exception for protectionism in the case of a need to provide imperative protection for newly developed industrial branches.[12] This protection must, however, be of a selective character and may, thus, concern only selected types of production. It must also be limited in time, that is temporary. According to this way of thinking, a policy of protecting newly developing industries is necessary due to the need to protect them against a flow of technologically advanced goods from abroad, produced in large series, cheaper and better in quality. Without such protection, domestic production would not be able to cope with competition by imported goods (this was the experience of Polish electronics in the 1990s when after the removal of protectionist barriers the industry was totally destroyed). After reaching maturity, when the newly developed industry is capable of competing with foreign products under free market conditions, protection ceases to be necessary and must be withdrawn, because instead of helping it would have a destructive influence on producers, discouraging them from competing on their own.

The choice of protection of this kind entails, first of all, the need to decide what types of new production should be developed and whether they should necessarily be covered by protection. Highly industrialized countries extend such protection to branches generating scientific and technical progress, assuming they cannot be dependent on foreign countries in a given domain. Less developed countries traditionally protect practically all new industries. The long duration of this protection is its main drawback. For a number of different reasons these industries are not capable of coping with competition on the part of products from highly industrialized countries under free market conditions.[13] That is why supporters of the free trade policy highlight the necessity of selective development of less developed countries.

Another justified exception to the free trade policy is the need for counteracting unfair competition. This takes place when different forms of stimulating production and exports, leading to unjustified growth of the competitiveness of offered goods, are applied abroad. They include dumping, market disruption and export subsidizing. They disrupt the functioning of a free market and free trade, exerting an adverse effect on the utilization of factors of production and eventually decreasing the efficiency of production and weakening economic growth.[14] They improve the situation in the

---

12 Comp. E. Kawecka-Wyrzykowska, 'Polityka handlowa', in A. Budnikowski and E. Kawecka-Wyrzykowska, *Międzynarodowe stosunki gospodarcze*, op. cit., pp. 255–6.

13 Goods produced in less developed countries were worse in terms of quality, less reliable and worse in appearance even when the same technology and construction were used. The brand of the products as well as the place of manufacture were also of importance.

14 Comp. A. Budnikowski, *Międzynarodowe stosunki gospodarcze*, op. cit., p. 221.

country applying such solutions while, simultaneously, worsening the situation in the country against which they are applied.

In the literature on the subject, arguments exist allowing for the application of the protectionist policy to improve the terms of trade in the importing country. This finds its reflection, for instance, in the imposition of import duties to force foreign exporters to reduce prices. Such a policy can, however, be applied only by a country with a large market (the United States, the European Union) and a dominant position in international trade, since exporters must be so interested in maintaining their position on this market as to be reluctant to retaliate, which is particularly true of small and medium-sized enterprises.

Adherents of the free market and free trade policy are, on the other hand, critical of a number of other instances of protectionism, regarding them as unjustified and eventually loss-generating.

This concerns, in the first place, attempts to use a protectionist policy to increase employment by introducing restraints (e.g. customs duties) on imports. The growth of domestic production attained in this way makes consumption more expensive and leads to inefficient utilization of production factors (compare Figure 2.1).

The policy of limiting imports in order to improve the balance of trade is also generally criticized as it may result in limiting the demand for goods exported by the import-restricting country, which eventually has a negative impact on the its trade balance.

The protection of the domestic market from an influx of cheap imported goods in order to secure jobs against the competition of cheaper labour is also treated by proponents of the policy of free trade as harmful. In their opinion, a solution should be sought not in protectionism but in increasing labour efficiency, which is the best way leading to reduce prices and improve the competitiveness of domestic products. Labour can be paid better than abroad but if it is relatively more efficient, the manufactured products can successfully compete with imports.

Similar arguments are put forward against protectionism when it is used solely for social considerations. In this case, the point is to protect against foreign competition those industries which create jobs for the disabled without alternative employment. Articles manufactured under such conditions do not, as a rule, comply with world technical, qualitative and price standards. It is the consumers who suffers as they is deprived of the possibility of buying imported goods. In accordance with this approach, the best solution is to award disability and old age pensions or to direct the people concerned to other sectors of the economy (e.g. to the services sector) and open the domestic market to imports.

Protection of certain industries for reasons of national and cultural tradition are also considered a relic of the past by adherents of the free trade policy.[15] Symbols of these traditions are small peasant farms in Poland, producers of alcoholic beverages in Germany or kvas-producing plants in Russia. Their protection against foreign competition contributes to the maintenance of prices unjustified by efficiency and

---

15 Comp. ibid., p. 222.

makes consumption more expensive. Possibilities for the development of production of this type should be sought in reduction of production costs rather than in limiting access to the domestic market of competitive imported products.

Also, the argument concerning the necessity of providing the military sector with protection is not regarded as fully justified. In the opinion of free trade proponents, this argument might have had any value solely under conditions of an autonomic policy. In times of military alliances, far-reaching specialization and cooperation in production dependent on the comparative advantage of one country over another are possible also in this domain. Protectionism should, therefore, give way to a free market.

Summing up, adherents of the free trade policy treat protectionism as a necessary evil which can be used in exceptional circumstances, but to a limited extent and temporarily, in the form of a second best solution. Free market and free trade are always the first best solution. The costs of protectionism are borne, in their opinion, by unorganized and scattered consumers. The benefits of protectionism fall, on the other hand, to a few producers who can thus realize their particular interests. This means that a protectionist policy is pursued by the state, not so much in the name of social interest as in the name of highly particular, clearly addressed interests.

Apart from the contemporary liberal trend in economics which treats interventionism in economy and protectionism in foreign trade as an exception to the rule, there are also economists who believe that protectionism is today also an economic policy constituting an alternative to free trade.[16] It should take place also when foreign trade partners represent various levels of development, when one of them has modern industry and the other a raw material-agricultural structure of production. In this case, a free market leads to non-equivalent division of benefits from foreign trade, mounting unemployment in economically weaker countries, troubles with maintaining balance of payments equilibrium, trends towards petrifaction of the raw material-agricultural structure of production in countries with a lower level of economic development and, consequently, to the widening of the income gap between more and less developed countries. In such a situation, economically weaker countries should treat protectionism as an instrument enabling them to avoid these negative effects, at least to some extent.

The need for a protectionist policy appears also when partners are not equivalent in terms of volume and, in particular, when one of the parties is a monopolist while the other tries to enter the market. Without assistance on the part of the state, a small enterprise would have no chance to win an established market position. The

---

16 Comp. T. Kowalik, *Współczesne systemy ekonomiczne; powstawanie, ewolucja, kryzys* (Wydawnictwo Wyższej Szkoły Przedsiębiorczości I Zarządzania, Warsaw, 2000); A. Wojtyna, *Ewolucja keynesizmu a główny nurt ekonomii*, (PWN, Warsaw, 2000); J.A. Brander, B.J. Spencer, 'Protection and Imperfect Competition', in J.A. Brander, B.J. Spencer, *Monopolistic Competition in International Trade* (Oxford University Press, Oxford, 1984); P.R. Krugman, M. Obstfeld, *Międzynarodowe stosunki gospodarcze*, op. cit.

monopolist has a wide range of available means to prevent a small enterprise from entering the market and attaining any economic success there.

Protectionism is also used in the long-term strategy of gaining a market. This approach is based on the principle of imperfect competition in the international market, which is expressed by a monopolist position and the benefits connected with it. The winner is the one who occupies a dominant position of course at the expense of the partner. State protectionism (for instance, in the form of production subsidies) is in this case an instrument making it easier to gain a monopolist position and obtaining extraordinary profits, particularly in virtue of large scale of production.

Such an approach to protectionism rejects *ex ante* the classics' theorem about the existence of perfect competition on the international market and, consequently, about a fair distribution of benefits from international cooperation. Contemporary proponents of protectionism believe that such an assumption is pure illusion, only taking place when there are thousands of economic subjects with equal rights and balanced economy competing on the market, and not only on the part of consumption. If there ever was a situation close to this assumption it could have been at the initial stage of the creation of the classic theory of foreign trade. In the period of monopolist capitalism and nowadays, free competition has been replaced by competition between large transnational corporations taking advantage of all and any methods of winning the market, at different stages of product development, ranging from scientific research to sales. Rivalry of this type often lasts for years. The behaviour of Boeing and Airbus can serve as an example, the aviation market being actually divided between them. At the beginning of the 1990s, the share of Boeing in the sale of passenger planes was 60%, while that of Airbus was 30%. In 1998 Airbus outpaced Boeing in terms of orders for planes, gaining 52% of the total number.[17] The expansion of both firms on the world market proceeded with a significant participation of the interested states. The American government uses for this purpose the financing of aviation-related production for military purposes, while West European governments subsidize research and development. The scale of the subsidizing is, of course unknown to the public. However, both parties estimate that it is of strategic importance to the partner. Hence, also this form of protectionism is sometimes referred to as a strategic trade policy, since its outcome is to ensure a dominant (strategic) long-term position on the market to an enterprise.

Advocates of this type of protectionism argue that it eventually generates benefits. Through subsidizing research and development, the state uses taxpayers' money to give effects of scale and size of production series brought about by gaining an advantage on the market, as well as generating effects of scientific and technical progress achieved by the subsidized industry for the economy as a whole.[18]

---

17 Comp. A. Budnikowski, *Międzynarodowe stosunki gospodarcze*, op. cit., pp. 224–55.

18 Comp. P.R. Krugman, M. Obstfeld, *Międzynarodowe stosunki gospodarcze*, vol. 1, op. cit., pp. 150–52.

Contemporary adherents of protectionism also question the sense of the free market and free trade policy under conditions of differing levels of economic development. Comparative advantages in costs determined on the basis of these differences are often unfavourable for less economically developed countries since they petrify existing production structures, leading in the long term to a deterioration of terms of trade and decrease of benefits from international trade. That is why it is proposed to replace a statistically expressed comparative advantage with a dynamically expressed comparative advantage.[19] With the help of an industrial policy the state can adjust the statistical comparative advantage giving it the desired direction of change. This can be done using subventions, tax relief and other measures that the state can avail itself of to reduce production costs in selected industries. The state can also co-finance scientific research and development, facilitate access to technology and foreign credits. Consequently, the state can accelerate the development of production in certain sectors of the economy and production of specific goods, contributing to a decrease of production costs, acceleration of technical progress, upgrading of the quality and reliability of goods, and the like. Activities without chances of specialization under conditions of a statistical advantage in costs adopted as the base can become leading sectors of the economy under conditions of dynamic comparative advantages. That was the case in Japan and other newly industrialized countries that have built new sectors of the economy from scratch with state assistance, giving them the status of export specialties.

In summary, the policy of economic protectionism can be viewed in two ways, on the one hand as an inevitable evil and, on the other, as the best solution admissible temporarily exclusively to adapt the imperfections of existing conditions, unadjusted to the requirements of the free market and free trade mechanism. In this case, protectionist policy is applied only to ensure a possibly fastest adjustment of the existing conditions to the requirements of the free market and free trade. On the other hand, a protectionist policy can be treated as a permanent element of adjusting imperfections of the contemporary market, which is far from free market and free trade requirements. It is the stronger who wins in this market and, hence, this market abounds in such phenomena as concentration of capital, absorption of smaller enterprises by larger ones, and a drive towards monopolization of production. The state plays an important part in this process, supporting enterprises that have the opportunity to occupy a dominant position, or protecting smaller enterprises from being absorbed by the large ones.

The evaluation of protectionism depends on the point of view. Adherents of the free trade policy see in it mainly drawbacks, namely, weakening of the interest of enterprises in reducing production costs and growth of efficiency, decrease of interest by enterprises in technical progress, maintenance of inefficient production structures and, as a result – a deepening deficit of the balance of payments. Viewed

---

19 Comp. P. Bożyk, *Wymiana zagraniczna a dochód narodowy*, (PWE, Warsaw, 1968), p. 142; P. Bożyk, *Korzyści z międzynarodowej specjalizacji*, (PWE, Warsaw, 1972), pp. 63–70.

from this angle, state protectionist policy gives rise only to pathologies and should best be abandoned.

The second approach to protectionism perceives it as positive solutions adopted under conditions of imperfections of the contemporary market, in particular, as protection of the domestic market against destructive import competition, of domestic production against its destruction by stronger foreign firms, of the population against unemployment, and of the balance of trade against disequilibrium.

2.4.3. Mixed Policy

Current practice is influenced by both above doctrines, one of them taking a dominant position while the other moving to the background, depending on the period. Till 1980 the doctrine prevailing in economic policy gave priority to protectionism, since 1980 the free trade policy has moved to the forefront.

Regardless of these reshufflings in the majority of countries, including the highly developed countries, there are strong protectionist trends that temporarily intensify or weaken. Interest in protectionism depends on the state of market conditions in these countries and in the world as a whole. Under good market conditions, and, thus, a high economic growth rate, positive balances of trade and payments as well as lack of unemployment, protectionism tends to be restrained. Enterprises can then cope on the international market without state assistance. Under deteriorating market conditions and, in particular, in times of economic recession or crisis when demand slumps, unemployment grows and difficulties arise in maintaining equilibrium in the balance of foreign trade, a growing need exists for a protectionist policy on the part of enterprises. So it was in the second half of the 1970s and in the 1980s when, under conditions of the oil crisis, a number of West-European countries found themselves in trouble. Notwithstanding the long-term trends towards international trade liberalization, these countries applied a wide range of protectionist instruments in their economic policy (a period of so-called neo-protectionism). Also the 1990s witnessed periods of flat growth trends and drops in employment and demand connected with them. They were also accompanied by intensification of protectionism in international relations. Arguments varied, ranging from the necessity to counteract unfair competition and unfair trade practices to the need to protect the balance of trade and balance of payments, to counteract unemployment, and the like.

Like the economic policy, the currently pursued foreign economic policy is a choice between a larger or smaller dose of free trade and a smaller or larger dose of protectionism. This is illustrated in Figure 2.2.[20]

---

20 Comp. P. Bożyk, J. Misala, M. Puławski, *Międzynarodowe stosunki ekonomiczne*, op. cit., pp. 307–309.

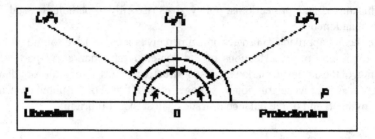

Figure 2.2. Possible Options of Foreign Economic Policy

Source: Author's own elaboration.

Liberalism Protectionism
This means that all practical solutions in this domain are of mixed character. The arrows in Figure 2.2 from the left to the right indicate increased injection of liberalism while those from the right to the left show increased injection of protectionism. The same phenomenon can be interpreted in two ways – as a growth of protectionism or a limitation of liberalism, everything depending on the starting point.

Discussion between supporters of liberalism and supporters of protectionism has been going on for several hundred years. However, it seems to revolve rather around theoretical considerations than economic reality. It is essential for both these points of view to define when one can talk about protectionism and when about liberalism. For fundamentalist liberals, protectionism already takes place when vector *P* moves to *P*1. Orthodox protectionists consider even a shift of vector *L* to *P1* a transition to liberalism.

The theory of economics does not tell explicitly when liberalism or protectionism occurs. It does not tell either that free trade is better than protectionism or that protectionism is better than liberalism in absolute terms. It only says that, under certain assumptions, liberalism has an advantage over protectionism and under others protectionism has an advantage over liberalism. Thus, which solution should be applied in practice depends on specific economic conditions.[21]

In other words, the choice between extreme liberalism and extreme protectionism is groundless as it would mean a choice between solutions that are not to be found in practice. Instead the principle of having as much free trade as possible and as much protectionism as necessary should be applied.[22] In economically developed countries with a mature market economy, the dose of liberalism can be much larger than in less developed countries with imperfect market mechanisms. In the first case, production structures are competitive enterprises, strong, well organized, easily winning in

---

21 See W.M. Corder, *Trade Policy and Economic Welfare*, (Oxford University Press, Oxford, 1974).

22 W.M. Corden, *International Trade Theory and Policy. Selected Essays of W.M. Corden* (Edward Elgar, London, 1992), p. 297.

competition on foreign markets without the need to resort to state protectionist assistance.

In the second case, the opposite situation occurs. The production structures of less developed countries are obsolete, uncompetitive, domestic enterprises that have no chance to win in competition, domestic markets are in the hands of foreign suppliers. Without state intervention these trends cannot be changed.

2.5. Goals of Foreign Economic Policy

The goals of foreign economic policy signify the selection by the state of specific priorities in economic relations with other countries. These priorities can be general or specific in nature. In the second case, they can be either quantitative or qualitative.

The general goals of foreign economic policy include, first of all, selection of the type of policy: free trade or protectionist, autonomic or contractual. This selection is by no means arbitrary, being determined by internal and external factors, mostly independent of the government pursuing the policy. For instance, systemic transformation exerted an essential influence on a change of general foreign economic policy goals, not only of the countries undergoing transformation, but also their external environment. On the one hand, conditions were created for the integration of the countries of Central and Eastern Europe with the European Union and, on the other hand, the idea of such integration with the countries of the former Soviet Union was abandoned.

The specific goals of foreign economic policy comprise quantitative and qualitative goals. A quantitative goal of foreign economic policy can be, for instance, an increase of the volume of exports or imports, attainment of a specific value of the balance of trade, balance of current accounts or balance of payments, increase of the size of foreign direct investments in the country or own investments abroad. A qualitative goal of foreign economic policy can involve improvement of terms of trade, i.e. obtaining more favourable (higher) prices in exports and (lower) prices in imports, revival of the economy and, thus, acceleration of its growth rate by increasing exports. The same group of goals includes also upgrading the quality and modernity of output through the import of technologies, know-how, licences, and the like.

The time horizon for the achievement of both general and specific goals of foreign economic policy is not uniform. Some of them can be reached within a short time while others in the medium or long term. In the short term (up to a year), a country can implement its quantitative goals, including increased exports and reduced imports, improvement of the balance of trade, and the like. In the medium term (from one year to five years) it is also possible to implement some quantitative goals, including improvement of the efficiency of foreign trade, upgrading of the technical level of production through imports of advanced technologies and licences, increased capital investments (foreign within a given country or the country's own investments abroad). Finally, in the long term (over five years), it is possible to carry out structural changes in the economy by increasing the share of a given country in the international division of labour, improvement of the balance of payments, and the like.

The goals of foreign economic policy are mutually interdependent, there being a feedback mechanism between them. Without achieving one goal it is impossible to achieve the other and vice versa. Frequently, there are contradictions between goals of foreign economic policy. This concerns both goals of the same time horizon and goals of different time horizons. Contradictions can also arise between quantitative and qualitative goals. The state must then choose the most important goals, focus on them and abandon the others. For instance, an increase of the volume of foreign trade is not, as a rule, accompanied by an improvement of terms of trade. Also difficulties with restoring equilibrium in the balance of trade must have, in the medium or long term, a negative impact on the quantitative development of commodity turnover, in particular, imports.

It is for these reasons among others that short-term goals of foreign economic policy frequently change and, simultaneously, may prove contradictory. Such a situation does not mean mistakes are made in the art of pursuing foreign economic policy. Variability and mutual contradiction of short-term goals of foreign economic policy are simply a frequent occurrence.

Unlike short-term goals, long-term goals of foreign economic policy should be fixed and mutually harmonized as they are of strategic character and determine the development of the economy of a given country. For example, an improvement of the balance of payments requires an improvement of the country's position in the international division of labour and, simultaneously, without an improvement of the balance of payments in the long term, the country's position in the international division of labour is impossible, for instance through a change of the commodity or geographical structure of foreign trade, development of cooperation in production, and the like. It is, therefore, impossible to abandon the implementation of one goal and focus solely on the other.

Invariability and harmonization of long-term goals of foreign economic policy are the fundamental principles of this policy, but when internal and external conditions of the development of international economic relations are not subject to radical changes. Otherwise, long-term goals of foreign economic policy should be evolutionary in character and, thus, adjust to these changes.

Medium-term goals of foreign economic policy are more stable and interdependent than short-term goals but, simultaneously, they are subject to more frequent changes and are less interdependent than long-term goals.

2.6. Means of Foreign Economic Policy

The means of foreign economic policy are adequate funds (financial resources) serving the state to reach its foreign economic policy goals. This is a definition that differs from the concept of means dominant in literature on the subject and used, as a rule, interchangeably with the concept of tools (instruments).[23]

In a market economy, the state can employ means to influence implementation of foreign economic policy goals in two ways: directly or indirectly. Direct influence concerns only the sphere of the economy that belongs to the state. In this field the state not only sets the goals of foreign economic policy but also decides on the means necessary to attain these goals. Although in a market economy state-owned enterprises are commercialised, which means a necessity to be controlled by the market logics, the state influences their behaviour through adequate selection of members of teams directly responsible for their management, among other ways. It can also apply to enterprises directly subordinated to the state, exceptions to generally compulsory rules, thus influencing their investment, production and trade decisions.

Indirect influence of the state on the behaviour of enterprises prevails in a market economy, since private enterprises that are not state property constitute an overwhelming proportion of all enterprises. In this case, the state cannot exert direct influence on decisions concerning foreign economic policy. It can, at best, indirectly support the activity of enterprises participating in foreign economic relations, availing itself for this purpose of the financial funds it holds. The state can use the funds to fuel economic subjects (enterprises, economic organizations) with means increasing their competitiveness on the international market. For instance, it can subsidize export-oriented production (in order to increase the volume of exports, improve the balance of trade or the balance of payments). Other forms of support for economic activity used by the state include credit relief given by state-owned banks to exporters of commodities and services, refunds of part of the interest on credits levied by commercial banks on investors, producers and exporters, insurance of credits contracted by exporters for the needs of exporting to high-risk countries. The state can, moreover, finance wholly or partially the import of licences or other forms of technical progress or refund part of the costs incurred by private enterprises.

In both cases (direct and indirect), the application of means of foreign economic policy to attain the goals of this policy makes sense only if a return of these means to the budget takes place within the time horizon (short-, medium- or long-term) adopted in advance. The state can spend the means encumbering the budget or drawing a special credit for this purpose. The return by enterprises of the means received from the state can take different forms, its basis being, however, a financial form expressed in domestic or foreign currency. Apart from that, there may also be a physical form, for instance an increased volume of exports or imports. Failure to meet this condition would signify that the expenditure of budget means for the implementation of the goals would be an ordinary loss. This results from the fact that means of foreign

---

23 Comp. J. Sołdaczuk, *Zagraniczna polityka handlowa*, op. cit., p. 269; A. Budnikowski and E. Kawecka-Wyrzykowska, *Międzynarodowe stosunki gospodarcze*, op.cit., p. 236; P.R. Krugman, M. Obstfeld, *Międzynarodowe stosunki gospodarcze*, op. cit., p. 127 and following.

economic policy should be only a temporary, not a permanent, form of supporting economic activity of enterprises in foreign relations, enabling them for instance to survive a period of poor market conditions, to improve management methods so as to raise the competitiveness of domestic production on foreign markets, and the like. Otherwise, the expenditure of budget resources would be devoid of any sense.

Put differently, the application by the state of the means of foreign economic policy should ultimately lead to increased income in foreign trade owing to a growth of the size of this exchange or improvement of its efficiency.[24] Improvement of the efficiency of foreign trade is of particular importance. The point is to improve the comparative advantage between a given country and other countries in the target period, with the help of the means applied in the initial period. For instance, under circumstances of a long-term deficit in the balance of trade, supporting exports with the help of financial resources from the state budget (subsidies, credit guarantees, insurance) can prevent a decrease of profitable imports. This support should, however, be only temporary and must be accompanied by steps aimed at raising the efficiency of the production of exported goods. Also, under conditions of a sudden deterioration of the profitability of exports (for instance, following a devaluation of the internal currency on an importer's market), support extended to exports with the help of means of foreign economic policy is a condition for the maintenance by exporters of their position on this market until the situation improves. Loss of these positions can be permanent, depriving the exporting country of long-term sales possibilities on this market.

2.7. Instruments Applied in Foreign Economic Policy

Instruments applied in foreign economic policy are carriers of information conveyed by the state to subjects participating in economic relations with other countries, to achieve the goals of this policy. These carriers include elements of the economic mechanism operating in a given country, being a derivative of its socio-economic system. They must be adjusted to the ownership relations prevailing in this country, the character of economic subjects which make production, investment, export and import decisions.[25]

In a market economy system based on the institution of private ownership, economic decisions, including those concerning relations with foreign countries are made by individual enterprises. The state cannot, thus, influence them by administrative commands and bans. It can do so only in exceptional cases, acting in the name of overall social interest, forbidding the development of production or imports of goods harmful to health, creating a threat to the natural environment, and the like. The state can also temporarily ban export of goods being in short supply

---

24 Comp. P. Bożyk, 'Pojęcie dochodu z międzynarodowego handlu towarami i usługami', in P. Bozyk, J. Misala, M. Puławski, *Międzynarodowe stosunki ekonomiczne*, op. cit., pp. 81–90.

25 Comp. J. Sołdaczuk, *Zagraniczna polityka handlowa*, op. cit., p. 267.

from the country, from the point of view of satisfying domestic needs (foodstuffs, raw materials, particularly those of strategic character). It can also impose restrictions or a ban on the import of some technologies constituting means of the country's defence, including armaments. The state can also restrict in an administrative manner imports of, for instance, products harmful to health, drugs which do not comply with treatment standards in force in a given country, foodstuffs which do not meet sanitary standards, plants and animals from territories affected by dangerous diseases.[26]

Instruments applied in foreign economic policy can be divided into macro- and microeconomic. With the help of macroeconomic instruments the state creates general conditions for the development of economic activity in a given country as well as economic relations with foreign countries. The consequences of the application of macroeconomic instruments are universal, affecting all enterprises, also these which do not perform economic activity involving foreign countries. In this sense, microeconomic instruments are addressed to enterprises participating in economic relations with foreign countries. They can, simultaneously, concern all these enterprises or only some of them. Their role is to increase and decrease the profitability of cooperation with foreign countries.

---

26 J. Sołdaczuk, *Zagraniczna polityka handlowa*, op. cit., p. 268.

Chapter 3

Macroeconomic Instruments Applied in Foreign Economic Policy

3.1. The Concept of Macroeconomic Policy

Macroeconomic policy is the influence of the state on the economy as a whole and, in particular, on national income, consumption, investments, savings, revenues and expenditures of the state budget, trade balance and balance of payments, demand for money and supply of money, employment and unemployment, and the like.[1] Macroeconomic policy, thus understood, covers income policy, price policy, monetary policy, fiscal policy, credit policy and others.[2] It gives primary attention to stimulating economic growth, limiting inflation, eliminating unemployment, balancing the state budget, counteracting disequilibrium in the balance of payments, in particular in the balance of current accounts.

Macroeconomic policy is characterized by a comprehensive influence on the behaviour of economic subjects, which means that it gives rise to phenomena both desirable and undesirable from the point of view of the state.[3] Moreover, the obtained effects differ in the short and in the long-term, both positive and negative for internal equilibrium. Thus, macroeconomic policy does not allow phenomena which would be exclusively positive to be highlighted, and to eliminate negative phenomena.[4]

---

1 Comp. B. Begg, S. Fischer, R. Dornbusch, *Ekonomia*, op. cit., vol. 2. p. 14; M. Nasiłowski, *System rynkowy. Podstawy mikro- i makroekonomii* (Wydawnictwo Key Text, Warszawa, 1996), p. 20.

2 Comp. J. Kaleta, 'Polityka gospodarcza', in *Encyklopedia Biznesu*, vol. 1 (Fundacja Innowacja, Warszawa, 1995), pp. 628–35.

3 M. Nasiłowski, *System rynkowy*, op.cit., p. 22.

4 Literature on the subject distinguishes, apart from macroeconomic policy of the state, also meta-economic and meso-economic policy. In this meaning, meta-economic policy is the state influence on social factors, system of values, basic scheme of political and economic organization, ability of subjects to formulate strategy and policy.

According to this approach, macroeconomic policy embraces budget policy, monetary policy, fiscal policy, foreign exchange policy, trade policy and competition policy while meso-economic policy embraces infrastructural policy, educational policy, industrial policy, environmental protection policy, export and import policy as well as regional policy. (Comp. M. Lubiński, *Proces integrowania się ze Wspólnotami Europejskimi jako czynnik wzrostu międzynarodowej konkurencyjności polskiej gospodarki* (IRiSS, Warsaw, 1995), p. 37).

This is particularly important under conditions of parliamentary democracy when a government carrying out economic policy on behalf of the state strives for social approval in order to have its mandate extended in subsequent elections. Negative side effects of the pursued policy become a threat to the implementation of this goal. Consequently, governments tend to avoid a challenging macroeconomic policy which is likely to generate not only positive but also negative results, in particular, when the latter arouse social discontent. The point is not to give the political opposition arguments which it could use in subsequent elections. Excessive caution in economic policy obviously limits the ability to implement efficiently and effectively the positive targets set.[5]

Macroeconomic policy exerts a direct or indirect impact on economic relations with other countries. The scale of this impact depends on the extent to which a given economy is open. In an open economy it is much wider than in a closed economy. This is illustrated in Figure 3.1.

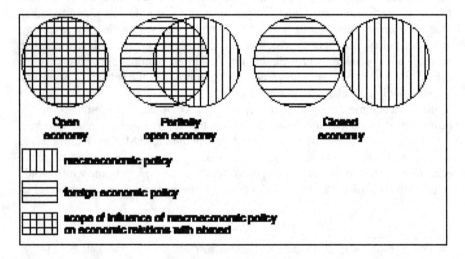

Figure 3.1. The Scope of the Influence of Macroeconomic Policy on Economic Relations with Abroad

Source: Author's own elaboration.

In a fully open economy, domestic-market oriented economic activity is integrated with foreign-market oriented activity, both being treated alternatively by economic subjects. Thus, acting on these subjects, macroeconomic policy affects their operations both on the domestic and foreign markets, being consequently integrated with foreign economic policy. In a closed economy, foreign economic

---

5   Comp. M. Nasiłowski, *System rynkowy. Podstawy*, op. cit., p. 29.

policy is autonomic in relation to macroeconomic policy shaping economic activity on the domestic market.

The most important instruments affecting economic relations with other countries include the exchange rate policy, the interest rate policy, the monetary policy, the fiscal policy, the income policy and the budget policy.[6] They are used by the state to influence the pace of development of economic links with abroad, shape the structure of these links and the ensuing economic benefits.

3.2. Exchange Rate Policy

3.2.1. Devaluation, Revaluation, Depreciation, Appreciation

The exchange rate is an instrument of macroeconomic policy, which enables the state to influence both economic relations with other countries and the internal economy.

The state can use the exchange rate to ensure equilibrium in the balance of payments, a change of the exchange rate as a conversion rate in relation to currencies of different countries being equivalent to a change of the price which has to be paid in a given currency to purchase one unit of another country's currency. The value of this price is determined by the supply of foreign currencies and the demand for them. The kinds of foreign currencies available on the money market of a given country are ensured by exporters of goods and services as well as by other economic subjects having foreign currencies and trying to exchange them for the domestic currency (e.g. foreign investors interested in the purchase of shares, bonds or in green-field construction in a given country).[7] Demand for foreign currencies on the money market of a given country is dictated by importers of goods and services as well as by subjects which must make foreign payments (domestic investors in foreign markets, foreign enterprises repatriating dividends, and the like). If the demand for foreign currencies exceeds their supply, the balance of payments is negative and, conversely, a surplus of the supply of foreign currencies over the demand for these currencies gives rise to surpluses in the balance of payments. In both cases the state can intervene on the money market by changing the exchange rate. This is justified when a deficit or a surplus of the balance of payments persists over a longer period of time and cannot be changed using other instruments of economic policy.

In the case of a long-term balance of payments deficit, the state devaluates the domestic currency, that is raises the exchange rate of the foreign currency into the domestic currency. After devaluation, the price of the foreign currency expressed in the domestic currency rises and hence more has to be paid in the domestic currency for a foreign currency unit. Devaluation thus makes domestic goods cheaper on

---

6   Comp. P. Bożyk, J. Misala, M. Puławski, *Międzynarodowe stosunki ekonomiczne*, op. cit., pp. 296–304.

7   Comp. ibid., p. 233; K. Lutkowski, 'Kursy wymiany walut', in *Encyklopedia Biznesu*, op. cit., p. 463; J. Sołdaczuk, Z. Kamecki, P. Bożyk, *Międzynarodowe stosunki gospodarcze. Teoria i polityka* (PWE, Warszawa, 1987), p. 115.

foreign markets. For example, when the domestic production cost of product x equals to 100 zlotys and the exchange rate is 4 zlotys to the dollar, it pays to sell product x on a foreign market for at least 25 dollars. After devaluation of the zloty by 25% and the setting of a new exchange rate at 5 zlotys to the dollar, the profitability of exporting product x increases by 25%. At a domestic production cost of 100 zlotys, exporters are already satisfied with a foreign price above 20 dollars. As a result, exports grow because a larger number of foreign buyers are willing to pay a price higher than 20 dollars rather than above 25 dollars. This reasoning is of course true if the price elasticity of demand on the foreign market is equal to or higher than unity. The situation in import changes in the opposite direction. Prior to devaluation, domestic prices of imported goods are lower than after devaluation, which means that the demand for them on the domestic market is higher than after devaluation. At an exchange rate of 4 zlotys to the dollar, imported product x purchased abroad for 10 dollars costs at least 40 zlotys on the domestic market while after devaluation it costs 50 zlotys.

The impact of devaluation on the balance of trade is determined by the development of nominal (price) terms of trade and real (volume) terms of trade. In the first case, when devaluation gives rise to deterioration of nominal terms of trade, the balance of trade deteriorates. When this balance is expressed in the domestic currency, terms of trade deteriorate due to a rise of domestic prices of imported goods. On the other hand, when the balance of trade is expressed in a foreign currency, a deterioration of terms of trade results from a decrease in prices of foreign goods exported by the devaluation-making country. In the second case, when devaluation results in an increase of the quantity of exported goods and a decrease in the quantity of imported goods, real (volume) terms of trade improve.

The effects of devaluation depend, however, on which of the phenomena prevails, a deterioration of nominal terms of trade or an improvement of real terms of trade. If real terms of trade deteriorate faster, the balance of trade deteriorates and, conversely, if real terms of trade improve faster than nominal terms of trade deteriorate, the balance of trade improves.

This is determined, on the one hand, by the flexibility of domestic demand for imports and foreign demand for exports and, on the other hand, by relations between foreign prices of exported goods and domestic prices of imported goods. The flexibility of both foreign demand for exports and domestic demand for imports can vary significantly, ranging from a value of below unity to a value higher than unity. In accordance with the Marshall-Lerner condition, a devaluation gives rise to an improvement of the balance of trade when the sum of flexibility of the foreign demand for exports and domestic demand for imports is higher than unity, of course provided the influence of nominal terms of trade is neutral.[8] If the sum of flexibility of foreign demand for exports and domestic demand for imports is lower than unity,

---

8   See: A. Marshall, *Money, Credit and Commerce* (Macmillan, London, 1929), p. 354; A. Lerner, *Economics of Control* (New York 1947), pp. 378–9.

devaluation can cause a deterioration of the balance of trade. When the sum of the two equals unity, the impact of devaluation on the trade balance is slight.

Naturally, when the impact of nominal terms of trade on the balance of trade is not neutral but influence it in a positive or negative way, the Marshal-Lerner condition must be adjusted. This concerns notably a situation when domestic exporters do not lower the prices of their products on foreign markets after devaluation of their currency, while foreign exporters lower prices of their products on the market of the country devaluating its internal currency (in order to maintain competitiveness). In this situation, nominal terms of trade do not deteriorate and may even improve.

In the case of a prolonged balance of payments surplus, the state revaluates its domestic currency, that is lowers the exchange rate at which a foreign currency can be exchanged for a domestic currency. After revaluation, the price of the foreign currency expressed in the domestic currency drops and, consequently, less can be paid in the domestic currency for a unit of the foreign currency. As a result, revaluation makes domestic goods relatively more expensive on foreign markets. In the example studied, at a domestic production cost of product x of 100 zlotys and an exchange rate of 4 zlotys to the dollar, a price higher than 25 dollars obtained abroad is a prerequisite to export. A 25% revaluation of the domestic currency up to 3 zlotys to the dollar means that a price of at least 33.3 dollars must be obtained for the same product on the foreign market. Under conditions of price flexibility of demand on a foreign market equal to or higher than unity, this leads to a drop of sales. Simultaneously, revaluation of the domestic currency makes imported goods relatively less expensive on the domestic market. Prior to revaluation, importing an article of 10 dollars value costs at least 40 zlotys but only 30 zlotys after revaluation. Hence, revaluation leads to the elimination of a balance of trade surplus.

Due to the fact that a small number of countries boast long-term balance of payments surpluses, revaluation is applied more rarely than devaluation. It serves, first of all, to ensure internal equilibrium, in particular, to reduce inflation.

Both the two principal goals of revaluation, the attempt to reduce inflation and to limit payment reserves, are closely connected since balance of payment surplus contributes to an exacerbation of inflationary trends. Foreign means of payment gained abroad and resold to the state for the domestic currency are in this case greater than the means of payment purchased by importers. As a result, a surplus of the domestic currency develops on the market, generating increased demand in relation to the supply of goods and services, followed by a growth of inflation. This, of course, occurs only under conditions of economic recovery. When market conditions are poor, and thus under conditions of high unemployment and unutilized production capacities, a positive balance of payments performs a positive function as it creates additional demand and increases production and employment.

From this point of view, revaluation must be carried out under strictly defined conditions since, revived market conditions and an additional flow of money can generate negative phenomena in the form of a surplus of demand and acceleration of inflation. As a result, exports slow down while imports increase and the market witnesses an additional supply of goods and services. This in turn generates deflationary phenomena in the economy, reflected in a reduction of output and a decline of employment. Simultaneously, nominal terms of trade improve as revaluation makes domestic goods more expensive on foreign markets and foreign goods less expensive on the domestic market. More favourable nominal terms of trade contribute to an improvement of the balance of trade and, consequently, also the balance of payments. Positive effects of an improvement of nominal terms of trade depend, however, on negative effects connected with a deterioration of real terms of trade and, thus, on the change in the quantity of exported and imported goods.

Real terms of trade depend on the flexibility of foreign demand for exported goods and domestic demand for imported goods. If this flexibility is high, real terms of trade deteriorate neutralizing the positive effect of improvement of nominal terms of trade and giving rise to a deterioration of the balance of trade. If the flexibility of foreign demand for goods exported by a given country and of domestic demand for imported goods is low, the effect of a deterioration of real terms of trade can be smaller than the effect of an improvement of nominal terms of trade. Finally, when the flexibility of foreign demand for goods exported by a given country and of domestic demand for imported goods are mean, then the balance of trade can remain unchanged in spite of a revaluation. Basing on the reasoning of the Marshall-Lerner condition, a deterioration of the balance of trade takes place only when the sum of the flexibility of foreign demand for goods exported by a given country and the elasticity of domestic demand for goods imported by the country is higher than unity (with the assumption of nominal terms of trade equal to unity).

Depreciation, that is a spread-in-time reduction of the exchange rate, is an instrument of state policy geared to ensure equilibrium in the balance of trade by making exports cheaper and imports more expensive.

Appreciation of the internal currency, that is a spread-in-time rise of the exchange rate, is primarily an instrument to combat inflation. It can be applied when no difficulties exist connected with maintaining equilibrium in the balance of trade and balance of payments, since it relatively increases prices of goods exported by a given country and decreases prices of goods imported by the country, producing a deterioration in the balance of trade and the balance of payments.

In an open economy, both devaluation and revaluation as well as depreciation and appreciation signify not only a change in the domestic prices of imported goods but also prices of goods manufactured solely for the domestic market by increasing or decreasing domestic prices of imported raw materials and materials for the production of cooperative elements, technologies, and the like. Unlike in a closed economy, where internal prices are not linked to foreign prices, in an open economy the exchange rate is a price-creating parameter on the domestic market. It is, thus, a parameter which affects the allocation of factors of production, encouraging international cooperation in some domains and discarding such cooperation in others, in favour of imports.[9] The consequences of devaluation and revaluation are, therefore, much wider than their influence on the balance of trade and balance of payments. Devaluation increases the scope of specialization on the foreign market, broadening the range of profitable goods. Revaluation gives rise to opposite consequences, narrowing the scope of profitability.[10]

The impact of a change of the exchange rate on economic growth proceeds, moreover, not only through exports and imports of goods and services but also factors of production. Devaluation makes foreign capital more interested in investing in the devaluation-making country, since a foreign investor receives more units of the domestic currency for one unit of the foreign currency than before devaluation. This makes an investment relatively less expensive to finance. On the other hand, revaluation not only makes foreign investments more expensive but, simultaneously, negatively influences the size of the repatriated dividend. For example, at an exchange rate of 4 zlotys to the dollar, a profit of 100 m zlotys gives a dividend of 25 m dollars, while at an exchange rate of 5 zlotys to the dollar it gives a dividend of only 20 m dollars.

The consequences of a change of the exchange rate are, however, different in the long and the short term. A side effect of devaluation is a growth of inflation generated by rising prices of imported goods. This has an adverse influence on economic growth and, consequently, on the balance of payments. Revaluation also exerts a negative impact on economic growth, discouraging foreign capital from investing in a revaluation-making country, thus weakening growth trends, which leads to disequilibrium in the balance of payments in the long-term.

3.2.2. Exchange Rate Systems

Forms of state influence on the exchange rate depend on the exchange rate system effective in a given country. A large number of such systems are known from practice. However, some have already become history while others still remain of interest to different countries. Two of these systems are of interest from the point of view of the analysed subject, namely the systems of stiff and floating exchange rates.[11]

The system of stiff exchange rates, which can be divided into the system of exchange rates adjusted from time to time, the so-called adjustable peg, and the system of crawling exchange rates, the so-called crawling peg, allows for possible devaluation or revaluation without disturbing the parity. It differs at this point from the system of fixed exchange rates which were in force under conditions of the system of a gold, bar-gold and foreign exchange-gold currency, when a change in the exchange rate required a change of the parity of the currency.

---

9   J. Sołdaczuk, Z. Kamecki, P. Bożyk, *Międzynarodowe stosunki gospodarcze*, op. cit., p. 116.

10   K. Lutkowski, 'Kursy wymiany walut', op. cit., p. 463.

11   Ibid., pp. 463–5; P. Bożyk, J. Misala, M. Puławski, *Międzynarodowe stosunki ekonomiczne*, op. cit., pp. 234–5.

The Bretton Woods system, in force in 1944–73, can serve as an example of an adjustable peg. In accordance with the articles of agreement of the International Monetary Fund, an organization set up to monitor the functioning of the Bretton Woods system, exchange rates could fluctuate within a 1% band up or down from the official rate. If these limits were exceeded, governments were obliged to intervene on the market so as to counteract the developed situation. Intervention could involve (in case of need) also devaluation and revaluation of the domestic currency. Great Britain, for instance, devalued the pound sterling twice – in 1949 by 30% and in 1967 by 14.3%. Devaluation or revaluation was justified by a long-term disequilibrium in the balance of payments. Short-term imbalances were counteracted by purchases of currencies in short supply or sales of currencies available in excess. To be able to make such interventions, countries had to maintain foreign exchange reserves and were, in case of need, assisted by the International Monetary Fund.

The stiff exchange rate systems include also the crawling peg. In this case a change of the exchange rate is not made from time to time but frequently (for instance, daily), being programmed and announced. The causative factor underlying these changes is high inflation, the stiff crawling peg being used in high-inflation countries. Unlike the adjustable peg system, the crawling peg system disaggregates a devaluation (caused by inflation) into a large number of small changes of the same character. Its aim is to prevent foreign exchange speculations (escape of the domestic currency into a foreign currency or conversely).

In the system of floating exchange rates, the state does not set an official exchange rate but leaves its shaping to market forces.[12] Thus, if the supply of foreign currencies on the market of a given country increases (export soars, foreign direct capital investments or portfolio investments grow), then with a flat or more slowly growing demand for foreign currencies, there is a gradual reduction of the exchange rate of foreign currencies against the domestic currency (an appreciation of the domestic currency), meaning that fewer units of the domestic currency are paid for a unit of a foreign currency. Conversely, when the supply of foreign currencies on the market of a given country decreases without being accompanied by a growth of demand for them, the exchange rate of foreign currencies into the domestic currency goes up (depreciation of the domestic currency), which means that more units of the domestic currency must be paid for one unit of the foreign currency. Thus, improvement of the balance of payments contributes to an appreciation of the domestic currency while its deterioration has a reverse effect.

When the rate of inflation in a given country is slower than abroad, exported goods become relatively cheaper than imported goods, which favours growth of exports and reduction of imports. This gives rise to an appreciation of the domestic currency and a depreciation of foreign currencies. A new exchange rate makes exports more expensive and imports cheaper and, consequently, equilibrium is restored in the balance of trade.

---

12 K. Lutkowski, 'Kursy wymiany walut', op. cit., p. 465.

A faster rate of inflation in the country than abroad means that exported goods become relatively more expensive while imported goods cheaper, which favours a decrease in the growth rate of exports and a rise in the growth rate of imports. As a result, the supply of foreign currencies is smaller and of domestic currencies larger, which results in depreciation of the domestic currency and appreciation of foreign currencies. A new exchange rate makes exports relatively cheaper on foreign markets and imports relatively more expensive on the domestic market. And, consequently, equilibrium is restored in the balance of trade.

This kind of a mechanism of purely market-determined changes in the exchange rate is rarely encountered as it is exposed to speculative changes animated by foreign exchange players with the purpose of making extraordinary exchange rate-related profits. Therefore, in practice, a state (central bank)-regulated exchange rate is applied. This finds its reflection in the purchase of foreign currencies when their growing supply threatens depreciation of the internal currency, more expensive exports and cheaper imports and, consequently, a deterioration of the balance of trade. Conversely, when a decreasing supply of foreign currencies on the domestic market poses a danger of depreciation of the domestic currency, and hence accelerated inflation and its other negative consequences, the state (central bank) can use the foreign exchange reserves it holds and increase the supply of foreign currencies on the domestic market, thus preventing a change in the exchange rate.

3.3. Interest Rate Policy

As an element of macroeconomic policy, the interest rate policy plays an equally important role as the exchange rate policy in shaping economic relations with other countries, the two policies being actually closely interrelated.

The interest rate is the relation existing between the charge paid for using capital or the amount obtained for making capital available (as a rule during one year) and the size of the capital. It is an important instrument to influence economic growth, on the one hand, and the balance of trade and the balance of payments, on the other.[13]

The interest rate should be considered from the point of view of both the lender and the borrower. For the former, the interest rate is the measure of the return on making capital available. The lender is thus interested in its highest level. The borrower is in an entirely different situation. Looking for financial capital, he is interested in the lowest possible interest rate. The limit of profitability for both parties is the income rate on production, trade and service activity, current or investment. The higher the income, the more willing the borrower is to pay a higher interest rate. Also the lender, knowing the value of the rate of income from production or investment, demands an adequate interest rate on the lent capital. When the productivity of the physical capital decreases, the borrower loses interest in access to capital, while the lender is ready to accept a lower interest rate on the capital made available.

---

13 Comp. P.R. Krugman, M. Obstfeld, *Międzynarodowe stosunki*, op. cit., p. 47; P. Bożyk, J. Misala, M. Puławski, *Międzynarodowe stosunki ekonomiczne*, op. cit., p. 299.

In a relatively short time, a rise of the interest rate increases the willingness and tendency to save and deposit capital in banks as well as other financial institutions, simultaneously reducing interest in drawing credit as with a fixed rate of profit on economic activity, a rise of the interest rate decreases benefits resulting from the use of credit in conducting this activity. At the same time, however, a rise of the interest rate hampers inflation as the growing interest in saving and depositing income in banks reduces consumption and, consequently, the demand for both domestic and imported goods. Due to a declining demand on the domestic market, producers become more interested in exports. As a result, a rise of the interest rate leads to an improvement of the balance of trade and, consequently, an improvement in the balance of current accounts.

In the long term, a rise of the interest rate exerts a varied influence on the situation in the economy and in the balance of payments. By hampering inflation, it accelerates economic growth, stimulates modernization of production, makes exports more interesting and the supply of domestic goods more competitive in relation to imports. It thus leads to an improvement of equilibrium in the balance of trade. On the other hand, simultaneously, a rise of the interest rate leads eventually to a deterioration of the balance of trade since it diminishes the interest of domestic economic subjects in broadening their activity basing on credit.

A reduction of the interest rate triggers an entirely reverse economic processes.

In the short term, it reduces interest in saving and thus increases demand on the domestic consumer and investment market. As a result, it reduces the readiness of domestic producers to expand exports (due to increasing demand on the domestic market). Simultaneously, it increases the demand for imported goods. In effect, inflation goes up and the balance of trade deteriorates. Meanwhile, on the other hand, a reduction of the interest rate increases the interest of economic subjects in drawing credits for the development of production and investment activity and, thus, stimulates economic growth.

In the long term, a reduction of the interest rate exerts a multidirectional influence on economic growth and balance of trade. Growth of inflation hampers economic growth and adversely affects the balance of trade. Simultaneously, however, the growth of economic activity caused by cheaper credit makes the exports more attractive and increases the competitiveness of domestic goods in relation to imported goods. It, thus, improves the balance of trade.

Summing up, the interest rate policy cannot be conducted unilaterally. For instance, a need to reduce inflation should not mean an immediate rise of the interest rate as it can give rise to long-term negative effects in the form of a weakening of the rate of economic growth and a deterioration of the balance of trade although, in the short term, the balance of trade should improve. Simultaneously, on the other hand, a need to accelerate the rate of economic growth may not be perceived as equivalent to a reduction of the interest rate, since it would result in a rise of inflation and deterioration of the balance of trade.

If banks reduced the interest rate to below the rate of profitability on material capital (the so-called natural rate, also referred to as the equilibrium rate), then the demand for credit would increase to a level exceeding the existing savings.[14] Production and investment activity would then grow to unjustified dimensions, which would push up inflation.[15] Simultaneously, on the other hand, if banks raised the interest rate above the equilibrium rate, then part of the savings would not be used, owing to a decreased demand for credit and the rate of economic growth would drop in an unjustified way while inflation would give way to deflation. Hence the conclusion is that the bank interest rate (referred to as the market interest rate) should be equal to the natural rate (equilibrium rate).

As an inflation-reducing instrument, the interest rate can be used in two ways, direct and indirect. In the first case, the dependence between a change of the interest rate and a change in inflation as well as between a change of the interest rate and a change in market conditions must be determined. In practice, these dependences are hard to determine being, moreover, variable over time.

Consequently, in attaining the inflation-related target, the interest rate is more and more frequently used indirectly, called the strategy of direct inflation target. It was first introduced by New Zealand (in 1990), followed by Chile (1991). In total, in the 1990s, the strategy of the direct inflation target was applied by 17 countries, including Canada, Great Britain, Sweden, Austria, Brazil, Mexico, Columbia, the Czech Republic and Poland. In 2000, the strategy of the direct inflation target was implemented by Switzerland, followed by the European Central Bank.[16]

When a direct inflation target is determined, the principal attention is given not to determining the relation between a change of the interest rate and a change of the inflation rate but to determining a specific level or scope of inflation as the target to which the monetary policy, including the interest rate policy, is subordinated. In this case the interest rate is, thus, one of the elements of macroeconomic policy which serves to attain the inflation target. It plays a generally important role in the achievement of the set inflation target and its future level is determined, as a rule, on the basis of correlations with past inflation.

A side effect of the strategy of direct inflation target is the inability to use the interest rate policy to influence market conditions, its changes being exclusively a result of the implementation of the inflation target. Thus, experience shows (e.g. in Poland) that the attainment of the direct inflation target can be accompanied by a simultaneous decline of economic activity. Therefore, if a reduction of inflation is assumed, the interest rate policy is subordinated exclusively to this target, excluding its possible change with the intention to revive the economy.

---

14 Comp. K. Wicksell, *Geldzins und Guterpreise* (Jena, 1898), p. 9.

15 M. Kucharski, S. Raczkowski, J. Wierzbicki, *Pieniądz i kredyt w kapitalizmie*, 2nd edn (PWE, Warsaw, 1973), pp. 408–409.

16 Comp. P. Szpunar, *Polityka pieniężna. Cele i warunki skuteczności* (PWE, Warsaw, 2000), pp. 183–96; W. Siwiński, 'Bezpośredni cel inflacyjny i kurs walutowy', *Ekonomia*, no. 5, 2002, p. 3.

In practice, a change of the basic interest rate (discount rate) by the central bank can be (but need not be) accompanied by a change of the interest rate by commercial banks. As a rule, commercial banks change the interest rate on deposits immediately, while the interest rate on credits is changed later. Moreover, significant differences exist between the two rates, the interest rate on deposits being lower than the interest rate on credits.

Indirectly, the policy of a change of the interest rate exerts a significant impact on the interest of foreign capital in investments in a given country. A real growth of incomes on deposits in the domestic currency encourages foreign capital to make deposits in this currency and, conversely, a decline of real incomes on deposits in the domestic currency contributes to an outflow of foreign capital. Consequently, the balance of capital turnover changes, followed by the balance of payments. A comparison of the income possible to be achieved in virtue of interest requires, however, knowledge of the predicted changes in the exchange rates of individual currencies and relations between these changes. Devaluation of a given currency (the same as its appreciation) leads to a reduction of the real income on deposits in a given currency, independent of the interest rate and, conversely, revaluation (like appreciation) leads to a growth of the real income on deposits. This is followed by an increase or a decrease of interest in holding deposits.

3.4. Monetary Policy

Money is all and any means of exchange and means of payment, the ability of which to pay is unlimited both when goods or services are bought and when financial liabilities towards a creditor, a bank, central budget, local budget, and the like are settled. It performs an essential role both in the economic policy of individual countries and in their foreign economic policy.[17] As a measure of value, means of circulation, means of payment and means of accumulating reserves, money facilitates the process of exchange, also including international exchange. Without money, the scale of this exchange would be much smaller and its costs much higher. Simultaneously, money facilitates the development of other forms of economic activity, including production, scientific and technical research, and the like. Without money, cooperation in production, investments, science and technology on an international scale would be impossible.

In a market economy, the monetary policy is pursued by the central bank.[18] Its primary functions include the emission of money and regulation of money supply. It also holds the cash reserves of private banks and extends loans to them. The central bank settles state expenditure, gathers state treasury funds and gives the state different loans in case of need. Finally, the central bank holds the foreign exchange reserves of the state and is responsible for the exchange rate of the domestic currency in relation to other currencies.

---

17 Comp. M. Nasiłowski, *System rynkowy*, op. cit., p. 246.
18 J. Kaja, *Polityka gospodarcza. Wstęp do teorii*, (SGH, Warszawa, 2001), p. 80.

In conducting the monetary policy, the central bank avails itself of two methods, direct and indirect.[19] In the first case, it applies administrative instruments such as setting the interest rate, the exchange rate, the size of deposits or credits, or other restraints imposed on commercial banks. In the second case, it applies market instruments affecting the behaviour of subjects on the financial market.

Direct instruments guarantee high effectiveness in reaching the set targets of the monetary policy. Their drawback is, however, the fact that they lower the efficiency of the financial market. Look, for instance, at credit limits applied when the interest rate proves an instrument insufficient to regulate the demand for credit.

Indirect instruments are taken advantage of when the monetary market is well developed and balanced and the role of the central bank consists solely of stimulating individual segments of the monetary market and not of posing barriers to specific transactions. The principal indirect instruments of the monetary policy of the central bank include obligatory reserves, open market operations and credit-deposit transactions.

Simultaneously, central banks of individual countries monitor the volume of cash money as well as bill of exchange deposits drawn by private banks, since excess of money in circulation in relation to the supply of goods and services gives rise to inflation expressed in price rises. A deficit of money in circulation causes deflation (limiting effective demand), decline of prices and halt in economic growth. Both these phenomena adversely affect the economy, each of them having a different impact on the balance of trade.

Within a short time, the excess of money in circulation and inflationary phenomena connected with it exert a negative influence on the balance of trade. Exported goods become relatively more expensive and less competitive while imported goods are relatively cheaper and more competitive. A deficit of money in the economy acts in the opposite way, contributing to the improvement of the balance of trade. These are, naturally, short-term effects. In the long term an excess of money can improve the balance of trade accelerating the rate of economic growth, while a money deficit can worsen the balance of trade, thus weakening the rate of economic growth.

It is thus clear that monetary policy in an open economy cannot be pursued without taking into account the need to ensure balance of trade equilibrium. When a deficit of the balance of trade tends to show a long-term upward trend, the central bank should not pursue a deflationary policy, raising simultaneously the value of the internal currency in relation to foreign currencies (appreciation or revaluation of the currency). In a converse situation, when surpluses in the balance of payments tend to grow in foreign trade, the central bank can pursue a policy of difficult money (money shortages) contributing to the growth of the value of money in relation to other currencies. This is particularly true of a situation when there is a need to combat inflation.

Failure to take account of the needs of equilibrium in the balance of trade (or in the balance of current accounts with other countries) in the pursued monetary policy

---

19 P. Szpunar, *Polityka pieniężna*, op. cit., p. 59.

(for instance, giving priority to combating inflation rather than to the need to ensure equilibrium in the balance of trade) can lead to a collision between goals of internal and foreign economic policy and, in consequence, to mounting costs of economic growth.

The monetary policy can undergo some adjustment when external equilibrium is determined not only by the balance of trade or other components of the balance of current accounts but also by the balance of capital turnover and, thus, on the assumption of international mobility of not only goods and services but also factors of production, in particular, capital. The monetary policy must be closely linked to the interest rate policy, the exchange rate policy, the price policy and the income policy.[20] For example, a rise of the interest rate causes a decline of the demand for money while a rise of prices causes a reverse situation. Thus, the monetary policy pursued in the first case should differ from the policy pursued in the second case.

To sum up, a rational monetary policy is a very complex and difficult task. It must reconcile the needs of the internal economy and those of external equilibrium, the needs of economic growth and those of counteracting inflation.

3.5. Fiscal Policy

Fiscal policy is the shaping by the state of taxation rules and, consequently, affecting the structure of people's income and expenditure. In most general terms, direct taxation and indirect taxation, can be distinguished: the former covering income tax, property tax as well as tax on legacies and donations while the latter covers value-added tax, excise duty, customs duty and other charges.[21] Both types of taxes can perform different functions.

Direct taxes levied on individual income as well as income from enterprises reduce their ability to finance consumer and investment expenditure. On the other hand, they increase the consumption and investment abilities of subjects subsidized by the state budget. In this way the structure of demand changes. By paying income tax, individual taxpayers as well as corporate-tax payers reduce their demand for some goods while the state allocates the obtained budget revenues to creating demand for other goods. Assuming that higher taxes are paid by subjects with the greatest income, this reduces their consumption demand for goods from the so-called upper end of the market (including luxury goods). The fact that the state subsidizes mass consumption, health care and the poorest groups of society from the budget increases the demand for basic kinds of goods. The income tax paid by enterprises decreases the possibilities of the latter to increase output and investments, increasing, on the other hand, state expenditure on these purposes. However, these are not the same products as the state most frequently develops infrastructure, which is, as rule, not done by private enterprises.

---

20 See P.R. Krugman, M. Obstfeld, *Międzynarodowe stosunki*, op. cit., p. 71.
21 Comp. J. Kaja, *Polityka gospodarcza. Wstęp do teorii*, op. cit., p. 83.

Indirect taxes are also an instrument to change the structure and size of consumer and investment demand. They push up prices of individual goods and services in a different way, thus contributing to diversification of demand, with higher tax rates reducing demand more than lower tax rates. The state can, therefore, use indirect taxes to stimulate the demand for some goods and stifle the demand for others. Simultaneously, higher indirect tax rates increase state budget revenues to a larger extent, thus creating redistribution possibilities.

The policy of reducing taxes (direct and indirect) for subjects in the highest income categories increases, primarily, their investment abilities (assuming that consumption needs in these groups are fully satisfied), and, thus, contributes to a growth of production and investments. In the long term it, therefore, leads to increased export possibilities and reduced imports, since quantitative growth of production, its technological and qualitative modernization constitute the best way of improving the balance of trade.

Simultaneously, the policy of reducing taxes for subjects with the lowest income leads to increasing their consumer demand. It, thus, contributes in two ways to a deterioration of the balance of trade, firstly through a growth of demand for domestic goods, which decreases exports and, secondly, through a growth of demand for imported goods. At the same time, the balance of trade deteriorates in the long term due to a growth of inflation.

From the point of view of the balance of trade equilibrium, the policy of reducing taxes for subjects with the highest income and raising (freezing) taxes for subjects with the lowest incomes would, thus, be the best solution. This policy, in the form of a flat tax rate, has been introduced in a number of countries (for instance, in Russia). To pass from tax rates differentiated and progressive in relation to the level of income, to a flat tax rate is a most complex issue, due to social opposition.

3.6. Income Policy

Income policy is the influence of the state on the real incomes of the population and, thus, on wages, non-wage incomes and prices.[22] This policy can be conducted in a direct or indirect way.

Directly, the state can notably influence the public sector, setting the wage rates in force as well as prices of goods supplied by this sector. This concerns, in the first place, the section of the public sector that is monopolized. One of the forms of the policy of direct state influence is minimum and maximum prices fixed, for instance, for foodstuffs. This policy can also affect the private sector. Apart from prices and wages, the state can, moreover, shape directly the non-wage incomes of the population, including old age and disability pensions.

Prices and wages in the private sector are regulated by the state indirectly, taxes being the most important instrument in both cases. A policy preventing the

---

22 Comp. ibid., p. 91.

infringement of free market principles, in particular counteracting monopolization, is also of significance. The instruments applied to this end include customs duties as well as para- and non-tariff instruments. They can serve the state to reduce competition, which helps maintain a high level of prices, or they can help increase competition forcing domestic producers to reduce prices. Instruments of indirect influence on prices also include charges and surcharges of different types, purchase by the state of production surpluses which destabilize the market (primarily farm products), and the like.

The income policy of the state remains closely linked to foreign economic policy. By preventing a growth of prices on the domestic market, the state can enhance the competitiveness of exports and, hence, its growth at the same time offsetting an excessive growth of imports. Thus, the income policy contributes to an improvement in the balance of trade. The wage policy of the state can also affect the balance of trade. The policy of reducing the growth of wages favours improvement in the balance of trade while the absence of such a policy exerts a reverse impact.

3.7. Budget Policy

Budget policy is a derivative of all the remaining elements of macroeconomic policy, including the exchange rate policy, the interest rate policy, the monetary policy, the fiscal policy, the income policy. Therefore, there must be, by assumption, full harmony between these policies.

Budget policy is the influence exerted by the state on revenue and expenditure, regardless of the level of the political and administrative structure. The budget is the state's financial plan, for the implementation of which executive bodies are responsible. Approved by an act of parliament, the budget is a binding directive for the government, at least as regards expenditure, because its level cannot be exceeded without authorisation.

Budget expenditure comprises, on the one hand, the financing of those sectors of the economy, the development of which falls directly within the scope of state duties and, on the other hand, subsidizing the social sphere. In some market economy countries, the state budget subsidizes also selected economic activity in which private subjects are reluctant to become involved.

Budget revenue comprises direct taxes, namely, personal income tax and corporate tax, as well as indirect taxes imposed on goods paid by their buyers.

In the case of a budget deficit, that is when expenditure is higher than revenue, the principal aim of the state policy is to balance the budget by eliminating excessive expenditure or obtaining additional revenue. The most commonly used form of covering a budget deficit is, however, a loan contracted by the state, being a form of public debt. Loans of this type can be taken directly on the credit market or take the form of the issuance of securities sold subsequently also on this market. Another practice consists of selling state bonds to the central bank. All this encumbers the expenditure side of the state budget. Put differently, public debt is nothing but cumulated expenditure from the past, too high in relation to revenue, which encumbers the budget in the future. Unfortunately, expenditure on public debt service does not help pursue any policy (economic, social, foreign economic policy, and the like). Public debt service is part of so-called stiff expenditure on which the government has no influence.

Evaluation of public debt requires identification of the elements of the past budget deficit. Such a deficit can have its roots in excessive budgetary expenditure on maintaining central organs of legislation (parliament and president), executive bodies (government and ministries), public security and national defence sectors, as well as on education, health care, culture and science. Moreover, public debt can result from excessive social expenditure (old age and disability pensions, unemployment benefits, and the like). Finally, public debt can be the consequence of exorbitant subsidizing of state-owned and private subjects (assuming the form of an industrial, technological, structural policy, and the like).

Counteracting the accrual of public debt requires, therefore, restriction of all the above-mentioned or only selected types of budgetary expenditure, on the one hand, and an increase of budgetary revenue, usually through higher taxes, on the other. The choice of possibilities depends on many factors. A reduction of expenditure on maintaining legislative or executive power depends on the their size and consent for reduced spending of this kind (e.g. for reducing remuneration received by parliament deputies, members of government and state administration of other levels). Economies in education, health care and culture depend on the level of development of these sectors. It should be borne in mind that, in the long term, economies of this type bring about a number of adverse effects. A reduction of expenditure on public security and national defence depends on the condition of internal order and security as well as external obligations (for instance, from participation in pacts or defensive agreements). Economies in the social domain give rise to social discontent and may lead to a loss of legislative and executive power. Finally, cuts in expenditure on subsidizing economic subjects adversely affect the growth of production and exports.

Two entirely different approaches to budget policy can thus be noticed in the long term – the first emphasizes reduction of expenditure, especially on social purposes and subsidies for economic subjects, and the second seeks possibilities of ensuring budget equilibrium in taxes (high and effectively levied).[23] Both solutions have their merits and drawbacks. The former, creating possibilities of reducing taxes, favours accelerated economic growth but leads to the pauperization of part of society. The latter prevents social anomalies but exerts an adverse effect on economic growth.

Simultaneously, these entirely different solutions have a different impact on the development of economic relations with other countries, in particular, on the balance of trade.

A reduction of expenditure on social purposes has a positive effect on inflation and balance of trade as it decreases demand, including the demand for imported goods.

---

23 Comp. ibid., p. 90.

Thus, it offsets growth of prices and creates potential possibilities for increasing exports.

A reduction of expenditure on subsidizing economic entities (e.g. on export subventions) has a positive effect on inflation, though it simultaneously limits export possibilities, exerting a negative influence on the balance of payments.

At the same time, a reduction of expenditure has a positive impact on long-term growth, provided the reduction concerns people with the highest incomes. A reduction of taxes for social groups with the lowest incomes contributes to a growth of inflation and has a negative impact on the balance of trade.

A growth of budget expenditure on social purposes under conditions of a concurrent growth of taxes leads, on the one hand, to accelerated inflation and, on the other hand, hampers this inflation. Higher taxes reduce possibilities of financing consumption, while a growth of social expenditure acts in the opposite direction. Simultaneously, a growth of taxes limits possibilities of financing economic growth. Thus, in the long term, it exerts a negative influence on the balance of trade.

Budget policy should, consequently, take into account both the goals of internal policy and the goals of foreign economic policy, both current and long term. The task of harmonizing these policies is extremely difficult and practically impossible because they are mutually contradictory. Consequently, a policy of radical cuts in budget expenditure or a substantial rise of taxes can often lead to undesired changes in the rate of economic growth, in the rate of inflation, in the balance of trade deficit and sometimes even in the balance of payments.

Chapter 4

Microeconomic Instruments Applied in Foreign Economic Policy

4.1. The Concept and Types of Microeconomic Policy

The concept of microeconomic policy is used herein to mean the influence of the state on individual sectors of the economy and occasionally on specified economic subjects. The scope of microeconomic policy covers industrial policy, farm policy, investments policy, technological policy, educational policy, transport policy, environment protection policy, foreign trade policy, and the like.

Microeconomic policy is characterized by its clearly defined addressee and clearly formulated targets. It does not affect sectors and entities which are outside its scope of interest.

Microeconomic policy can serve the attainment of short- and long-term targets. In the former case, the point is to defend the existing position currently occupied by a given economic sector while in the latter the aim is to improve this position. This means that microeconomic policy can be protective or expansive in nature.

Under free market conditions, microeconomic policy is of marginal significance as it is treated as inconsistent with the principles of the system and infringing the logics of its functioning. Nevertheless, in practice, it is applied by many countries, especially when they find themselves in a difficult economic situation.

Microeconomic policy should be closely harmonized with foreign economic policy. In the short term, it is foreign trade policy, one of the sectors of microeconomic policy, that is the instrument to ensure this harmony. In the long term, microeconomic policy should be harmonized with foreign capital, migration, technological and other policies.

Industrial policy involves the influence of the state on the competitive position of individual industrial sectors. It may find its reflection in supporting expansion or in maintaining the existing position of these sectors.

Another form of support may consist of extension by the state of preferential investment credits, facilitation of access to modern technology (through foreign exchange credits or supportive treaty policy). A policy promoting and supporting the development of a given industry should bring about its increased competitiveness on the domestic and international market, among others by improving the efficiency, modernity and quality of the manufactured products.

A conservative industrial policy manifests itself in the protection of production against competition, by subsidizing this production or by preventing the expansion of foreign products. A conservative industrial policy does not prevent in the long term the elimination of the protected industrial production from the market as this production is deprived of any chance to survive under open economy conditions.

The expansive and the conservative industrial policy both should be pursued with internal (domestic) and also external development conditions taken into account. The expansive policy should thus take account of trends in the scope of technological progress and changes in the structure of industry observed in world economy, as well as the need to protect the natural environment, and the like. Conservative policy must bear in mind changes in the structure of demand on the domestic market, size of unemployment, level of production costs in the protected industries, and the like. Conservative policy should be temporary in character.

Farm policy consists of influencing the development of agriculture and its competitive position in relation to other sectors of the economy. It may be geared to maintaining the existing competitive position of agriculture or to improving it. In the first case, one can speak of a conservative farm policy, in the second of an expansive farm policy.

The aim of conservative farm policy is to ensure parity of incomes in agriculture and in industry, which prevents migration from agriculture to industry, to maintain the required level and structure of farm production, to prevent fluctuations of farm products prices. The aim of expansive farm policy is to increase or limit the size of agricultural production, to change the structure of this production, to improve its efficiency and raise its competitiveness in relation to other sectors of the economy. In the case of both conservative and expansive farm policy, the competitiveness of agriculture in other countries is an important point of reference which affects the efficiency of farm exports and imports.

To implement its farm policy aims the state applies a wide array of instruments, including taxes, prices, surcharges, credits, central purchases and storage of farm products, restricting the area of land under cultivation as well as tariff, para-tariff and non-tariff instruments of foreign trade policy. The point is that farm policy must be harmonized with export and import policy, which may find its expression in reducing imports of competitive foodstuffs and supporting exports of domestic farm and food products.

Investment policy involves state influence on the development of individual sectors of the economy. It can generate an accelerated growth rate in one sector and retarded growth rate in other sectors. In this sense, investment policy can be offensive or defensive.

In an offensive policy, the state can avail itself of preferential investment credits, tax relief, credit guarantees, foreign exchange credits, and the like. On the other hand, a defensive policy can take the form of higher tax rates, liberalization of import policy and increased competition on the part of foreign goods, extended depreciation periods, and the like.

Technological policy consists of the state's impact on the directions and rate of technological progress, resulting in diversification of this progress, which implies that it is faster in some sectors and slower in others. Technological policy thus prevents fortuitousness of technological progress.

This policy can assume different forms ranging from support for the development of scientific and technical research, through importing licences and technologies, developing scientific-technical cooperation with other countries, training specialists in different countries, to common scientific and technical research with foreign countries.

In this comprehension an instrument of technological policy is the growth of outlays for scientific research, state policy focusing on financing selected directions of research, selective import of licences and scientific documentation and a resultant growth of foreign exchange expenses.[1]

Technological policy should be harmonized with investment policy and industrial policy as well as with foreign trade policy since it is an instrument of structural changes in production and foreign trade. Hence, it requires concentration on directions of development that create possibilities to improve the competitiveness of domestic products, on the one hand, while taking into account changes occurring in world economy, on the other.

Educational policy involves the influence of the state on the level and structure of education in a given country. The influence can be direct or indirect in nature. Direct influence consists of financing education, issuing decrees determining educational requirements, and the like. The state's indirect influence on the development of education consists of informing the organizers of education on world trends in educational progress, requirements of the economy towards education, and the like.

The state's direct responsibility for the development of education concerns, in the first place, compulsory education. The state is here obliged not only to finance it but also to ensure proper accommodation and staffing. The state also decides on the directions of this education.

A slightly wider scope of the state's direct responsibility concerns the non-compulsory education (secondary and university level). The state partly finances the development of this part of the educational system, takes care of its qualitative level and directions of education (bearing in mind global advances and requirements of the domestic economy).

Educational policy is of a selective character, which means that the state can support the development of some directions of education to a greater extent than others. It can also contribute to the abandonment of specific forms and directions of education.

Transport policy consists of the influence exerted by the state on the development of the transportation infrastructure, production, export and import of means of transport and also on the rules of passenger and cargo carriage. The influence can also be direct or indirect.

---

1 Comp. G. Monkiewicz, J. Monkiewicz, J. Ruszkiewicz, *Zagraniczna polityka naukowo-techniczna Polski; diagnoza, uwarunkowania, kierunki* (Wyd. Ossolineum, Warsaw, 1989), pp. 146–63.

The state can determine directly the structure and forms of transportation links, including road, rail, air, sea and other links, bearing in mind trends in technological development, needs for professional and production activation of specific geographical regions, protection of the natural environment, and the like. By directly affecting the development of transport, the state can finance construction of different communication links, including motorways and expressways, railway lines, airports, railway stations and sea ports.

Indirectly, the state can influence the development of transport through the privatization of part of the transportation infrastructure, crediting the construction of transportation links (e.g. motorways), determining the rules of passenger and cargo carriage, shaping prices and costs of carriage. An important role in this process is played by the introduction by the state of technical and social standards for domestic carriers and foreign firms using the transportation network belonging to a given country. This is achieved through carriage quotas, different types of taxes and other transport-related charges.

Transport policy remains closely related to foreign trade policy, making it easier or more difficult to conduct this policy. The lack of a well-developed road or rail infrastructure, airports, sea ports, border trans-shipment stations adversely affects development of foreign trade, migration of the population and other forms of international links.

Environment protection policy consists of promoting the development of production, consumption and trade in harmony with the environment as well as limiting economic activity having an adverse effect on the environment.

It is thus essential to influence production, so as to eliminate production where effects are difficult or impossible to remove. Bans and commands are the instruments used by the state to reach this goal. When the contamination of the natural environment can be prevented, the state ensures that any production started should be accompanied by the construction of plants and equipment eliminating or significantly reducing the emission of toxic substances, for example, filters counting emission of toxic gases into the atmosphere, sewage purification plants, removal of other post-production wastes, re-cultivation of degraded land, and the like.

Apart from influencing production endangering the natural environment, the state can also limit or eliminate the consumption of goods adversely affecting the environment (e.g. cars without catalytic converters, freon-based fridges, and the like). This is done by bans, commands as well as import policy, credit policy and price policy. Finally, the state can contribute to better protection of the natural environment through its foreign trade policy acting on the flow of goods, capital and people on the international scale, which is expressed in preventing imports of goods having a negative impact on the natural environment, reducing foreign investments which distort ecological balance and counteracting the import of services having a negative impact on the natural environment.

Policy of foreign trade (foreign trade policy) signifies the influence of the state on commodity relations with foreign countries and thus on the volume and structure of exports and imports, on the balance of trade, efficiency, and the like.[2] It avails itself of tariff, para-tariff and non-tariff restrictions.

4.2. Tariff Instruments (Customs Duties)

4.2.1. The Concept and Types of Customs Duties

The concept of customs duties refers to charges imposed by the state on goods crossing the customs border. Customs duty is the equivalent of tax increasing the budget revenues of the state. It raises the price and burdens the consumer (the buyer of the product) with additional costs.

From the historical point of view, customs duty is the oldest instrument of the state's foreign economic policy (more precisely, trade policy). At the early stages of development of foreign trade, it was commonly applied and constituting the main source of budget revenues for the state. In the course of time, its role has diminished.

Customs duties can be divided according to different criteria. In terms of the way of determination, customs duties can be divided into those imposed in proportion to the value of goods, their quantity or also the value and quantity of goods taken together. The importance of individual types of customs duties classified according to this criterion changed over time. In times of good market conditions, the role of value-related customs duties gained importance, while in times of poor market conditions the role of (specific) quantity-related customs duties increased. The state has, thus, been able to influence foreign trade. Nowadays, in connection with a decline of the importance of customs duties and assortment diversification in commodity exchange with abroad, the importance of quantity-related customs duties keeps decreasing in favour of value-related duties (also referred to as *ad valorem* duties).

In terms of the direction of the movements of goods, customs duties can be divided into import, export and transit duties. Import duties are put on goods brought into a given country in order to protect the balance of trade, the level of internal prices or domestic production against foreign competition. Import duties can also be applied for other purposes of the state's economic policy, such as increase in budget revenues (fiscal purposes), as an instrument of discriminating foreign partners or in order to give them preferences. Export duties help the state to shape the volume and directions of exports. They are imposed in the first place on articles that have guaranteed long-term sales on the market of one or more countries (e.g. a given country is a monopolist in their production and export). In particular, this concerns a situation in which a given country uses customs duties to regulate export delivery to the international market depending on the market conditions. In times of poor market conditions when prices display a downward trend, the state introduces export duties to encourage enterprises to export goods with the aim of reducing their supply,

---

2   See above, 2.1. 'Definition and Features of Foreign Economic Policy'.

and thus, contribute to the growth of international prices, on the one hand, and accumulate a larger quantity of goods to be sold in times of good market conditions, at much higher prices, on the other. Naturally, this is possible in relation to goods which can be stored (e.g. raw materials) and their supply to the international market is controlled by exporters from a given country. Customs duty is also put on goods in short supply on the exporter's internal market to reduce their import, frequently at higher prices. Transit duties are charged on goods in transit through a given country. In practice, they are no longer applied, this being banned by international agreements. Moreover, countries are not interested in limiting transit, which can bring considerable profits.

In terms of the functions that customs duties perform in the economy they can be divided into protective and fiscal. Protective duties protect domestic production against foreign competition. This goal is achieved by augmenting the price of the foreign product on the domestic market by the customs rate. The higher this rate is, the more comfortable the position of the manufacturer of the domestic product. Protective duties are applied in particular to protect newly developing production against competition. Application of this duty only makes sense when it is temporary. Over a longer period of time this duty discourages enterprises from technological and technical progress, adversely affecting their prices, quality and up-to-dateness of output. Import duties introduced to protect the level of internal prices are referred to as expansive duties. They are frequently applied when production in a given country is monopolized and customs duties serve to protect the monopoly price. Fiscal duties, on the other hand, are used to provide the state with adequate budget revenues from the import of goods, levied, as a rule, on goods not manufactured in the country and on goods of a relatively low price flexibility. When this is low, the level of customs duties can be higher than when price flexibility is high.

As regards the level of customs duties, they can be divided into minimal and maximal. Minimal customs duties are the duties in trade with countries that enjoy the most favoured nation clause (MFNC), which is given bilaterally or multilaterally in the form of a commitment to treat the partner no worse than another most favoured nation. Once country 1 grants the most favoured nation clause to countries 2 and 3, any reduction of duty made by country 1 in trade with country 2 is automatically transferred to the relations of country 1 with country 3 vice versa. Maximal duties are applied in trade with countries which have not been granted the MFNC. Thus, these duties are, in principle, higher than minimal duties.

From the point of view of the treatment of the partner, customs duties can be divided into preferential and discriminatory. Preferential duties are lower than minimal duties and are applied in trade with countries which enjoy preferential treatment better than guaranteed by the most favoured nation clause. When the preferential customs rate is set at a zero level, the so-called customs preference is said to arise. Preferential duties are an exception to the most favoured nation clause, meaning that countries which have been granted the most favoured nation clause are not entitled to them. An example of such preferences can be found in the mutual treatment of countries belonging to an integration grouping of the free trade area

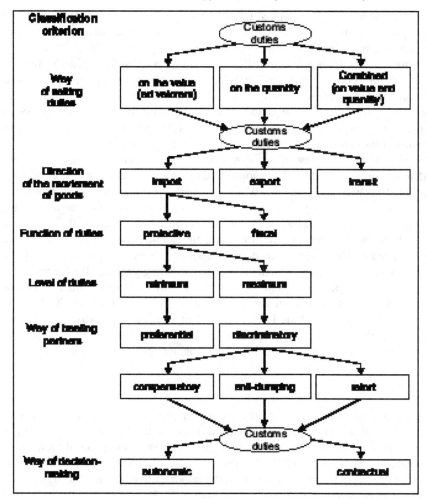

Figure 4.1. Classification of Customs Duties

Source: Author's own elaboration.

or customs union type as well as in the treatment of less developed countries. The preferential duties used in relations with less developed countries can be divided into two groups: those of a lower level – in relation to the least developed countries – and those of a higher level – to the remaining less developed countries. In both cases, basic customs duty is a point of reference.[3] Discriminatory duties are higher than

---

3 Comp. M. Guzek, *Międzynarodowe stosunki gospodarcze. Zarys teorii i polityki handlowej* (Wydawnictwo Wyższej Szkoły Bankowej, Poznań, 2001), p. 220.

maximal duties. They are applied towards countries which are treated worse than average, which means that the discriminatory duty is higher than basic duty. The reasons for the application of discriminatory duties vary, with political, systemic and security considerations heading the list. The most spectacular form of discriminatory duties are retort duties used as a form of retaliation for unfriendly economic actions of a country or a group of countries. Discriminatory duties also include compensatory duties used to neutralize the economic effects of subsidies applied by a foreign exporter. Finally, anti-dumping duties are designed to offset the negative effects on imports of the consequences of exports below production costs.

From the point of view of decision-making, customs duties can be divided into autonomic and contractual. An autonomic duty is introduced by a unilateral, non-consulted decision of a country. While this method seems simple and practically applicable by every country, in reality it usually encounters counteractions on the part of other countries, which offset, in consequence, the effects of the autonomic duty. In the past, the practice of introducing autonomic duties was the main reason for so-called customs wars between two or a larger number of countries, which often lasted for years. That is why autonomic duty is increasingly replaced with contractual duties agreed on between countries. Arrangements of this kind (often taking the form of agreements) determine the level of the imposed customs duty, its duration, item differentiations, and the like. They lead to bilateral or multilateral 'binding' of customs duties, consisting of mutual interdependence between levels and other elements of which the customs tariffs of different countries are composed.

4.2.2. The Economic Mechanism of Import Duties

The introduction of a customs duty on an imported product or raising its level contributes to the growth of the domestic price of the product, thus making it more expensive in comparison with other products. From the point of view of the domestic buyer, this is essential. The payer of the duty is, however, of no importance, whether the foreign exporter or the domestic importer. In each case, the higher price exclusively encumbers the domestic consumer.

The consequences of the rise of the domestic price of the imported product can vary, depending on the flexibility of demand for the product as well as on the possibilities of substituting the imported product with a product manufactured in the country (price flexibility of the domestic supply of import-substituting products).

In the first variant it may be assumed, for the sake of simplicity, that the imported product does not have a domestic equivalent and thus cannot be substituted with domestic production. The economic consequences of the introduction of customs duty (or its increase) in this case depend solely on the level of the duty and on the flexibility of the domestic demand for the imported product. The effect is a drop in demand for this product. The higher the level of the introduced duty, the higher becomes the rise of the domestic price of the imported product and the larger the decline of the demand for it. Simultaneously, the higher the price flexibility of the demand, the greater is the negative effect on the demand.

If *ep* (price flexibility) of demand equals unity, then it is only a rise of duties that gives a drop in domestic demand. This dependence is at the same time directly proportional. The higher the level of the introduced duty, the larger the rise of the domestic price and the larger the drop of the demand for the product.

The introduction of a duty of *AA'* (i.e. raising the domestic price by 20%) will result in a drop of the domestic demand for product *x* of *CC*; with price flexibility equal to unity (*ep* = 1), *CC'= AA'*, and thus a decrease of the domestic demand for product *x* is identical to the growth of the domestic price of the product caused by the introduction of the duty. A further rise of the duty of *A'A"* (i.e. of another 30%) causes a decline of the domestic demand for product *x* of *C'C"*; with *ep* = 1, *C'CC"* = *A'AA"*, that will give a drop of demand of 30%.

It is extremely simple to conduct foreign economic policy (in this case in the form of foreign trade policy). It becomes a little more difficult when the price flexibility of the demand for the imported product is higher or lower than unity.

When the flexibility of demand is greater than unity (*ep*>1), a rise of the domestic price of the imported product *x* of *AA'* (to *OA'*) will produce a decline of the domestic demand for this product of *CC'2*, with *CC'2>AA'* and *CC'2>CC'*.

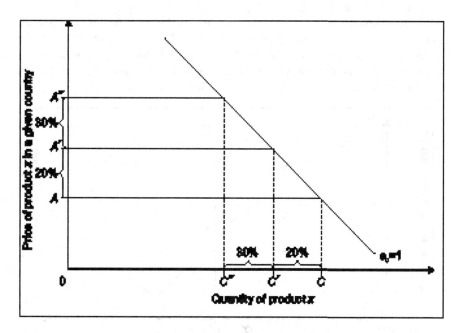

Figure 4.2. The Economic Effects of the Introduction of Customs Duty on an Imported Good with the Price Flexibility of the Demand Equalling Unity

Source: Author's own elaboration.

When the flexibility of demand is lower than unity ($ep<1$), a rise of the domestic price of the imported product x of AA' (to OA') will produce a decline of the domestic demand for this product of $ep'l$, with $CC'l<AA'$ and $CC'l<CC'$. With $ep>1$ and $ep<1$, it is much more difficult to conduct foreign economic policy (foreign trade policy). With $ep>1$, even a slight change of the domestic price produces a significant drop of demand, while with $ep<1$, the drop of demand is insignificant even in the case of a considerable change of the domestic price. This means that in both cases customs duty should be imposed or changed in a more cautious way.

Summing up, a successful customs policy requires the knowledge of the flexibility of domestic demand for the imported product because the customs rate (or the same change of the customs rate) can generate radically different effects on the domestic market depending on the value of this flexibility.

In the second variant we assume that in the country under discussion conditions exist for the development of production competitive in relation to the imported product x. Therefore, it becomes more complicated to conduct a customs policy as it must take into account not only the price flexibility of demand but also the price flexibility of supply (Ep). This flexibility can be equal to unity ($Ep=1$), can be higher than unity ($Ep>1$) or lower than one ($Ep<1$).

Let us assume for the sake of simplicity that both the price flexibility of demand and the price flexibility of supply equals unity ($ep=1$, $Ep=1$). An identical (like in the previously discussed case, change of the domestic price following the introduction of a customs duty or its increase) will, however, produce in this case different changes in the market situation than it was previously. This is illustrated in Figure 4.3.

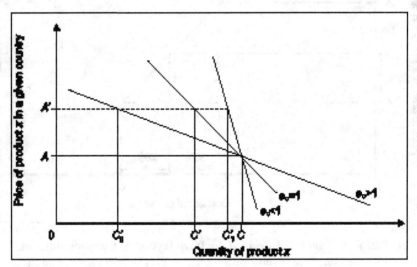

Figure 4.3. The Economic Mechanism of the Import Duty with Assumed Price Flexibility of Demand Higher or Lower than Unity

Source: Author's own elaboration.

With the adopted assumptions, a rise of the domestic price of product *x* of *AA'* (value of customs duty) will produce a decrease of the demand for the imported product *x* of *CC'* (with *CC'= AA'*) and an increase of the domestic supply of this product of *DD'* (with *DD'=AA'*). This means that the proportions of the domestic market supply with imported products and with products of domestic production have changed in comparison with the initial state.

In the initial period the total demand for product *x* on the domestic market amounted to *0C*, with domestic production covering only *0D* of this demand with imports as much as *DC*, that is the majority. A rise of the domestic price of product *x* to *0A'* (of *AA'*) caused a decline of the total demand for product *x* to *0C'*. At the same time, the domestic production of product *x* went up by *DD'* (to *0D'*). Thus, in total, the share of domestically manufactured goods in the market increased while the share of imported goods decreased.[4]

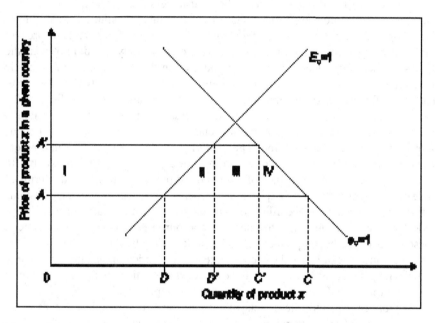

Figure 4.4. Economic Mechanism of Import Duty Assuming that *ep*=1 and *Ep*=1

Source: Author's own elaboration.

The costs of this operation encumbered consumers. Their total loss is defined in the figure as areas marked as: I + II + III + IV. The sum of these areas symbolizes greater expenses incurred by consumers for the purchase of smaller quantities of

---

4   Comp. P.R. Krugman, M. Obstfeld, *Międzynarodowe stosunki*, op. cit., pp. 136–8.

product x ($0C'<0X$). Part of the losses borne by consumers constitutes the income of domestic manufacturers, the remainder being transferred to the state budget.[5]

Producers benefit from their additional profits (marked as area I) resulting from the increase of the production of product x of DD'. If customs duties were not introduced and the domestic price of product x did not increase by AA', domestic production would not increase and would equal $0D$. This would take place if the introduction of the duty led solely to a rise of domestic prices of imported goods. Unfortunately, this rarely happens. As a rule, in such a situation prices of both imported goods and domestically manufactured goods go up.

The state budget receives the additional expenses of consumers marked in the figure as area III. Their size is the product of the customs rate (AA') and the size of the import of product x ($C'D'$). Thus, the higher the customs rate, the higher the budget revenues.

The areas of triangles II and IV reflect customers' losses connected with the commencement of more expensive domestic production to substitute cheaper import (II) as well as the social cost resulting from the reduction of purchases of product x (IV). If the government did not introduce the customs duty and did not raise the domestic price of product x, the incurred outlays on the development of domestic production substituting imported goods could be used more effectively. Therefore, adherents of a free market and free trade believe that consumers' losses defined by the areas of triangles II and IV are absolutely unnecessary and result from the limitation of international trade. It should be, consequently, avoided at any cost. The adherents of protectionism represent a different point of view on this question. In their opinion, the introduction of the customs duty can, first of all, force the foreign exporter to reduce the foreign exchange price of the imported product x. In effect, the terms of trade of the importing country improve. The benefits of the country imposing customs duty on product x include, according to them, the freedom of the state to use increased budget revenues, for instance, to finance social purposes (combat unemployment, for social benefits, health protection, and the like). Finally, the introduction of the duty or the increase of its level can contribute to acceleration of the rate of economic growth and generate additional benefits connected with this growth, in particular in the form of increased employment and reduced unemployment.

No wonder then that the effects of introducing a customs duty are assessed differently by different economic subjects. They are unanimously criticized by foreign exporters, especially those representing highly industrialized countries, offering goods competitive on the world market, since customs duties introduced, in particular, by small and medium-sized countries constitute an obvious loss for them, because they only reduce the market and the resultant benefits. This negative attitude is shared by consumers in the duty-introducing country as they must not only bear increased expenses on the purchase of the duty-encumbered goods but are also offered worse quality domestic goods in the place of better quality imported

---

5   Comp. A. Budnikowski, E. Kawecka-Wyrzykowska, *Międzynarodowe stosunki gospodarcze*, op. cit., p. 234.

ones. The attitude of domestic manufacturers, especially of new goods, is, on the other hand, positive. Without protection against imports, the development of new production in a country with a lower level of development would never be possible. Naturally, this protection must be temporary and short term, allowing the domestic manufacturer to achieve technical, qualitative, marketing and other efficiency.

The introduction of import duty-related benefits and losses discussed above depend on the price flexibility of the demand for product *x* as well as on the price flexibility of the supply of this product. These two types of flexibility hardly ever equal unity and, moreover, are different for different products. That is why, unlike in the previously considered variant, it is first assumed that the price flexibility of demand is changeable. This is shown in Figure 4.5.

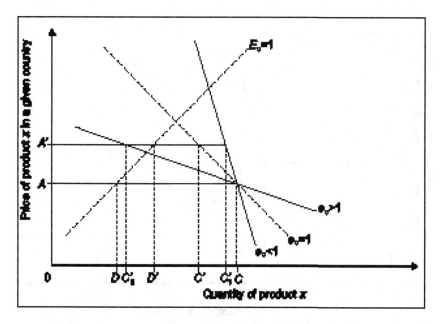

Figure 4.5. The Economic Mechanism of the Import Duty, Assuming a Diversified Price Flexibility of Demand for the Imported Product *x*

Source: Author's own elaboration.

The broken line represents the system of the price flexibility of demand and supply equalling unity transferred from Figure 4.4, while the continuous line represents the price flexibility of demand higher or lower than unity.

When the price flexibility of demand is higher than unity (*ep>1*), a rise of duty of *AA'* produces a drop of demand for the imported product *x* of *CC'2*, with *CC'1>CC*.

As a result, instead of *0C'* of product *x*, the demand absorbs only *0C'2* of the product, with *0C'2* being *C'C'2* lower than *0C'1*.

In the case when the price flexibility of demand is lower than 1 (*ep*<1), a rise of duty of *AA'* produces a decrease of the demand for the imported product *x* of *CC'1*, with *CC'1< CC'*. This decrease is lower than in the case when the price flexibility of demand equals unity. This means that instead of *0C'* of product *x*, the domestic demand absorbs *0C'1* of the product, with *0C'1* being *CC'1* higher than *0C'*.

Put differently, knowledge of the price flexibility of demand for the imported product is essential to conduct the correct customs policy because it is the value of this factor that determines the development of the situation on the market.

Figure 4.6. will in turn present the changeability of the price flexibility of domestic supply.

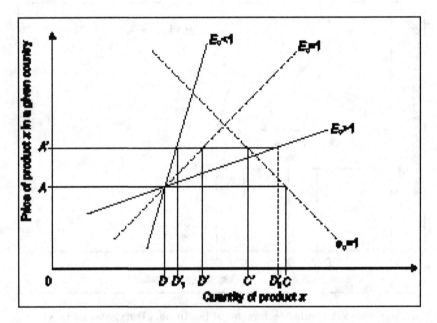

Figure 4.6. The Economic Mechanism of Import Duty, Assuming a Diversified Price Flexibility of Domestic Supply of Product *x*

Source: Author's own elaboration.

The broken lines represent the price flexibility system for demand and supply equaling unity transferred from Figure 4.4, while the continuous lines represent the price flexibility of supply higher and lower than unity.

In the case when the price flexibility of supply is higher than unity (very flexible supply), the growth of the domestic production of product *x* amounts to *DD'2*, with *DD'2>DD'*. In the case when the price flexibility of supply is lower than 1 (poorly flexible), the growth of the domestic production of product *x* amounts to *DD'1* (Figure 4.6).

Put differently, in order to conduct the proper customs policy it is essential to know both the price flexibility of the demand for the imported product which we want to encumber with a new or higher customs duty and the price flexibility of the supply of the import-competing, domestically manufactured product.

Such a mechanism is triggered when the foreign supplier does not reduce export prices in response to the introduction of an import duty and, thus, when the supplier has an alternative internal or foreign market. This concerns, in particular, relations between a big and a small country. To give an example, let us assume that the countries involved are the European Union (EU) and Albania. It would be difficult to expect the EU to reduce prices of the goods they exported to Albania in response to an increase of import duties by that country. The Albanian market is of too small importance for the EU and the latter would certainly be able to find other alternative markets.

The effects of the introduction of an import duty are, however, different when it is a small country that is the foreign supplier, with a big country being the recipient. Let us assume, for instance, that it is Albania that is the exporter and the European Union the buyer of Albanian products. It would be difficult for Albania to find a market alternative to the EU market. That is why it is more than likely that in response to the introduction by the EU of a customs duty, Albania will decide to reduce prices of its goods exported to the EU market. In effect, in spite of the imposition of a customs duty, the internal price on the EU market will not change. This means that the foreign exporter will bear the whole burden of the import duty. The terms of trade for the importing country will improve, on the other hand. This phenomenon is referred to as customs incidence.

Improvement of the terms of trade of the importing country is of essential influence on the balance of customs duty introduction related benefits and losses (compare Figure 4.7).

In accordance with Figure 4.7, with the adopted assumptions, the introduction of a customs duty of *AA'* should be accompanied by a decrease of domestic demand for the imported product *x* of *CC'* as well as growth of the domestic supply of the product of *DD'*. If the foreign exporter is not interested in a change of this kind, they decide to reduce the price of product *x* imported by a given country by *AA''*, with *AA''=AA'*. In effect, the importing country improves its terms of trade and derives from it additional budget benefits amounting to: *AA''* (reduction of the price of the imported product *x*) multiplied by *C'D'* (size of import). Thus, the benefits are the function of the level of the customs rate and the volume of the import of product *x*.

The foreign exporter's readiness to reduce the price of product *x* depends, first of all, on the price flexibility of supply. The lower the flexibility (and, thus, when the flexibility *ep* curve is steeper), the more willing the foreign exporter is to reduce the foreign exchange price of the offered product. Simultaneously, the price flexibility of the demand for the imported product *x* in the importing country is also of significance – the lower the flexibility and, thus, the steeper the curve of the demand, the less interested the foreign exporter is in reducing the foreign exchange price of the offered product and vice versa.

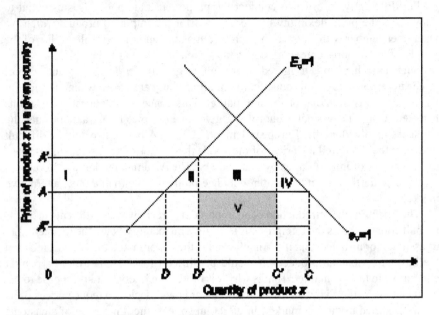

Figure 4.7. Benefits of Customs Incidence

Source: Author's own elaboration.

Put differently, customs incidence appears only in specific economic conditions, namely, when the importer is a large country and the exporter a small country for which the importer's market is of decisive importance and, simultaneously, when the price flexibility of supply is low and the price flexibility of demand is high. If these conditions are not satisfied, the importing country should not expect a reduction of the price of the imported product by the foreign exporter.

4.2.3. Economic Effects of Reducing Customs Protection

Reduction of customs protection can generate far-reaching changes in the structure of foreign trade since it gives rise to the emergence of new flows of trade while, simultaneously, eliminating the existing flows in relations with countries which have not been covered by the reduction of protection. Literature on the subject refers to the economic effects of the reduction of customs protection as to the effect of trade creation and the effect of trade diversion.[6]

---

6   Comp. P. Bożyk, J. Misala, *Integracja ekonomiczna*, (PWE, Warsaw, 2003), pp. 94–6.

The effect of trade creation expresses itself in the growth of the volume of trade among countries that abolished customs protection in mutual trade. Prior to the abolition of this protection all countries used to satisfy their own market demand with domestic production not encountering foreign competition as customs-duty-encumbered imported goods were more expensive. The removal of customs duties meant that own production by more expensive manufacturers became unprofitable due to the possibility of importing cheaper articles from neighbouring countries. As a result, comparative advantages increased and mutual trade grew.

The effect of trade diversion finds reflection in an increased share of the countries that reciprocally reduce customs protection in their overall trade at the cost of the share of other countries which have not been covered (following diversion in the sources of purchase of specified goods from countries with lower costs but higher prices, including customs duty). The diversion effect thus stems from differentiation of the scope of difficulty in access to the market. The countries which have reduced mutual customs protection enjoy easier access than countries which have not been covered by this protection reduction.

The effects of trade creation and trade diversion can appear, in particular, when the countries involved establish a free trade area or a customs area.

A free trade area is characterized by the elimination of customs duties between member countries, with a simultaneous maintenance of autonomy in the determination of customs rates in relations with non-member countries. The essence of the trade creation effect in a free trade area lies in the emergence of a new flow of international turnover following their total liberalization. Certain goods which could not be exported previously when individual countries pursued an autonomic customs policy, their prices including customs duties being higher than domestic prices, become objects of mutual trade in conditions of an established free trade area. Without customs encumbrance they are cheaper than goods manufactured in individual countries. In effect, a new flow of trade develops, the stronger it is, the higher the level of abolished customs duties and the larger the differences in production costs. Let it be assumed that in conditions of an absence of customs preferences, countries 1 and 2 satisfied their needs with respect to product x with their own production, country 2 manufacturing it at less cost. The customs duty imposed by country 1 on the import of this product made it, however, much more expensive (above the production costs in country 1). The establishment of a free trade area changed this situation entirely. Domestic production ceased to be profitable for country 1 as opportunities for less expensive import from country 2 appeared. The effect of trade creation depends on the price flexibility of demand for imported goods and the price flexibility of supply in the exporting country. The higher the flexibility, the better and larger the effect of trade creation.

The nature of the trade diversion effect in a free trade area consists of the growth of the share of the area-establishing countries in their mutual trade, following diversion in the purchase sources of specified goods from countries with even lower production costs, but remaining outside the scope of granted preferences. The effect stems from the differentiation of customs duties. Inside the preferential areas they are abolished, while outside they are still applied.

Let us assume that three countries (1, 2, 3) differ in the production costs of product x. Country 1 has the highest production costs, country 3 has the lowest. Under conditions of lack of a free market area, country 1 imports product x from country 3. When, however, customs preferences appear between country 1 and country 2, directions of trade change. Country 1 stops importing from the previously cheapest country 3 and begins to import from country 2, which is relatively cheaper than country 3 after the abolishment of customs duties.

The effect of trade diversion depends on a lot of additional factors, including the price flexibility of demand and the price flexibility of supply of product x. In the case when the flexibility of demand for product x exported by country 3 is low, the trade diversion effect will be smaller. Consumers on the market of country 1, which granted customs preferences to country 2 within a free trade area will still seek goods exported by country 3, only reluctantly substituting them with import from country 2. In much the same way, in the case of a high flexibility of supply in country 3, the trade diversion effect will be smaller because manufacturers of product x exported previously to the market of country 1 can easily reduce its output or direct it towards an alternative market. Another phenomenon which determines the scale of the trade diversion effect is the customs incidence. The exporter of product x from country 3 on the market of country 1 can reduce the export price by the full value of the customs rate (or its part). The competition conditions will then remain unchanged (or will change only partly) in relation to the situation prior to the mutual extension by countries 1 and 2 of customs preferences within the framework of a free trade area.

A customs union is characterized not only by full liberalization of mutual trade between member countries but also by an additional unification of the level of customs rates in relation to the non-member countries.

In conditions of a free trade area, the trade creation effect and the trade diversion effect can become distorted due to diversified customs tariffs for the same goods in individual countries constituting a free market area in relations with non-member countries. Countries with the lowest customs rates can import part of their goods from non-member countries instead from the countries forming a free trade area. Moreover, these goods can be subsequently re-exported to the countries of a free trade area that have higher customs tariffs in trade with non-member countries. This is likely especially under conditions of an absence of the country-of-origin rules with respect to goods.

A customs union excludes practices of this kind, introducing a uniform customs tariff in relations with non-member countries, which means that both the trade creation effect and the trade diversion effect cannot be distorted. At the same time, the allocation of resources within a customs union improves. In a less effective country, production resources are withdrawn from anti-import production and shifted to other types of production, including pro-export production. Simultaneously, consumption also improves as the level of domestic prices drops (to the level of prices in the customs union). This is reflected in the growth of the volume of goods purchased by consumers within the framework of the customs union and, moreover, not only the goods manufactured by member countries of the union but also by countries from outside the union. This signifies that the trade creation effect within a customs union leads to increased benefits in production, trade and, eventually, also in consumption on the scale of the entire world economy.

In contrast to the effect of trade creation, the trade diversion effect can lead to the deterioration of production and trade conditions both within a customs union and also outside it. The point is that it limits the export possibilities of high-efficiency countries which remain outside the customs union. At the same time, it raises the costs of imports covered by consumers, who are forced to pay more for goods delivered within the framework of the customs union than they would pay were there no customs union. This means that the trade diversion effect within a customs union leads to improvement of the terms of trade only when it creates trade between member countries of the union and also creates rather than limits trade in relations with non-member countries. The latter results in increased imports from non-member countries and, thus, also their exports which trigger the export multiplier mechanism and lead to the development of intra-sector trade.

In practice, however, that happens very rarely, in particular when the non-member countries are small and medium-sized countries. As a rule, the establishment of a customs union is accompanied by the phenomenon of customs incidence leading to an improvement of terms of trade in member countries and a deterioration of terms of trade in non-member countries. Only when the non-member country is a large country of dominant importance in the import of product x, the trade diversion effect need not be accompanied by a worsening of the terms of trade of the non-member country.

4.3. Para-Tariff Instruments

4.3.1. The Concept of Para-Tariff Instruments

The concept of para-tariff instruments of foreign economic policy refers to restrictions on foreign trade which are not customs duties but produce the same effects as customs duties. These are, thus, 'nearly' tariff instruments, starting the same or similar mechanism as the customs duty mechanism. Subventions are the only exception to this definition as they do not generate effects identical with those of customs duties and serve to stimulate exports rather than limit imports.

Para-tariff instruments (with the exception of subsidies) lead to the rise of the price of an imported product and reduce its competitiveness on the internal market of the importing country.[7] In this sense, para-tariff instruments can replace or complement

---

7   See: J. Sołdaczuk, Z. Kamecki, P. Bożyk, *Międzynarodowe stosunki*, op. cit., p 217; A.J. Klawe, A. Makoc, *Zarys międzynarodowych stosunków*, (PWN, Warsaw, 1981), p. 302.

customs duties. This is extremely useful given the fact that the importance of customs duties in foreign economic policy is marginal.

Unlike customs duties, para-tariff instruments are not considered by international trade regulating institutions as complying with the market economy principles and, therefore, in this sense, are illegal. Nevertheless, in practice, they are often applied as being more effective and easier in comparison with customs duties.[8] Moreover, they are not universal in nature, which means that do not concern all participants in foreign trade. As selective instruments, they cover only certain economic subjects and selected goods. This causes them to be treated as discriminatory. A large part of these instruments are applied in an overt manner which makes their exemplification more difficult and increases uncertainty in mutual relations.

Para-tariff instruments are, at the same time, easier to apply than customs duties as any adjustment or change of the customs tariff requires complex and time-consuming legislative procedures at a parliamentary level, while introduction of para-tariff restrictions lies within the competence of the executive authorities. Moreover, the autonomy of individual countries in the scope of the customs policy has been seriously restricted as a result of commitments resulting from membership in international organizations of different kinds. On the other hand, the countries in question often enjoy unrestricted freedom of action as regards para-tariff instruments which are treated as internal barriers used to regulate internal economic phenomena, generating only indirectly effects of foreign trade.[9] This approach generates difficulties in bilateral and multilateral relations between countries reducing or eliminating of these barriers, allowing their discretionary manipulation with the purpose of reaching the desired benefits.[10]

The most important para-tariff instruments include compensatory amounts, fiscal charges, special charges, subventions and others.

4.3.2. Variable Levies

Compensatory amounts (variable levies) are the difference between the lower price of the imported product and the higher, fixed and state-guaranteed internal price of the domestically produced product. The internal price is something of a threshold price, while the import price includes the cost of transport, customs duty and other encumbrances levied on the product carried into the country. The principal aim of variable levies is to raise the price of the imported product to the level of the domestic product price in order to impose equal competitiveness. In other words, the aim of

---

8   Comp. J. Wieczorek, 'Znaczenie środków i barier pozataryfowych dla polskiego eksportu na rynkach rozwiniętych krajów kapitalistycznych', *Monografie i Opracowania*, no. 273, 1989, p. 59 and following.

9   M. Guzek, *Międzynarodowe stosunki gospodarcze*, op. cit., p. 229.

10   See: B. Kiesiel-Łowczyc, 'Protekcjonizm w handlu zagranicznym w teorii i historii myśli ekonomicznej. Przyczynek do analizy polityki handlowej rozwiniętych krajów kapitalistycznych' (University of Gdansk, PhD thesis, no. 18, Gdansk, 1974), p. 92 and following.

variable levies is to prevent the import of a given product at a price lower than the internal price, guaranteeing sustainable profitability of the domestic production of a given product, indispensable and durable in the long-term.[11]

Variable levies are characterized, primarily, by the variability in which they differ from customs duties which should, in principle, be stable during the validity of the customs tariff. The changeability of compensatory amounts is the derivative of price fluctuations on the international market of imported goods.[12] When prices are not reduced, compensatory amounts grow, otherwise they decline because the point of reference, i.e. internal prices, is constant, as shown in Figure 4.8.

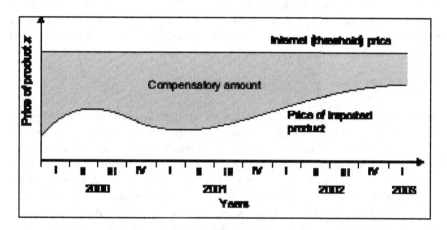

Figure 4.8. Variable Levies in a Given Country under Conditions of a Constant Internal Price and a Variable Price of the Imported Product on the International Market

Source: Author's own elaboration.

Variable levies are applied together with or instead of the customs duty. In the first case, they are imposed when the price of the imported product together with the customs duty is still lower than the internal price. These levies are characterized, primarily, by their high effectiveness in eliminating the competition of foreign products. That is so because in the case of compensatory amounts there is no escape, since any reduction of the price of the imported product only pushes up the compensatory amount while the importer of a customs-duty-encumbered foreign product can only reduce the foreign exchange price by the equivalent of the customs

---

11 Comp. M. Guzek, *Międzynarodowe stosunki gospodarcze*, op. cit., p. 237.

12 P. Bożyk, J. Misala, M. Puławski, *Międzynarodowe stosunki ekonomiczne*, op. cit., p. 320.

duty (which leads to neutralization of the duty). In effect, compensatory amounts lead to fast development of domestic production of goods to which they are applied.[13]

4.3.3. Fiscal Charges

Fiscal charges are applied on goods not manufactured in the importer's country in order to increase budget revenues.[14] The scope of goods covered by fiscal charges includes, in the first place, goods of a low price flexibility of demand. A growth of the domestic price of these goods does not, therefore, limit the demand for them and in some cases even pushes it up. More rarely, the charges are used to protect the balance of payments and, thus, in relation to goods of a high demand flexibility or having domestic substitutes. Charges of this type are, as a rule, levied on so-called luxury goods (high quality cars, perfumes, and the like).

4.3.4. Special Charges

Contrary to fiscal charges, special charges are applied, as a rule, on imported goods having their domestic substitutes. Their principal aim is, thus, to limit imports in order to protect the domestic market and domestic production against foreign competition as well as to maintain balance of payments equilibrium. Special charges are, consequently, used mainly on imported goods which are characterized by a high price flexibility of demand. Special charges include, for instance, consular charges, stamp duty charges, statistical charges, administrative charges and others. That is why these charges are often interpreted as payment for services rendered by the state administration apparatus in favour of subjects dealing with foreign trade. Special charges are at the same time para-tariff barriers only when they are out of proportion in comparison with the state-provided service. Otherwise, they should not be treated as such barriers.[15]

---

13 In the European Union compensatory amounts cover farm and food products, constituting the foundation of the common agricultural policy. Threshold prices there used to change annually while compensatory amounts used to fluctuate practically all the time. Only in 1995, on the basis of international agreements, compensatory amounts in mutual trade between WTO member-countries were replaced with a customs equivalent. They are, however, still used in trade with countries which are not WTO members. In Poland, compensatory amounts were introduced only in 1994. After becoming a WTO member, Poland replaced the compensatory amounts with a customs equivalent. (comp. M. Guzek, *Międzynarodowe stosunki gospodarcze*, op. cit., p. 227).

14 J. Sołdaczuk, Z. Kamecki, P. Bożyk, *Międzynarodowe stosunki*, op. cit., p. 219.

15 Comp. M. Guzek, *Międzynarodowe stosunki gospodarcze*, op. cit., p. 241.

4.3.5. Taxes

Taxes in the importing country can also be regarded as para-tariff instruments when taxes on to imported goods differ from the taxes applied to goods manufactured in a given country. Otherwise they are not regarded as restrictions.

Internal taxes performing the function of para-tariff instruments can, first of all, directly burden the importer's profit. Thus, in formal terms, they do not increase the price of the imported product on the domestic market. In effect, however, they do so although with some delay in respect of subsequent import deliveries since the channelling of part of the foreign exporter's profit to the state budget of the importer reduces interest in exports and tends to push up the price of the product exported to the importer's; in that manner it lowers its competitiveness in relation to domestic goods and eventually eliminate it from the market.

Internal taxes can also be indirect in nature and contribute to reducing the importer's profit by raising the internal price of the imported product. Such taxes become para-tariff instruments when they apply to imported goods only or when taxes on imported goods are higher than taxes on domestic goods. In such cases, internal taxes of an indirect character reduce the competitiveness of imports and favour the development of domestic production. In accordance with the General Agreement on Tariffs and Trade (GATT) rules, indirect taxes can be refunded in the exporting country in the amount imposed by the importer (to avoid double taxation as exporters also pay taxes in their home countries). Such a procedure is, however, not envisaged with respect to direct taxes, exporters exposed to such taxes thus being in a relatively worse situation.

Both direct and indirect taxes can be applied selectively and, thus, with respect to selected imported products (in the case whenever they constitute a threat to domestic production). Apart from these, taxes can also be imposed that encumber all imported goods in the same way (so-called border taxes).

4.3.6. Import Deposits

Import deposits constitute another import-restricting instrument as they make imported goods more expensive on the internal market of the importing country and, in particular cases, exert a positive influence on shaping its terms of trade. The concept of import deposits signifies the state burdening the importer with the obligation to pay into a special interest-free account an amount proportional to the volume of imports. The deposit remains in the account for a definite period of time specified in advance, to be returned to the importer unless aggravating circumstances emerge (e.g. when the importer fails to cover the costs of a claim on the part of the buyers of imported goods). Since the deposits are interest-free, the importer incurs losses as he must commit his own financial resources, resigning from income which they could generate if otherwise utilized. The losses are even greater when the importer does not have his own financial resources and must avail himself of credit, the interest on which increases import costs. All this hikes the internal price of the imported product and, thus, limits the demand for it. Sometimes, to counteract this phenomenon, the importer reduces his own profits, lowering the foreign exchange price. In this way he improves the terms of trade of the deposit-introducing country. Import deposits are diversified in scope. They can encumber a single product or a wide range of imports. As a result, burdening of importers with their negative effects can vary in scope.

4.3.7. Increase of the Customs Duty Assessment Base

One of the para-tariff barriers is also to employ as the base of customs encumbrance the internal price in the importing country instead of the foreign trade price, amounting so an arbitrary increase of the customs duty assessment base. It is practised in a situation when the internal price is higher than the import price. As a result the customs encumbrance on the imported product increases and, consequently, its competitiveness declines. Moreover, the importer is unable to counter a restriction of this kind, since a reduction of the import prices does not create such a possibility and a change of the internal price remains beyond his scope.[16]

4.3.8. Tariff Quotas

Tariff quotas are yet another para-tariff instrument eliminating or lowering customs rates to a specific import level. They define the maximum volume of duty-free import or lower-customs rate import. They may apply to all exporters to a given country or only to some of them (e.g. exclusively from the European Union countries). Exporters from outside the fixed quota must pay standard customs rates applied by a given country on deliveries as a whole. As a result of the application of tariff quotas, the part of imports covered with them is cheaper than the remainder by the value of the customs rate. Put differently, tariff quotas are a form of a privilege determining the size of imports on preferential terms. They do not, however, restrict the size of import at the effective customs rate. This results in the difference between them and qualitative restrictions (belonging to the group of non-tariff restrictions).

Tariff quotas are used, first of all, when the introducing country wants to open only part of its market to foreign exporters, leaving the rest to domestic manufacturers. This can be done when the volume of domestic output does not correspond to the size of the market or in order to supply this market partly with better quality,

---

16 In accordance with the GATT rules (and now the World Trade Organization) an arbitrary increase of the customs assessment base is forbidden. Nevertheless cases of the application of this restriction have taken place, especially in relation to countries which are not members of this organization. The United States, for instance, set on the basis of their internal prices customs duties on chemical products while Canada did the same on potatoes. India and Pakistan also used the same way to set customs duties on a number of goods. While Canada was forced to change this method under the pressure from the GATT, India and Pakistan avoided it. (comp. M. Guzek, *Międzynarodowe stosunki gospodarcze*, op. cit., p. 243.

more advanced or less expensive products. Customs-tariffs-encumbered imported products would not be competitive in relation to domestic products. Simultaneously, the abandonment of customs duties in relation to imports as a whole would restrict the possibilities of selling domestic products.

4.3.9. Standards

Para-tariff restrictions include, in addition, technical, sanitary, veterinary, phytosanitary, ecological and other standards of all types introduced by the importing country. However, they perform their restricting function only when they exceed the universally effective standards forcing foreign manufacturers to bear additional outlays in order to meet enhanced requirements on the importer's market. They push up production costs and prices and, thus, reduce the competitiveness of such exports in relation to domestic products.

Frequently, the importing country introduces the duty to hold special certificates confirming the required standards and issued exclusively by the institutions of a given country, posing a significant difficulty for the importer.

The fact that regulations vary from country to country constitutes particular problems for exporters, and are often contradictory. They must not only be familiar with them but also programme the volume of output diversified in terms of the requirements in proportion to sales possibilities. Another source of trouble is also the changeability of the valid standards proceeding in different directions.

The problem of the unification of standards was first taken up by the Tokyo Round of the GATT. It resulted in the conclusion in 1970 of an agreement on this issue, which lays down that technical standards as well as life and health protection standards should not constitute a restriction to international trade and expose exporters to additional expenses. However, this principle was not recognized as obligatory for all signatories of the agreement. During the Uruguay Round of the GATT some countries reverted to the subject, demanding a wording of the agreement to make it obligatory for the signatories. After long debate, such an agreement was forged and the countries which signed it were bound to adjust their standards to international standards.

The procedure of the unification of standards and regulations on the international scale made it easier for exporters to overcome the barriers involved, though it did not remove their effects on competitiveness in relation to domestic production in the importer's country. On the other hand, the procedure simultaneously encountered a number of difficulties resulting from the need to subordinate national standards to international standards. Some economically developed countries contended that they could not lower their standards bearing in mind the good of customer, the technological level of production and protection of the natural environment. Less developed countries, on the other hand, argued that the adopted international standards were too strict for them. The subject was debated for several years during the Uruguay Round.

4.3.10. Subsidies

The hitherto discussed para-tariff instruments of foreign economic policy concern exclusively imported goods. They are applied to reduce their competitiveness or simply eliminate them from the internal market. Apart from such instruments, the group of para-tariff instruments also includes subsidies. The notion of a subsidy, as used in this text, will denote the assistance granted by the state to domestic manufacturers to lower production costs, to upgrade the technological or qualitative level of production, and the like. Subsidies can be divided into two basic groups: domestic subsidies and export subsidies.

Domestic subsidies serve to maintain or increase the domestic output of a specific product for different reasons (social, defence, technological, ecological) The most frequent reason for their application is, however, to counter imports of substitute products as the subsidizing of domestic production causes a decrease of prices and a resultant increased competitiveness. Also in this regard, subsidies perform a function similar to the function of the remaining para-tariff instruments. The policy of subsidizing domestic production is sometimes referred to as industrial policy. However, it is simultaneously an instrument of foreign economic policy because of its impact on imports.

Export subsidies, on the other hand, serve to improve the competitiveness of exported goods. The notion of export subsidies should be understood as benefits extended by the state in favour of enterprises producing for export and selling their output abroad. They express the difference between a higher domestic price of the product and its lower price on the foreign market. Subsidies include, among others, premiums, exemptions and facilities granted to exporters by the state in order to reduce export costs.[17] Put differently, subsidizing enables exporters to lower prices on the foreign market without reducing their profits (in order to increase the competitive power and the volume of exported products).

Export subsidies are applied for a number of reasons. Firstly, they are used in order to export commodity surpluses which cannot be sold on the internal market and can, thus, generate limitation of output, growth of unemployment, and the like. Secondly, they are applied in order to utilize fully production capacities and growth of employment. A third use is to counteract a balance of trade deficit (through the development of export). The application of export subsidies is also connected with certain negative side effects. First of all, they fuel inflation in the exporting

---

17 See: P.R. Krugman, M. Obstfeld, *Międzynarodowe stosunki*, op. cit., p. 139 and J. Sołdaczuk, Z. Kamecki, P. Bożyk, *Międzynarodowe stosunki*, op. cit., p. 223.

In accordance with the WTO agreement on subsidies and compensatory measures which contains the results of the Uruguay Round on multilateral trade negotiations published in Marakesh (15 April 1994) export subsidies included: a financial contribution of the government or any public institution in the form of a direct flow of means (donations, loans, capital contributions, credit guarantees), cancellation or non-collection of taxes and other encumbrances of this kind, provision by the governments of assets and services. (comp. M. Guzek, *Międzynarodowe stosunki gospodarcze*, op. cit., p. 234).

country. At the same time they also reduce the interest of producers and exporters in reducing production costs, investing in technological progress, raising the quality of production. Moreover, subsidies change proportions in the distribution of the gross national product among different social groups.

Export subsidies affect prices in a way different from the influence of customs duties.[18] Customs duties make the imported product more expensive on a given country's internal market (Figure 4.9) raising its price by the value of the duty and, thus, restricting demand and stimulating the development of domestic production. On the other hand, subsidies make the product exported by this country cheaper on the world market. With the price $0A$, the internal demand on the market of a given country is $0C$ (consumption), production is $0D$ and export CD. If, however the price of product x on the international market is $0A'z$ and is, thus $AA'z$ lower than the internal price, then a prerequisite for profitable export is the obtainment by the enterprise of a state subvention of value not lower than $AA'z$ for one unit of the exported product. If the subvention takes the form of a possibility to raise the domestic price of product x from $0A$ to $0Ak$ and thus by $AA'k$, then a given country witnesses an overestimation of the volume of the demand for and output of product x. The volume of output will increase from $0D$ to $0D'$ (by DD'), the volume of internal demand will decrease from $0C$ to $0C'$ (by CC') and the export volume will increase from CD to $C'D'$ (and thus by CC' plus DD', that is by the equivalent of the growth of the domestic output of product x and the drop of the internal demand for this product) (compare Figure 4.9).

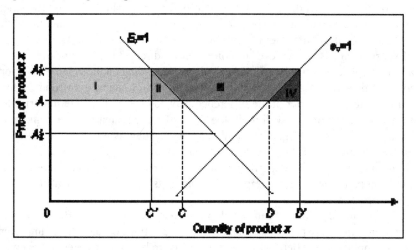

Figure 4.9. The Economic Mechanism of Export Subsidies with $ep=Ep$

Source: Author's own elaboration.

---

18 See A. Budnikowski and E. Kawecka-Wyrzykowska, *Międzynarodowe stosunki gospodarcze*, op. cit., pp. 235–6 and P.R. Krugman, M. Obstfeld, *Międzynarodowe stosunki*, op. cit., pp. 139–40.

How can the balance of losses and gains connected with an operation of this kind be presented? Subsidies benefit producers and exporters first of all, because as a result of subventions domestic production goes up and so do exports (this can be seen in areas II, III and IV). On the other hand, consumers lose (areas I + II) because subventions push up the domestic price of product x. The state also loses (II + III + IV). Areas II and IV reflect disruptions in consumption and production identical to those which can be seen in the case of the introduction of customs duties on imported goods (compare Figure 4.4).

Losses generated by the application of subsidies also include a deterioration of terms of trade. This results from the reduction of the price of product x on the international market from $0A$ to $0Az$ following the appearance of a subvention. The size of these losses depends on the scale of the reduction of the price and volume of exported products x. Apart from the losses incurred by the exporter, there are also losses incurred by the importer (country 2) which are borne by manufacturers of goods competing with those imported from a given country being subsidised by the exporter. Cheaper import eliminates part of the more expensive manufacturers from the market of country 2. It is, however, unfair competition as it does not result from lower production costs in country 1 but from state aid. Consumers in country 2 gain as they can purchase products which are cheaper (though subsidized by country 1).

As long as subsidies bring country 1 benefits in the form of rising exports, country 2 will not introduce customs duties or compensatory amounts (under pressure from its own producers competing with imports). Consumers in country 2 will, on the other hand, benefit from imports (cheaper than domestic production) until intermediaries balance the price of the subsidized product on this market to that from before application of the subvention.

Export subsidies are divided into direct and indirect.[19] Direct subsidies consist primarily in paying exporters specific premiums depending on the volume of exports reached. This is the longest used form.[20] In addition, they can be granted in the form of a refund to the exporter of the difference between the highest internal price and the lowest world price as well as in the form of out-payments towards financing foreign market research, gaining new customers, advertising, and the like. It is characteristic of direct subsidies that they can be easily detected by foreign partners and, in consequence, the importing countries can easily neutralize them with the help of compensatory duties, compensatory amounts or other instruments of foreign economic policy.

Indirect subsidies have been developed mainly to make their detection more difficult and protect exporters against neutralizing actions on the part of importers. They are applied in a variety of forms, some of them being abandoned in the course of time only to be replaced by new ones coming into practice. The general feature of direct subsidies is that they take various forms of exemptions and facilities reducing

19 See: Z. Kamecki, 'Pozataryfowe narzędzia polityki handlowej w kapitaliźmie', in J. Sołdaczuk, Z. Kamecki, P. Bożyk, *Międzynarodowe stosunki*, op.cit., p. 223.
20 A. J. Klawe, A. Makać, *Zarys międzynarodowych*, op. cit., p. 318.

costs of production and making easier to export. Indirect subsidies can be, broadly speaking, divided into three main groups: fiscal facilities, credit facilities and exporters' benefits connected with financing by the state of expenses of a marketing nature.

Fiscal facilities consist primarily of tax relief given by the state to enterprises producing for export or exporting. Their form can be diversified (reduction of tax on wages or profit, reduction of the taxable profit, for instance, due to the granted right to accelerated depreciation). Fiscal facilities also include the refunding to the exporter of the customs duties on the imported raw materials and cooperative elements used in export-oriented production, the right to the development of this production in duty-free zones and the resultant advantages given by utilizing duty-free imported machinery and equipment, materials and semi-finished products.

Credit facilities include, first of all, reduction of the interest rate on credits granted to the exporter by the state or an extended grace period on such credits. In cases when the exported obtained a credit from a private bank, the credit relief can consist of the state covering part of the interest on the credit from budget resources. The state can also give the exporter guarantees in the case when the latter delivers his products to a foreign buyer not for cash but on credit. A possible default on the part of the importer to repay such a credit encumbers the state budget, not the exporter.

The group of subsidies referred to as benefits from the state coverage of the exporter's marketing expenses embraces, in the first place, the organization and funding by the government of commercial centres (e.g. commercial counsellors' offices) which are entrusted with collecting and disseminating information concerning sales opportunities of goods exported by a given country. This group of subsidies also includes the organization by the state of exhibitions, fairs and promotion events of different types, which are geared to promote and facilitate the exports of goods.

Apart from the three basic groups of indirect subsidies, additional solutions are sometimes applied. They are, however, not of a universal character but concern specific situations. One of them can involve a freeze by the state of the level of internal prices. In such a case, the exporter can obtain consent to raise the internal price of the exported product so as to be able to sell the product abroad at a lower price without diminishing his total income. Foreign exchange restrictions constitute another specific situation. The exporter can in such a case receive permission to use part of foreign exchange revenues to finance, for instance, the import of procurement goods (or other goods).

Adherents of a free market and free trade consider all and any subsidies as harmful to the economy as, according to them, they generate net losses to the subsidy-applying country and distort relations of outlays between individual countries, thus reducing possibilities of deriving comparative advantages from global international trade.[21]

GATT and presently the World Trade Organization (WTO) seem to represent a less radical attitude. Though GATT strove to eliminate subsidies, it admitted a number

---

21 Comp. A. Budnikowski, *Międzynarodowe stosunki gospodarcze*, op. cit., p. 206.

of situations in which they could be legally applied. This concerned, primarily, domestic subsidies. The GATT rules (Articles VI, XVI and XXIII) allowed for the application of production subsidies supporting the restructuring of the economy, combat unemployment, level differences in regional development, protection of the natural environment, development of scientific research. There was, however, one essential prerequisite: the subsidies should not infringe the interests of other countries.

On the other hand, GATT provided for much more radical rules as regards export subsidies. Article XVI obligated countries introducing such restrictions to inform partners publicly about their scope and influence on international trade. Whenever export subsidies infringed the interests of other GATT countries, the latter were authorized to apply compensatory customs duties offsetting the action of the subsidies.

GATT's stance was upheld by the WTO, in accordance with which, subsidies can be divided into three groups: forbidden, allowed conditionally and allowed without limitations. The first group includes export subsidies, because, in the opinion of the WTO, they are ineffective for the exporter and harmful to the importer, as well as domestic subsidies, the granting of which is made dependent on the use in production of exclusively raw materials and semi-finished products of domestic origin. The group of conditionally allowed subsidies embraces domestic subsidies which do not infringe the economic interests of other countries and, in particular, those which do not contribute to restricting imports to the subsidies-applying country. Finally, the third group of subsidies (allowed without limitations) involves the state subsidizing research in enterprises, scientific and research entities and universities, the subsidizing of backward regions and natural environment-protecting ventures. A non-discriminatory character is a prerequisite to the classification of a subsidy to the group of unconditionally allowed subsidies. This means that such subsidies cannot be restricted to a given enterprise, branch, group of enterprises or to an industry branch. Anyone who, for instance, starts production which accelerates the development of a backward region will automatically receive a subsidy.

4.3.11. Dumping

Dumping, that is selling a product below the internal price on the exporter's market and, in an extreme case, below production costs in the exporting country, produces effects similar to export-subsidizing. The difference lies in the subject which applies this form of protectionism. While subsidies are government financed and encumber the budget, dumping is financed by enterprises on their own account.

The principal aim of dumping is to gain or maintain the importing country's market by reducing the export price and defeating the competition. On the international market this is regarded to be an unfair practice as it destroys competitors not by increasing the efficiency of production, improving quality or better marketing but by passing the burden of part of production- and sales-related costs onto domestic consumers.

Literature on the subject distinguished three forms of dumping: sporadic, aggressive and permanent.[22] Sporadic dumping is a temporary, often accidental, phenomenon which appears, for instance, when owing to record crops an enterprise wants to sell abroad surpluses of goods above the annually offered quantity when crops are average. It then reduces the export price to attract an additional buyer of good when a perishable is offered. Once a surplus of this kind is sold, the exporter returns to the previous price level. Sporadic dumping is naturally a threat to producers in the importer's country but it soon ends. Domestic producers can urge the government to introduce anti-dumping duties. However, they usually resign from such actions because they are short lasting and do not recur periodically.

Aggressive dumping is a deliberate, well-thought out strategy intended to eliminate competitors from the market, gaining a monopoly position and eventually raising prices permanently. Thus, the initial slump of prices below the production cost changes into an increase resulting in extraordinary monopolist profits. Aggressive dumping is an example of universally condemned, unfair competition, qualifying for the anti-dumping duties.

Permanent dumping is practised by enterprises enjoying a monopoly position on the market, the principal aim being to win new markets, increase production series and thus reap profits. In this case, domestic enterprises keep selling their goods abroad below production costs in order to win additional buyers. This is justified when the price flexibility of demand on the domestic market is below unity (low flexibility demand) while on the foreign market it is above unity (high flexibility demand). In this manner higher prices can be maintained on the domestic market than on foreign markets.

Domestic producers threatened with dumping by foreign exporters strive to eliminate the negative effects of dumping and create equal conditions for competition. This is, as a rule, achieved by means of anti-dumping duties introduced by affected states. The notion of anti-dumping duties covers charges imposed on imported goods to liquidate the difference between dumping prices and prices of these goods on the exporter's market or their production costs plus a reasonable profit. For these reasons, to prove that dumping is practised is extremely difficult, requiring much time and complicated procedure, particularly true when an exporter does not sell his goods on the domestic market.

The effects of dumping vary depending on the economic subject. The benefits, in the first place, go to consumers in the importer's country, in particular, when the dumping-practising foreign exporter does not intend to take over of the importer's entire market and raise prices. Its effects for producers in the importer's country are, however, clear. Dumping is particularly harmful to the importer's country when it constitutes a threat to the development of the domestic industry by decreasing the demand for goods manufactured by this industry, changing of customers' behaviour, and the like.

---

22 Comp. T. Walther, *The World Economy* (John Willey and Sons, New York, 1997), pp. 180, 250; W. Ethier, 'Dumping', *Journal of Political Economy*, vol. 90, no. 31, 1982.

4.4. Non-Tariff Instruments

4.4.1. The Concept of Non-Tariff Instruments

The concept of non-tariff instruments has not been defined explicitly so far. This results from the fact that non-tariff instruments are extremely diversified and numerous, some of them becoming extinct while new ones emerge. In English they are referred to as non-tariff measures, non-tariff barriers, non-tariff restrictions, non-tariff distortions, non-tariff obstacles[23] and the like. In their majority, they are administrative restrictions, other than customs duties and para-tariff instruments. Their function is directly to reduce commodity trade, in particular, in terms of volume. Non-tariff instruments can affect foreign trade only indirectly, through the price mechanism. They avail themselves directly of the form of a command or a ban. Their advantage is they are highly effective.

Non-tariff instruments (like para-tariff instruments) are applied selectively, being thus discriminatory in nature. A decision to impose them need not be made by legislative authorities. The fact that these measures can be adopted by executive authorities considerably shortens the decision-making time and makes them more flexible. A prevailing part of non-tariff instruments is applied discretely, all being applied as internal barriers.

The most important non-tariff restraints include import and export bans, quantitative restrictions, voluntary export restraints, agreements on voluntary export restraints, foreign exchange restrictions, government purchases, trade.

4.4.2. Import and Export Bans

Import and export bans, also referred to as embargos, are the most restrictive form of non-tariff restrains. These bans can be introduced for political, sanitary, ecological, economic and other reasons. They consist of a legal ban forbidding specified trade operations, movement of citizens of a given country or other countries, sailing of ships under a given country's own flag or foreign flags. As a rule, an embargo is imposed for security reasons although there can be other underlying reasons. It appears in periods of political tensions as a result of decisions by the administration of one country, a group of countries or international organizations (including the UN).

4.4.3. Quantitative Restrictions

Quantitative restrictions are less restrictive than an embargo. The notion of quantitative restrictions (often called quotas) refers to a state determination of the volume of imports or exports which cannot be exceeded annually (or over other

---

23 See: J. Wieczorek, 'Znaczenie środków i barier pozataryfowych dla polskiego eksportu', op. cit., pp. 47–8.

period of time). A quantitative quota can be set at a zero level (a ban on imports or exports), it can also be set at a level higher than the actual level of import or export. In the majority of cases, however, quantitative restrictions are set somewhere between the two extremes.

The main reasons for quantitative restriction of imports include protection of domestic production, need to shift demand from imported goods to domestic goods, need to counteract a balance of trade deficit, sanitary considerations or security considerations. Quantitative restrictions in exports are much less frequent. In this case, the main reasons include the need to counter the export of goods in short supply on the domestic market, security considerations (for example, prevention of export of arms to a hostile country), the need to use retaliatory measures against a country which applies unfair practices towards the exporter. Quantitative restrictions can also be an expression of the determination to maintain domestic prices of certain goods at a level lower than world prices.

Quantitative restraints in foreign trade generate effects of two kinds. Firstly, they reduce the supply of imported goods to the domestic market or exported products to foreign markets. Secondly, they usually lead to a growth of prices, in particular, when the demand for the goods subject to these restraints is of a low flexibility, non-tariff restraints being in this aspect similar to para-tariff restraints.

Among the adverse effects of the application of import quotas mention must also be made of tolerance of low-efficiency of domestic production due to lack of or insufficient foreign competition. The introduction of quotas shifts part of production from more efficient foreign producers to less efficient domestic producers. It is ultimately the consumer who is the loser in this case because the consumer must pay a higher price, a better quality imported good being substituted with a domestic good being of poorer quality, as a rule.

Quantitative restrictions can be applied in two forms: global (also referred to as stiff) or bilateral (also referred to as flexible). Global quotas are set by governments autonomically and expressed by maximum import volumes for individual goods from all or some countries. They do not change during the period of their validity. Bilateral quotas are dependent on the partner's concessions and, thus, change over time. Consequently, they are fixed at different levels with respect to individual countries.

In accordance with GATT rules, quantitative restraints were deemed to be more restrictive than customs duties and were thus treated as instruments of foreign economic policy, more disruptive to the functioning of a free market and free trade than customs duties. As a result, quantitative restrains were forbidden by GATT and, hence, GATT's tenacious attempts to convert these restrains into customs duties. Nevertheless, GATT allowed the application of quantitative restraints in exceptional situations, in particular, trade with countries outside GATT. The WTO took over the GATT settlements and tries to put them into practice.

4.4.4. Import and Export Licences

Import and export licences serve to monitor quantitative quotas. The notion of import licences covers permissions issued by state authorities to import a specified quantity of a particular product. As a rule, licences are accompanied by import quotas, though they are sometimes given to exporters when there are no quantitative restrictions in force to allow the state to monitor imports. Occasionally, quantitative restrictions are set but fail to be revealed to the parties interested. This implies import licensing without formal introduction of quotas. Practices of this kind serve to monitor the scope of links with foreign countries and to refuse the granting of a license in case of need.

In a situation when quantitative import restrictions are used, the total of the licences granted to interested enterprises cannot exceed the quantitative quota. The licences are distributed until the fixed limits are exhausted. In practice, the state sometimes halts issuing licences despite the fixed quota not yet being exhausted. In such a case, a quota lower than previously announced is unofficially fixed (e.g. due to a deterioration in the economic situation).

In the short term, quantitative quotas and import licences are highly effective instruments of protecting domestic production against foreign competition, protecting the balance of trade or countering internal market disruption. In the long term, however, they generate numerous adverse economic phenomena. By isolating domestic producers from foreign competition, they lead to less efficient production methods, with higher costs, lower quality and less advancement. Protection of the internal market against foreign suppliers tends to give rise to an upward trend in prices and even to a mounting scarcity of certain goods. On the other hand, protection of the balance of trade remains effective as long as similar instruments of economic policy are not applied abroad.

4.4.5. Voluntary Export Restraints

Non-tariff foreign economic policy instruments include also voluntary export restraints (VER) which are, from the formal point of view, introduced by a country limiting its export. This is, naturally, done at the importer's request. The exporter agrees to such a solution in order to avoid more severe import restraints.

Voluntary export restraints began to be applied in the 1960s and became widespread in the 1970s and the 1980s. There were two reasons for this: massive export of cheap industrial goods from Japan and newly industrialized countries, mainly to the American and West European markets, on the one hand, and an obvious decline of the importance of customs duties in restricting access to the internal market in developed countries due to the fast progressing customs-lowering process (mainly as a result of GATT negotiations), on the other. American and West European industries were, consequently, faced with the necessity to find new instruments and methods to protect themselves against competition. Voluntary export restraints filled this gap very well and, moreover, while not being forbidden by GATT, they were simultaneously very effective.

Voluntary export restraints lead to a reduction of the supply of a given article to the importer's market and, consequently, to a rise of its price. It is, therefore, consumers who suffer most as they are forced to bear higher purchase costs. Foreign exporters are also losers as they must restrain the size of their deliveries and volume of output. This, in turn, has a negative impact on production costs. A positive effect for exporters is that they can raise prices on the importer's market (following the reduced supply). The final result depends, however, on the price flexibility of demand on the importer's market. If it is high ($ep>1$), the price rise creates a danger of losing the market. On the other hand, domestic producers in the importer's country benefit, as the demand for domestic industry products increases following the reduced supplies of imported products and their higher prices.

4.4.6. Voluntary Restraints Agreements

Voluntary Restraints Agreements (VRA) are a form of voluntary export restraints. They concern, as a rule, so-called sensitive goods and are concluded between an exporter and an importer for a period specified in advance. More often than not, the exporter is forced to conclude such an agreement, being otherwise exposed to even more severe restraints (e.g. import quotas).

Both voluntary export restraints and voluntary restraint agreements have not been directly covered by GATT prohibitions (they were not yet in use when the GATT text was agreed). Therefore, for a long time they gave the countries interested in their application much greater freedom of action than quantitative restraints. They were often used selectively, which gave them a discriminatory character. Only in the agreements of the GATT Uruguay Round that came into force on 1 January 1995, both types of 'voluntary' restraints were forbidden. Since that time conclusion of such agreements is forbidden and those set in the past should be abandoned.[24] The prevailing part of 'voluntary' restraints concerns textiles, cars and steel. Interestingly, losses incurred by consumers and the state budget related to the existence of these restraints were in two-thirds of cases transferred in the form of profit to the exporter's country, while in one-third they benefited producers in the importer's country.[25]

4.4.7. Foreign Exchange Restraints

Foreign exchange restraints are another non-tariff instrument of foreign economic policy. The notion of foreign exchange restraints refers to a complete or partial abolition of the freedom of foreign exchange turnover. In times of economic crises,

---

24 See: A. Budnikowski, E. Kawecka-Wyrzykowska, *Międzynarodowe stosunki gospodarcze*, op. cit., pp. 245–6.

25 See: J. Michałek, *Polityka handlowa. Mechanizmy ekonomiczne i regulacje międzynarodowe* (PWN, Warsaw, 2002), pp. 234–6.

especially payment crises, the role of foreign exchange restraints increases, while under conditions of harmonious growth, foreign exchange restraints give way to free convertibility of currencies and their unrestrained international transfer.

Under conditions of foreign exchange restraints, currency transfers on an international scale are subject to monitoring or are entirely taken over by the state, expressed in the obligation to resell foreign exchange earned abroad to banks authorized by the state (as a rule, the central bank). Simultaneously, payments to foreign countries can be made solely after state permission is granted.

The scope of foreign exchange restraints can be diversified physically and geographically. In the first case, they can apply to the total or part of commodity foreign turnover, e.g. one or several commodity groups, while in the second case – to all or only some foreign partners. The scope of foreign exchange restraints is also closely linked to the scope of limitations in the convertibility of the currency of a given country. The latter can be internal or external as well as total. When foreign exchange restraints concern all foreign currencies, all payment titles and all economic entities, the currency of a given country is fully inconvertible (both internally and externally). On the other hand, when the foreign exchange restraints concern selected foreign currencies, selected payment titles or selected economic subjects, the currency of a given country is only partially inconvertible (internally or externally). One can speak of internal inconvertibility when persons, enterprises and institutions of a given country are not freed to exchange their currency into foreign currencies. External inconvertibility is a situation in which foreign persons, enterprises and institutions are not allowed to exchange the internal currency of a given country into other currencies.

Under conditions of foreign exchange restraints, specific forms of international settlements came to be applied, ranging from barter and compensation transactions to payment and clearing agreements.

Barter transactions consist of the exchange of one good for another item. They are made in kind and, thus, without the participation of foreign exchange. A barter type exchange is used in situations particularly difficult for one or both partners, when a shortage of foreign means of payment does not allow for any other form of settlement.

Compensation transactions consist of linking exports and imports of a more than a single article. They can take the form of a full or partial compensation. Full compensation occurs when the exchange is balanced without the participation of foreign exchange. Partial compensation requires the use of foreign exchange to settle part of the exchange which has not been balanced in kind. While allowing the scope of exchange to be widened in relation to barter transactions, compensation transactions do not lead to full utilization of the partners' abilities, limiting them to their weaker side.

Payment agreements allow for some scope of foreign exchange settlements specifying the limit for the transfer of foreign exchange in global terms or according to sector-specified payment quotas. Payment agreements are applied when countries pass from full foreign exchange restraints to the convertibility of currencies. They help systematically increase the share of turnover settled in foreign exchange, simultaneously reducing the part mutually compensated with goods. Eventually, exchange as a whole comes to be settled in foreign exchange.

Clearing agreements consist of settlements between countries by virtue of exports and imports being made in the national currencies of each of the partners to the clearing, These settlements do not involve foreign exchange. They can be bilateral or multilateral. In the case of multilateral settlements, clearing significantly widens the scope of international exchange compared with bilateral clearing, which is limited by the weaker partner's abilities, allowing for multilateral compensation of balances.

4.4.8. State Trade

State trade is a non-tariff instrument of foreign economic policy consisting of state monitoring of the production and sales of certain goods, in particular such as alcohol and alcohol products, tobacco and tobacco products, arms and weapons, among others. The very existence of the state monopoly is not, in itself, a non-tariff restraint. It becomes such a restraint only when the state extends its control into imports and exports, subordinating them clearly to the interests of domestic producers. In practice this means elimination or limitation of sales of imported goods as well as promotion (through subsidies) of the export of domestic industry products. Under conditions of liberal foreign economic policies, the role of state trade has decreased significantly, though in some countries (e.g. newly industrialized or less developed) it still plays a significant role.

4.4.9. Government (Public) Purchases

Government purchases (also referred to as public) can also constitute a serious non-tariff restraint of foreign economic policy. This is, however, the case only when they give preference to domestic goods even if they are more expensive than imported ones.

Government purchases cover budget expenses of government institutions and agendas. They involve the financing of group consumption (social welfare institutions, schools, kindergartens, military) as well as support for loss-making enterprises, for production considered to be growth-oriented, scientific research in strategic sectors (aviation, space exploration, high-speed railways, and the like).

Only rarely does the government approve and announce publicly relevant regulations obligating purchase of domestic instead of imported goods (in order not to be accused of applying discriminatory barriers). Thus, formally, everything is done under conditions of free competition and equal treatment of domestic and imported goods. In fact, however, the government gives preference to domestic goods for a variety of reasons (to combat unemployment, to restructure the economy, to support technical progress).

In some countries (for instance, the United States), regulations explicitly command the government to purchase domestic goods until imported goods become adequately cheaper (imported military equipment must be, for instance, 50% cheaper than domestic equipment to be considered in government purchases). In smaller countries instructions of this kind are not published in order to prevent any accusation of non-tariff restraints in the form of government purchases. Priority is given to goods manufactured in a given country, potential importers not even being informed of an opportunity to submit an offer.

4.4.10. Local Content Rules

The so-called local content rules are yet another non-tariff restraint, committing domestic producers to use a certain specified percentage of raw materials and materials as well as semi-finished products of domestic production. This has a negative impact on import. Where it not obligatory, the domestic producer would certainly use imported components which are frequently less expensive and of better quality.

Local content rules are, as a rule, accompanied by tax relief offered by the state to producers who substitute domestic components for imported ones, in the form of tax exemptions and financial subventions. This is an incentive necessary from the point of view of the competitiveness of the final product. The use of better and cheaper raw materials and materials and, in particular, of more advanced, imported semi-finished products makes the product more competitive than it is when imported components are substituted by domestic ones. Without tax exemptions and financial relief, the final product manufactured with the use of domestic components would require greater protection against imported final products being its substitutes and it would have to be subsidized in exports.

This practice is common in less developed countries where production developed, for instance, on the basis of foreign direct investments makes use of components manufactured by the domestic industry. This is particularly true of car production. Also in Poland, foreign car manufacturers are obligated to use domestic components.

The benefits for a country applying practices of this kind are expressed, primarily, in countering the imbalance in the balance of trade. A country can in this way combat unemployment, increasing the incomes of the population and triggering multiplier effects. The drawback is that it hampers technological progress, which often concentrates only on the production of assemblies, sub-assemblies and parts and, thus, decreases the competitiveness of domestic products on foreign markets. In turn, it slows down the economic growth rate and exerts an adverse influence on the balance of trade.

Local content rules are treated as a manifestation of non-tariff protection which primarily increases the benefits drawn by domestic manufacturers of assemblies, sub-assemblies and parts used for the production of the final product. It ultimately means losses to the state budget, giving financial relief to producers of final products and lowering customs duties on imported components.

4.4.11. Rules of Origin

Whenever application of local content rules encounters difficulties connected with distinguishing between components of domestic production and imported ones, the so-called rules of origin can be used. They find application, notably, within economic areas whose members give one another certain preferences. Rules of origin define what part of the value of the good sold within the grouping must be added within this grouping. The point is to prevent goods imported from countries from outside the grouping from enjoying the preferences given one another by the members of the grouping. Requirements with respect to the share of the value added in the price of the final product vary from grouping to grouping, and are more or less restrictive. In the European Union, this share ranges from 20 to 50% (depending on the product) while in NAFTA the requirements are even more restrictive.

In accordance with the regulations in force, products originating from a given grouping are, first of all, those which are wholly manufactured within this grouping.[26]

Thus, as a non-tariff restraint, rules of origin perform, on the whole, a function similar to that of local content rules. While the main aim of local content rules was to protect one market, rules of origin protect the market of a group of countries. In both cases import is discriminated against whereas domestic production is given preferences. Again the losers are consumers who are deprived of access to cheaper imported goods, often more technologically advanced and of better quality, and also foreign producers whose sales market in the territory of one or more countries is limited. The benefits go to producers from one country or the integration grouping as a whole.

4.4.12. Minimum Export Requirements

Minimum export requirements posed by the state before domestic producers are yet another non-tariff restraint. They are applied by countries experiencing balance of trade difficulties, in particular less economically developed countries. The effect of

---

26 In the European Union the following groups of products are deemed to be wholly generated in the country: goods extracted from the land or from the seabed of a given country, collected plant products, live animals born and bred in the country, products obtained from live animals bred, from hunts, products of sea fishing and other products obtained from the sea outside territorial waters by vessels belonging to a given country, produced onboard factory vessels of a given country exclusively from fish products obtained by that country's vessels, second-hand articles collected in the country for recovering raw materials as well as wastes and scrap resulting from production in the country, goods manufactured in the country exclusively from the above-listed products. (Comp. M. Guzek, *Międzynarodowe stosunki gospodarcze*, op. cit., pp. 273–4).

the application of this restraint is similar to that of dumping. A domestic producer is bound to export and compete on a more difficult international market and does so at the expense of the domestic consumer, raising the price on the domestic market and lowering the export price. Thus, benefits to the domestic consumer decline, while the producer's benefits remain unchanged or even grow.

GATT rules did not cover local content rules, rules of origin and export requirements. At the time when GATT rules were formulated all the three types of restraints were not yet used in practice. The nation clause in force in GATT provided only a general definition of similar cases defending the presence of imported goods on the domestic market. It was only in the 1980s that less developed countries began to apply local content rules and export requirements while the developed countries – rules of origin. Each of these groups had their own interest in and expectations connected with the introduction of these restraints. One of the reasons for the phenomenon was the declining role of tariff restraints. The subject was taken up only by the Uruguay Round of GATT.

Summing up, the number of para- and non-tariff restrictions has grown with the passage of time and, in practice, has not yet been fully listed. Many restraints are concealed from foreign partners, some in the form of internal restrictions, only occasionally to cover imported products. This is connected with the almost complete abandonment by some countries of the use of customs duties, which has created a need for new foreign economic policy instruments. Simultaneously, clear trends have appeared towards the introduction of uniform standards for all participants in the international market, in the form of international policy.

Chapter 5

Globalization and International Economic Policy

5.1. The Concept of International Economic Policy

In comparison with foreign economic policy, international economic policy is a relatively new concept. It first appeared in the middle of the 20th century and has been gaining importance ever since, pushing foreign economic policy to the background.

The concept of international economic policy is understood herein as goals, means and instruments of this policy, similar or uniform on the scale of two or a larger number of countries. International economic policy may be of industry or geographical dimension. For instance, it may be pursued by producers (or consumers) of crude oil, copper, coffee, and the like. Also, the foreign economic policy of countries situated in the same region, for instance in Western Europe, North America or Southeast Asia may be of a uniform character. Numerous common features can be found in the foreign economic policy of less developed countries or highly developed countries as well. Economic policy pursued on a world scale as a whole is referred to as global policy. For the time being, the latter is only fragmentary and concerns selected sectors of the economy or certain economic problems (environmental protection, demographic growth, famine and nutrition, and so on. Attempts at conducting this policy are made by the United Nations Organization and some of its agendas.

The way leading to the development of international economic policy is coordination of the foreign economic policy of interested countries. According to R.N. Cooper, coordination of economic policy on the international scale is when every country adjusts its policy so as to reach its own goals without falling into conflict with the goals of the rest of the world.[1] According to him, the need for coordination can appear in the following circumstances: when there is a correlation between different economies and when uncorrelated actions of some countries would lead to losses in other countries. A transmission of the negative effects of the economic policy from one country to another would then take place, which would give it a character of the 'beggar-your-neighbour' policy. Examples of this can be

---

1   R.N. Cooper, 'Macroeconomic Policy Adjustment in Independent Economies', *Quarterly Journal of Economics*, vol. 83, pp. 1–24.

found in public and private actions increasing pollution of the natural environment, in some circumstances devaluation and other protectionist moves.[2]

Coordination of foreign economic policy can be made ex post or ex ante, and also take the form of a common economic policy.

Coordination ex post is the simplest form of developing international economic policy. It takes place when countries pursuing their own foreign economic policy exchange information about this policy from time to time. This form of developing international economic policy is known as consultations. Information obtained in the course of consultations can be used to make this policy closer. However, individual countries still pursue their foreign economic policy autonomously, though mutually adjusting their goals, means and instruments as the need arises. This very loose form of coordination of foreign economic policy as a rule concerns selected fragments and can be conducted on the scale of a limited number of countries or on the global scale. Thus, neighbouring countries in this way can coordinate environmental protection policy, employment policy and in this context migration policy, and the like. On the global scale, this is used to coordinate the policy of economic growth, of counteracting malnutrition, and the like.

Coordination ex ante of foreign economic policy is a more advanced form of developing international economic policy. In this case, international economic policy is the effect of agreements on goals, means and instruments of foreign economic policy reached in the past.

Coordination ex ante serves to neutralize the negative effects of the economic policy conducted by individual countries and can ensure benefits in place of losses to countries which have coordinated their national policy. Cases are very common of coordination of national economic policy by reaching a compromise when each country benefits with respect to one goal but loses with respect to another, though drawing net benefits. Coordination ex ante can be carried out using different methods. It can be undertaken ad hoc by agreeing on concrete goals (e.g. as regards the scope of tariff, para-tariff and non-tariff restrictions) and also take the form of institutionalized cooperation (in the form of contractual agreements of all kinds). The latter gives coordination a permanent character, to mention but the Bretton Woods System, Special Drawing Rights (SDRs) System, European Monetary System and many others. Some coordination agreements specify long-term recommendations to be followed in the national economic policy. It is for these reasons that institutionalised coordination is treated as a form of developing international economic policy, more effective than ad hoc settlements. It is quite common that ad hoc settlements precede institutionalized coordination or complement it when a change in the external and internal environment requires adjustment of institutionalised settlements.

The scope of ex ante coordination can be geography, problem or time determined. The geographical approach can be seen in the selection of countries interested in conducting international policy. The problem approach is reflected in the subject or

---

2   N. Acocella, *Zasady polityki gospodarczej*, (Wydawnictwo Naukowe PWN, Warsaw, 2002), p. 540.

industry scope of international economic policy. The time approach is expressed in the time horizon of international economic policy.

Common economic policy is the most far-reaching form of coordination of goals, means and instruments of foreign economic policy. Like coordination, it can be of a fragmentary character, concern individual areas of economic policy and, in some cases, this policy as a whole. The time horizon of the common goals can also vary, ranging from short term to long term. The largest number of features of the common economic policy is exhibited by international trade policy, reflected in the concluded agreements of a multilateral character. The scope of these agreements is geographically diversified, covering a few countries, a larger group of countries or all countries. Integration groupings are the best example of a common trade policy pursued by a few or more countries. A common trade policy pursued by a larger group of countries is evident in the policy of WTO (previously GATT), IMF, the World Bank and other such organizations. A policy common to all countries is pursued by the United Nations Organization.

5.1.1. Goals of International Economic Policy

The notion of international economic policy goals will be used to denote priorities in economic relations with foreign countries on the scale of a group of countries, region or globally. These priorities can be similar or common to a specific group of countries (for instance, members of an integration grouping, countries located in one territory, countries representing a similar level of economic development). In the case of economically developed areas such goals can include, for example, removal of the existing barriers to foreign trade (or opposing the introduction of new ones), the export of capital, restoration of equilibrium in the balance of payments and currency stability. In the case of less developed countries, the primary goals of international economic policy will include acceleration of economic growth, reduction of debt toward economically developed countries, improvement of terms of trade, and the like.[3] Some of these goals can be common to all countries, in particular the liquidation of barriers to international trade, reduction of the indebtedness of less developed countries, acceleration of the economic growth rate. The drive towards reduction of the indebtedness of less developed countries is, for instance, in the common interest of all countries, irrespective of the level of economic development, since this indebtedness has a destructive influence on the development of international trade of all countries.

International policy like foreign economic policy, also, has goals of a diversified time horizon, short term, medium term and long term. Market-condition-related goals (such as stabilization of prices, guaranteeing regular deliveries of raw materials and energy, countering a balance of trade deficit, and the like) have a predominantly short-term time horizon. The medium-term time horizon can be seen in attempts

---

3   Comp. J. Sołdaczuk, Z. Kamecki, P. Bożyk, *Międzynarodowe stosunki gospodarcze*, op. cit., p. 184.

to counter restrictions in foreign trade and accelerate economic growth. Structural goals (change of position in the international division of labour, transformation of the structure of production, change of the structure of exports, restoration of equilibrium in the balance of payments) have a long-term time horizon.

The international character of these goals can be seen in their growing similarity in individual countries following consultations ex post, coordination ex ante or finally the adoption of uniform goals by the interested countries. The growing international character of foreign economic policy goals depends on the interest of individual countries and, in particular, the benefits expected derived from such developments. The economic and political position as well as the bargaining power of individual countries is of no lesser significance as in the case of large countries with a major position in the world economy, international policy goals are similar to those of these countries' foreign policy. Small and medium-sized countries must, on the other hand, adjust the goals of their foreign economic policy to those of international policy. To give an example, Poland's accession to the Organization for Economic Cooperation and Development (OECD) was accompanied by subordination of Polish economic policy goals to those of the international policy of this organization, while the accession of the United States to this organization had very little influence on the goals of that country's foreign economic policy, since they mostly remained unchanged.

5.1.2. Means of International Economic Policy

Formulation of the goals of international economic policy does not signify they will be reached, even if foreign economic policy goals are subordinated to them. This is particularly true when a divergence exists between national and international goals. Assuming, for example, that a country is interested in increased foreign exchange revenues from exports of product x, because it suffers from a balance of trade deficit and thus wants to prevent growing imbalance. However, the growth of exports of product x leads to a drop of its international price, which has a negative impact on revenues of all the remaining exporters. To prevent that the interested countries agree to freeze their share in exports of product x at the existing level. While a drop of the international price and a fall of revenues from exports of product x (e.g. crude oil) is thus prevented, country A is forced to face payment difficulties in foreign relations. In exchange, country A can demand assistance from the interested countries in countering disequilibrium in the balance of trade. The organization which associates producers and exporters of product x must, therefore, have adequate means to support country A in countering payment difficulties, as otherwise it will not implement international policy goals when increasing exports of product x.

The concept of means of international economic policy is used herein to denote resources of goods or factors of production serving to reach the goals of this policy, treated in terms of material or value. The means are created from the funds of countries pursuing international economic policy. In this reviewed case, these would be the means created within OPEC (the Organization of Petroleum Exporting Countries) in the form of foreign exchange reserves, from which easy credit would be granted to country A. Sometimes, the means of international economic policy can assume a material form (raw material or capital reserves) easy to convert into finance.

Means of international economic policy can increase or decrease when implementing of the goals of this policy. They can also be used by all or only by selected countries. Finally, means of international economic policy may have to be returned or not by the countries benefiting from them.

Examples of various solutions in this field can be found in international commodity agreements having special funds connected with financing created stocks. Should the need arise, these stocks are sold creating financial means. Reserve funds are also held by the IMF and the World Bank. The European Union uses a special financial budget for this purpose financed by the member states, to support implementation of international policy goals. Practically all international centres pursuing a coordinated or common foreign economic policy in the form of international policy, operate according to similar schemes.

Means of international economic policy prove unnecessary when conducting a supranational policy, decisions taken then obligating member countries to proceed accordingly, instead of issuing recommendations addressed to member countries.

5.1.3. Instruments Applied in International Economic Policy

Apart from means to implement it, international economic policy also needs instruments of international economic policy, understood as instruments of foreign and, frequently, also internal economic policy coordinated by a group of countries, a region or globally. These instruments include, in the first place, international prices (e.g. prices of crude oil set by the OPEC countries), an international currency (e.g. SDRs, the euro) created by international organizations, maximum or minimum levels of tariff, para-tariff or non-tariff restrictions allowed in international trade, bans on exports or imports, and such like.

Instruments applied in international economic policy can be determined internationally or supranationally. In the first case, individual countries enjoy freedom and autonomy in mutually adjusting their policy. International settlements are made by international agreements and accords or through international organizations. The interested countries have the exclusive right to decide whether or not to sign them.

In the second case, the development of instruments applied in international economic policy assumes a supranational character. Taking place within integration groupings or trans-national corporations, the freedom of individual countries is significantly restricted.

5.2. Subjects of International Economic Policy

International economic policy is shaped by several groups of subjects: states, international economic organizations, transnational corporations, international cartels.

In many cases the influence of these subjects on international policy is intertwined. The influence of the state must obviously affect international organizations and transnational corporations just as the influence of transnational corporations, and international organizations is of no little importance for the state.

5.2.1. States

The role of the state in shaping international economic policy has undergone significant change with the passage of time. At the early development stage of this policy, states played a decisive, if not exclusive, role, However, the importance of international organizations and transnational corporations grew steadily. Nowadays, in many cases, the state plays only a secondary role.

This role tends to be, moreover, highly diversified, often dependent to a lesser extent on the size of a given country, its population or natural resources and to a greater extent on political, military and technological factors. Countries with a significant military potential, stable political systems, strong economy, playing an important role in international economic relations, exert a dominant influence on international economic policy since it is these countries which decide about a major part of international economic links. Instruments applied in their foreign economic policy constitute grounds for the development of instruments of international economic policy. This is particularly true of the United States, which plays a fundamental role in the development of the contemporary world international economic policy.[4]

The economically less developed countries with unstable political and social systems, participating in the process of coordinating foreign economic policy and developing international economic policy must immediately adjust to the parameters set by the countries playing a dominant role in the world.

The differentiated position of these two groups of countries is reflected in their role in shaping agreements, influencing the activity of international economic organizations, as well as in the position of their national enterprises in international relations.

States can participate in the development and implementation of international economic policy in two ways: directly, through governments concluding international agreements and accords or, indirectly, exerting an influence on international organizations and on enterprises participating in international cooperation.

International Economic Arrangements and Agreements
International economic arrangements and agreements can be concluded between two countries or a larger number of countries.[5] The agreements serve to define directions and forms of international cooperation, principles of settlements, ways of offsetting balances of trade and balances of payments, rules of credit policy, and the like. Such

---

4   Comp. W. Morawiecki, *Międzynarodowe organizacje gospodarcze. System organizacji międzynarodowych*, vol. 1 (PWN, Warsaw, 1987), pp. 42–6.

5   See: T. Łychowski, *Międzynarodowe umowy gospodarcze*, op. cit., p. 8.

agreements can, simultaneously, determine the ways in which economic policy is to be conducted and its instruments.

The role of agreements, a basic instrument of the state in shaping international economic policy, has evolved in the course of time, bilateral agreements being replaced with multilateral agreements. Moreover, agreements specifying in detail the scope and forms of mutual economic cooperation have given way to framework agreements formulating only basic principles of this cooperation. Finally, short-term, usually annual, agreements have been replaced with long-term agreements. This signifies that in the process of shaping international policy, states resigned from detailed, short-term annual agreements in favour of multilateral, framework and long-term agreements. These are not commodity agreements but economic agreements covering not only commodity exchange but also cooperation in production, finances, credits, science, technology and other fields. They contain, simultaneously, fundamental clauses determining mutual economic relations, and, in particular, reference to the most favoured nation clause, safeguard clauses (e.g. against market disruption), and the like. They differ drastically from traditional agreements and, consequently, they are referred to as economic treaties with increasing frequency.

Treaties on Economic Cooperation
Treaties on economic, industrial, scientific and technical cooperation focus their attention on equal mutual treatment of partners, particularly prevention of discrimination in market access. Treaties serve as a basis for establishing of different institutional forms of cooperation, including free trade zones, customs unions, common markets, and the like. Treaties can also provide grounds for granting countries interested economic preferences, for instance in the form of removal of customs duties or fixing customs tariffs at the lowest possible level. Treaties are also concluded with countries wishing to associate with already existing organizations.

Commodity arrangements
Apart from agreements and treaties on cooperation, states influence international economic policy also through commodity arrangements. The most important government commodity arrangements include international agreements: concerning sugar, cocoa, coffee, wheat, tin and wool. The first of these were concluded in the inter-war period, the majority were after the Second World War. Their participants include states which produce and export agricultural and mineral raw materials and also importers of these commodities. The main goal of their activity is to stabilize prices on the international market.[6]

The stabilization of prices can be achieved in many ways, the most important of which being the creation of a stabilizing reserve, establishing export quotas, reducing imports, and the like. Stabilizing reserves can be in kind or in cash and are created from members' contributions. In the form of cash, they are used to purchase raw

---

6 See: Z.M. Doliwa-Klepacki, *Encyklopedia organizacji międzynarodowych* (Wydawnictwo 69, Warsaw, 1997).

materials when prices of these raw materials on the international market are slipping, exceeding the earlier set bottom safety limit. In their physical form, the reserves are used when prices of raw materials grow and exceed the top safety limit. Part of the reserves are then put on the market to force prices go down.

An arrangement of this type is, first of all, the international sugar agreement signed for the first time in Brussels in 1931 and later in London in 1937. After the Second World War, till 1984, it was repeatedly signed and extended. The aim of the sugar agreement was to stabilize sugar prices on the international market, its instrument being imposition of quotas on the sugar exports. In practice, implementation of the sugar agreement was supervised by the International Sugar Organization, managed by the International Sugar Board. Depending on the level of world sugar prices (above or below the set band), the board changed export quotas to prevent excessive growth or fall of sugar prices. Simultaneously, the agreement obligated sugar-exporting countries to hold sugar reserves and sell them when a drastic surge occurred in the demand for sugar on the international market. Importers were obligated to reduce sugar purchases in countries not being signatories to the sugar agreement. Since 1984 the agreement has been replaced with a loose arrangement without the right to regulate sugar supplies.

Similar goals were pursued by the international cocoa agreement concluded in 1972. It was signed by countries being producers, exporters and importers of this commodity. Its aim was to balance the demand for and the supply of cocoa and, consequently, stabilize prices on the international market. This was to be by setting the minimum and the maximum price for cocoa and establishing a stabilization reserve (buffer stocks) in the form of the commodity and funds for its purchase. The mechanism of the agreement is similar to that of the previously discussed sugar agreement: when the price of cocoa drops below the minimum, funds from the stabilization reserve are used to keep buying this raw material until the price rises above the minimum. On the other hand, when the cocoa price exceeds maximum, material from the stabilization reserve is sold until the price drops below the maximum. The proper functioning of the international cocoa agreement is in the hands of the International Cocoa Organization (established on the basis of the said agreement).

The international coffee agreement was also set up to stabilize coffee prices. The agreement was signed in 1962 by coffee exporters and importers, its aim being similar to that of the international cocoa agreement, that is to maintain a balance between the supply of and demand for coffee. Export quotas are the principal instrument used to reach that. When coffee prices exceed the minimum or maximum level, export quotas change. On their part, importers are committed to limiting coffee purchases. Implementation of the coffee agreement is the responsibility of the International Coffee Organization, including the International Coffee Board.

Another arrangement: the international wheat agreement was concluded in 1933. After the Second World War a few such agreements were signed. In 1968 the wheat agreement was replaced with a grain treaty covering not only the principles determining international trade in grain but also a special convention on food aid.

The aim of the international wheat agreement is to stabilize world market prices by ensuring balance between market supply and demand. To this end, importers are committed to buying a specified quantity of wheat while exporters are committed to selling a specified amount when the world price exceeds the minimum or the maximum level provided for in the agreement. In case the price falls the minimum level, importing countries are obligated to purchase wheat at the minimum price from exporting countries until they exhaust the quotas set for them or until the price on the market rises above the minimum level. In the reverse case, when the price goes above the maximum level, exporting countries are committed to selling wheat to importers at the maximum price until exhausting the quota fixed for them or until the market price drops below the maximum level. The signatories of the wheat agreement have not yet reached consensus with respect to the creation of buffer stocks. Implementation of the international wheat agreement is handled by the International Wheat Board.

The international tin agreement was also concluded between exporters and importers of tin. It was first signed in 1931 and for the sixth and last time in 1982. The 1982 agreement remained in force for seven years. Its aim was to maintain balance between world market demand and supply.[7] It was to result in the stabilization of tin prices on international markets. As in the sugar agreement, stabilization reserves and export control were the instruments applied in the stabilization of prices. The international tin agreement led to the establishment of the International Tin Board responsible for implementation of subsequent tin agreements.[8] The board ceased to perform its functions in 1985 due to its inability to counter the growth of the world tin price above the maximum level, despite selling the entire stock of the metal from the stabilization reserve.

The international arrangement on wool had the same purpose as the above agreements. It was concluded in 1929 and led to the establishment of the International Wool Organization, associating producers and exporters of woollen yarn and textiles. Its role is limited to coordinating production and trade in woolen yarn and textiles. Unlike other raw materials agreements and arrangements, it takes no actions which would directly stabilize prices on the international market but attempts to limit their fluctuations by acting on wool-consuming production.[9]

5.2.2. International Economic Organizations

The declining role of individual countries in shaping international economic policy is accompanied by a growth of the importance of international organizations in this process.

---

7   See ibid., p. 226.

8   Ibid., p. 227.

9   Comp. P. Bożyk, J. Misala, M. Puławski, *Międzynarodowe stosunki ekonomiczne*, op. cit., pp. 336–9.

As subjects of international economic policy, international economic organizations can be divided into two groups: universal organizations and group organizations.[10]

Universal organizations encompass all or almost all countries. Participation in these organizations is voluntary and stems from the need to resolve problems requiring cooperation on the part of many countries. Economic problems of this kind include nutrition, economic growth, protection of the natural environment, technological progress and access to this progress, reduction of international debt, and the like. The universal character of international economic organizations is conditioned by not only their formal but also actual accessibility for all countries irrespective of their different levels of economic development, economic structure, economic potential, and the like.

Unlike universal organizations, group organizations are characterized by limited membership.[11] They associate only certain countries which meet special requirements. The selection criteria for members of such organizations are often formulated explicitly in their articles of association but most frequently follow directly from the aims and principles of a given organization. This concerns, in particular, organizations of an integration character. Integration groupings are guided primarily by the regional criterion, linking countries in the same area or at a distance not too remote from this area. They often pose requirements as to the level of economic development, complementariness of structures, and such like.[12] Gaining access to integration organizations is a long-term process and involves meeting a large number of political, social, institutional, production, technological conditions, etc. It usually proceeds in stages, starting from loose association and finishing with full membership.

The United Nations

The United Nations Organization (UN) is the main universal subject of international economic policy.[13] The UN is concerned not only with a large number of issues of a political character, concerning to peace and security. Economic questions also account for a significant part of this organization's activity, tackled in particular by two UN bodies, namely, the General Assembly and the Social and Economic Council.

The General Assembly is an international plenary body attended by representatives of all member states. At its ordinary, special and extraordinary sessions the General Assembly discusses almost all questions concerning the international economic

---

10 W. Morawiecki, *Międzynarodowe organizacje gospodarcze*, op. cit., pp. 83–7.

11 A.B. Kisiel-Łowczyc (ed.), *Współczesna gospodarka światowa* (Wydawnictwo Uniwersytetu Gdańskiego, Gdansk, 1997), pp. 45–8.

12 See: ibid., pp. 45–8.

13 See: K. Michałowska-Gorywoda, W. Morawiecki, J. Mulewicz, *Międzynarodowe organizacje gospodarcze. Główne organizacje powszechne i grupowe*, vol. 2 (PWN, Warsaw, 1987), pp. 5–23; A. Marszałek (ed.), *Gospodarka światowa* (Łódź, 1993), pp. 38–9; E. Latoszek, M. Proczek, *Organizacje międzynarodowe. Założenia, cele, działalność* (WSHiFM, Warsaw, 2001), pp. 62–98.

policy. Two special sessions of the General Assembly of the UN were devoted exclusively to economic issues, namely, the sixth session in 1974 and the seventh session in 1975, focusing on the developing principles of the New International Economic Deal. Among the resolutions then adopted there are two which are of particular significance The Declaration on the Establishment of the New International Economic Deal and The Charter of the Economic Rights and Duties of States.[14] Both attempted to subordinate the principles of international economic policy to the needs of less developed countries. The point was to extend to these countries a number of customs preferences in international trade, to increase the flow of financial aid from the developed countries to the less developed countries, to provide assistance in the industrialization of the less developed countries and so on. The idea underlying both these declarations was that the less developed countries should become the principal subject of international economic policy. The declarations both date from the very beginning of the raw-material-energy crisis initiated by a significant rise of crude oil prices, when the interest of the whole world was focused on the less developed countries.

The Social and Economic Council of the UN was established by virtue of the United Nations Charter as the body responsible exclusively for economic matters. It now associates 54 countries, its decisions taken by an ordinary majority of votes being of a recommendation character. The General Assembly chooses subsequent members. The division of member countries into individual regions is precisely defined. The Social and Economic Council issues part of its recommendations directly, though recommendations concerning major issues should be approved by the General Assembly. These major issues include actions taken by the Council in economic development and international cooperation. Since the Social and Economic Council deals with a wide range of issues, it has established several auxiliary bodies, including regional economic commissions, among others the European Economic Commission (EEC). The European Economic Commission is made up of all European countries as well as the United States and Canada. The primary attention of the EEC focuses on coordination of the member countries' foreign economic policy.

The General Assembly, the Social and Economic Council, regional commissions and other UN institutions concentrate on the ex post coordination of foreign economic policy providing a platform for the exchange of information between countries related to the pursued foreign economic policy. This is primarily the exchange of information in the widest possible extent, embracing all countries. It is, consequently, general in nature, focusing on such macroeconomic problems as growth, unemployment, nutrition and hunger, pollution of the natural environment and so on. The recommendations elaborated by the General Assembly, the Social and Economic Council or the regional commissions are thus also general in nature and do not obligate the member countries to subordinate to them. They inform governments on current development trends and the resultant consequences for the

---

14 See: K. Michałowska-Gorywoda, W. Morawiecki, J. Mulewicz, *Międzynarodowe organizacje gospodarcze*, op. cit., pp. 11–12.

future. The information is, therefore, often helpful and useful to governments and other subjects of foreign economic policy in making economic decisions.

There are a number of so-called specialized organizations connected with the UN. They include the IMF, International Bank for Reconstruction and Development (called the World Bank), WTO (and previously the GATT), and the United Nations Conference on Trade and Development, among others.

The International Monetary Fund
The IMF is an organization which plays a particularly important role in shaping international economic policy. It was established under an agreement reached by 44 countries during the Monetary and Financial Conference of the United Nations, held in Bretton Woods (in the US state of New Hampshire) on 1–22 July 1944. In accordance with the concluded agreement, the major aim of establishing the IMF was to restore free multilateral trade on the global scale. The instrument which was to help reach this goal was to be the introduction of internal convertibility of national currencies and stability of exchange rates. To this aim, the IMF undertook a variety of actions involving member countries, for example, the extension of credits to countries experiencing difficulties in balancing their balances of payments and the influence exerted on national economic policies to make them work towards reaching these balances.

It was the United States that was particularly interested in introducing convertibility of national currencies and stabilization of exchange rates (especially in Western Europe). The Second World War left the United States economically strengthened, with a strong internal currency, ready to introduce its convertibility into other currencies. Unfortunately, the domestic currencies in the remaining countries remained inconvertible and prospects for the early restoration of this convertibility were nowhere in sight, due to the enormous war destructions suffered by their economies. Moreover, there were fears that, in order to rescue their balance of payments, the countries in question might return to the practices of inter-war period, which took the form of recurrent devaluations of national currencies, high inflation and other negative phenomena. The IMF was to prevent such a danger, offering its member countries credit assistance to maintain equilibrium in the balance of payments, however, at the cost of sacrifices on the part of those countries in the form of adjusting the level of domestic consumption to the possibilities of their economies, development of export-oriented sectors of the economy and increasing exports, with long-term prospects for repayment of the debts incurred earlier.

The establishment of the IMF was simultaneously part of a wider economic programme designed to develop a new economic deal, in particular a new trade deal, based on resignation from setting of barriers to international trade, free flow of goods between countries and payment balance.

The principles of the IMF introduced in 1944 remained effective till 1969. In that period gold and the US dollar constituted the Fund's reserve means. However, rapid development of dollar-based international exchange in confrontation with a relatively slow growth rate of gold output gave rise to difficulties in the exchange of the American dollar to gold in relations between central banks (the convertibility of the dollar into gold by natural and corporate persons was suspended in the inter-war period). As a result, a new reserve means, the Special Drawing Rights (SDRs), was introduced as of 28 July 1969. Their parity was set at 0.888671 gram of gold and, thus, at the parity level of the American dollar. However, SDRs were not convertible into gold in relations between central banks.

Starting from July 1974, the value of the SDR was based on a basket of 16 currencies of the IMF members whose share in the world trade exceeded 1%. Between 1981 and 1998 the basket came to be composed of five (instead of 16) currencies (the US dollar, German mark, Japanese yen, French franc and the pound sterling). Since 1999 the basket is made up of four currencies: the American dollar (39%), the euro (32%), the Japanese yen (18%) and the pound sterling (11%). The value of SDRs is set daily on the basis of stock exchange quotations. They have the form of non-cash currency and do not require any physical coverage. The member countries decide on the value, time of emission, way of distribution and use of the SDRs by a majority of 85% of votes. The SDRs can be used to balance payments deficits, to conclude futures contracts, extend loans and settle other liabilities.

The introduction of the SDRs did not prevent the collapse of the Bretton Woods currency system in 1973 following the devaluation of the US dollar. In 1971 the United States suspended the dollar's convertibility into gold between central banks (due to difficulties in covering the demand for gold). Work to reform the international monetary system lasted till 1978. The new principles entirely eliminated gold as a means of accumulating reserves and offsetting balance of payments imbalances. Gold was replaced with the SDRs.

To sum up, during its existence the IMF prevented the pre-war currency anarchy being passed on to the post-war period. The system elaborated in Bretton Woods contributed, in the first place, to helping West European countries introduce in 1959 the internal convertibility of their national currencies, thus easing their balance of payments difficulties. The effects of the IMF policy with respect to the less developed countries troubled by recurrent currency crises, heavy foreign indebtedness, high unemployment and inflation were much less spectacular.

The International Bank for Reconstruction and Development
The International Bank for Reconstruction and Development (IBRD), commonly known as the World Bank, was established at the 1944 Bretton Woods United Nations Monetary and Financial Conference, the same which established the IMF. The basic tasks of the IBRD included supporting economic development and countering poverty in the less developed countries. In practice, it was to mean financing the reconstruction of Western Europe from war destruction and crediting autonomic investments aimed to initiate growth (primarily in less developed countries) which were of no interest to private capital as being of little profitability and which were, on the other hand, treated as preparing the way for such investment in the future. The first group of these tasks soon lost its validity owing to the assistance received by Western Europe under the Marshall Plan on much more advantageous conditions

than those offered by the World Bank. Thus, the main attention of the World Bank was directed to credit assistance for less developed countries experiencing balance of payments difficulties due to low economic growth rate, lack of an export-oriented sector etc. The investments financed by the World Bank included, notably, infrastructure-oriented ventures, including construction of roads, power stations, irrigation systems, schools and development of agriculture.[15] Simultaneously, the World Bank tried to encourage private investors to allocate their capital in those countries in which it financed autonomic investments by extending guarantees, participation in loans among other things.

The role of the World Bank has changed little since then. Nowadays, the Bank gives greater attention to supporting economic reforms, protection of the natural environment and supporting the private sector. This is accomplished through crediting ventures which enable the implementation of these targets, coordination of various forms of credit assistance directed to the countries being in the scope of interest of the World Bank, extending credit guarantees and offering the services of World Bank experts.

The World Bank is an international institution of a joint-venture character, with all its shares held by the member countries. The founders of the World Bank included 44 countries but nowadays their number approximates 200. The operations of the World Bank are financed from the Bank's own resources and from external funds borrowed by the Bank on the international credit market (for example, through the issue of bonds). The Bank also extends guarantees for loans contracted by the governments of the member countries, their banks and enterprises (with government guarantees) in commercial banks.[16] The World Bank is an institution complementary to the IMF, with the World Bank focusing on financing economic development in the less developed countries and the IMF extending loans to any member of the Fund, developing and less developed, suffering from balance of payments problems. Thus, in principle, the World Bank grants long-term loans while the IMF extends short-term loans.[17] Both these organizations play a significant role in shaping international economic policy, having at their disposal enormous financial resources and availing themselves of the principal instruments of international economic policy, such as the international currency and the international credit. The role of both these institutions increases in the course of time.[18]

The European Bank for Reconstruction and Development

The European Bank for Reconstruction and Development (EBRD) was established in 1990 (on the initiative of the French president, F. Mitterrand) as an institution

---

15 See: K. Zabielski, *Finanse międzynarodowe=* (Wydawnictwo Naukowe PWN, Warsaw, 1998), p. 315.

16 J. Sołdaczuk, *Współczesna gospodarka światowa. Struktura, mechanizmy, tendencje* (PWE, Warsaw, 1987), p. 57.

17 Comp. E. Latoszek, M. Proczek, *Międzynarodowe organizacje*, op. cit., p. 11.

18 See: K. Zabielski, *Finanse międzynarodowe*, op. cit., p. 324.

financing the economic development of Central and Eastern Europe countries. The principles of its organization and functioning resemble those of the World Bank. Thus, it is a joint-stock company associating 60 shareholders (58 countries as well as two institutions: the European Community and the European Investment Bank).

The primary aim of the EBRD is to support the transformation of Central and East European countries as well as the countries of the former Soviet Union, by financing economic ventures in compliance with the direction of this transformation. This concerns, notably, support for the development of the private sector and the financial sector with the help of the share Bank's capital,[19] made up of own and borrowed funds. The EBRD uses these funds to finance capital investments and offer credit guarantees. Loans of up to 5 million euro are extended for a period of 5–10 years, the public sector obtaining a credit for even 15 years. The interest rate on the credit is based on market principles.

The General Agreement on Tariffs and Trade
The General Agreement on Tariffs and Trade, established in 1947 and converted in 1994 into the World Trade Organization, was of exceptional significance for international economic policy. Its establishment was to prevent a return to protectionism in international trade – a widespread phenomenon in the inter-war period. GATT was a byproduct of the establishment of the International Trade Organization.

The United States, interested in the liberalization of international trade, in 1946 suggested establishing the International Trade Organization. Emerging victorious from the Second World War, with an extensively developed industrial potential, the United States faced difficulties with placing its production on the market, having switched its production potential from military to civilian purposes, since the American market was proving too small. Hence, the interest of the United States in growing exports. On the other hand, Europe, like other regions of the world, faced the destruction of the Second World War with unlimited needs but only slight export possibilities. Thus, to balance their balance of payments, European countries had to exert strict administrative control over imports and support exports.

The aim of the International Trade Organization was to achieve general liberalization of international trade, abolish all and any forms of discrimination and ensure all countries free and equal access to the market and to raw materials. Members of the International Trade Organization were to grant one other an unconditional most favoured nation clause and pledge gradually to reduce tariffs, lift quota restrictions and other para- and non-tariff barriers to international trade. The international conference convened in Havana (from November 1947 to March 1948), bringing together 56 countries, and resulted in the elaboration of the articles of agreement of the International Trade Organization (known as the Havana Charter) and in the formulation of the basic principles of development of international economic

---

19 This capital which amounted to 10 billion euro on the establishment of the Bank, is being constantly raised, amounting in 2003 to 29 billion euro.

relations, including the principles of concluding commodity agreements, principles of trade policy, and so on. These articles of agreement were signed on 24 March 1948 by 54 of the participants in the conference (except for Argentina and Poland). They were, however, ratified only by Liberia. The reason was the divergence of trade interests, particularly between the United States and the remaining signatories of the Charter. It was obviously still too early for liberalization of international trade in global terms.

The process of evolvement of the International Trade Organization was accompanied by negotiations on reducing customs tariffs in international trade, conducted by 123 countries which took part in creating the organization. The negotiations took place in Geneva in 1947 and concerned most important commodities. They resulted in agreeing on a list of so-called tariff concessions. Despite failure to ratify the International Trade Organization, the mutually negotiated concessions caused a temporary agreement to be signed which was to lose its effectiveness once the Havana Charter came in force. The agreement was called the General Agreement on Tariffs and Trade, adopted on 30 October 1947 and becoming effective on 1 January 1948 after signing by major participants in international trade. The International Trade Organization has never been ratified and so the GATT transformed from a temporary into a permanent agreement and remained in force for almost half a century.

The GATT had at its roots the logics of free trade and the conviction that liberalism was superior to other solutions in foreign and international economic policy.[20] Gradual elimination of barriers to international trade should lead, according GATT, to better utilization of the factors of production held by individual countries, acceleration of the growth rate of international trade and consequently to the growth of social prosperity. The principles of GATT presented in the preamble were thus based on the classical and neoclassical theory of international trade which assumed non-transferability of factors of production under conditions of an entirely free flow of goods on the international scale.

In accordance with the agreement, customs tariffs constitute the main restrictions to international trade and, thus, trade liberalization was to signify the gradual reduction of customs rates.

The document formulating the principles of procedure of the member countries consisted of four main parts. The first (Articles I and II) gave particular attention to the most favoured nation clause, the second focused on the national clause, the third (Articles XXIV–XXXV) on exceptions to application of the general principles and the fourth part on trade preferences.

The functioning of the General Agreement was based on four basic principles. The most important was the principle of non-discrimination consisting of the obligation of member countries to treat equally all partners belonging to GATT. This meant that any trade privilege given to one country was automatically extended to all member countries. Thus, the most favoured nation clause within GATT assumed a multilateral

---

20 See: A.B. Kisiel-Łowczyc (ed.), *Współczesna gospodarka światowa*, op. cit., p. 302.

character. This is said explicitly in Article I of the General Agreement. Moreover, it was of an unconditional character, which meant that all GATT members received privileges granted to others without any additional restrictions or requirements. In effect, the results of bilateral negotiations were automatically extended so as to cover all GATT countries. This constitutes departure from the inter-war practice when such an automatic extension of bilaterally given privileges to other countries did not take place although they also enjoyed the most favoured nation clause. This was particularly true of the United States. The multilateral principle of the most favoured nation clause was particularly advantageous for the less developed countries that obtained customs rates reductions as the outcome of negotiations between countries, without having to make concessions. They were, thus, called free riders. Simultaneously, however, economically strong exporters used this instrument to seize new markets, multiplying their incomes by virtue of growing production series and increasing scale of export deliveries.

The second, in terms of importance, was the principle of reciprocity. In accordance with it, GATT members were not obligated to grant concessions without obtaining reciprocal concessions from partners. That is why negotiations involved mutual exchange of equivalent concessions. In compliance with the reciprocity principle, countries newly joining GATT were obliged to hold negotiations with the member countries and grant them customs concessions equivalent to the concessions earlier granted each other by GATT countries. The General Agreement did not specify measures of the reciprocity of concessions. In initial negotiations the role of such a measure was performed by the scope of trade covered by tariff reductions, in subsequent ones it was the possible growth of trade taking into account the price flexibility of demand for the negotiated goods. In practice, most countries applied the criterion of the scope of trade covered by tariff reductions or the average level of the reduction of customs tariffs. Whenever the criterion of the scope of trade was adopted, the involved countries negotiated tariff reductions in one group of goods in exchange for tariff reductions in another (product by product).[21] After agreeing on the average level of customs rates reduction, the countries proceeded to agree on the general formula of percentage liberalization and applied it to all groups of goods.

Another important GATT principle is the national clause understood as the need to treat an imported product in the same way as a product manufactured domestically (Article III). This principle referred in particular to customs liabilities and regulations concerning sale, purchase, transport, distribution and use of the products on the home market, the purpose being to ensure non-discriminatory treatment of imported goods on the internal market. Consequently, after paying customs duty and being admitted to the internal market of a given country, the imported product should be treated in the same way as the domestic product. It should only differ in its price, quality, technical level, utility values, and the like, the choice being left to the consumer.[22]

---

21 Comp. J. Michałek, *Polityka handlowa*, op. cit., p. 122.

22 Comp. J. Kaczurba, E. Kawecka-Wyrzykowska (eds), *Polska w WTO* (Instytut Koniunktur i Cen Handlu Zagranicznego, Warsaw, 1998), pp. 20–23.

GATT principles also include exceptions to the principles of free trade The main exception here was the possibility to apply quantitative restrictions although GATT stated explicitly that only customs duties could be applied and allowed for the application of customs rates higher than the level negotiated by GATT countries only in the case of the necessity to protect the balance of payments or a 'young' domestic industry, to guarantee the security of the state or the health of the population. The application, additionally, of quantitative restrictions was allowed by GATT only when the application of protective customs rates did not bring the desired effects in countering the balance of payments deficit, protection of domestic industry, protection of the country's security or the health of the country's population.

The so-called 'grandfather' clause was the only exception. It permitted countries to maintain their national trade regulations differing from the GATT provisions contained in the General Agreement at the time of its entry. Put differently, a country acceding to GATT could simply not accept these regulations.

Another exception to the application of the general rules of the agreement was exempting the integrating countries from the obligation to grant most favoured nation clauses to countries from outside the integration grouping. For instance, countries setting up a free trade area or a customs union did not have to extend their mutual customs preferences to all other GATT countries, Also, trade between former colonies and the metropolis covered by mutual customs reductions or their elimination constituted an exception to the application of the General Agreement rules.

The main exception to the reciprocity principle was, however, the so-called Generalized System of Preferences. It exempted GATT member countries from transferring the preferential rates given to the less developed countries to other countries. The less developed countries, on the other hand, were not obligated to reciprocate with preferences.

Apart from these exceptions, all members of the General Agreement on Tariffs and Trade were obligated to subordinate their economic policy to the principles of international economic policy, common to all member countries. This concerned, in the first place, subordination of foreign trade policy.

GATT members were obligated to apply a uniform customs policy and to resign from para- and non-tariff instruments, in particular, from quantitative restrictions. In compliance with GATT principles, the tariff policy created conditions of transparency. Customs rates could be compared and negotiated on reciprocity principles, while other restrictions did not satisfy this condition.

Negotiations on the reduction of customs tariffs were held in the course of trade negotiations called rounds. There were eight such rounds.[23] Each succeeding one was longer, since the number of countries participating in the negotiations, as well as the list of goods subject to the negotiations, kept growing. The negotiations were an instrument of liberalizing international trade as they led to the reduction of customs

---

23 Comp. *Międzynarodowe organizacje gospodarcze i ich role w Unii Europejskiej* (Biblioteka Przedsiębiorcy, Centrum Informacji Europejskiej UkiE, Warsaw, 1998), p. 10

rates and obligated the participating countries not to raise customs tariffs above the level agreed in the course of the negotiations.

The first round of GATT was held in Geneva in 1947 and was attended by 23 countries. It had the character of bilateral negotiations between the main supplier on the 'product for product' basis. In total, the negotiations covered 44% of the overall value of world trade, with customs tariffs being reduced by 21.1%. The results obtained in the course of bilateral negotiations came to be extended, in compliance with the most favoured nation clause, to all GATT members. The negotiations did not cover, however, so-called 'sensitive' goods and, thus, goods for which import was a particular threat. This concerned especially foodstuffs and farm products, textiles, steel and steel products as well as coal and coal derivatives (e.g. coking coal). Excluded from the negotiations were also goods provided mainly by producers and exporters from countries not participating in the negotiations.

The second round of GATT was held in Annecy (France) in 1949, bringing much more modest results than the first round. Although it was attended by 33 countries, its negotiations covered only 3% of international trade and resulted in a reduction of the average level of customs duties of a mere 1.9%.[24] In the course of the first round the countries gave one other approximately 45,000 customs concessions, but the number extended by them during the second round was almost ten times lower and amounted to a mere 5,000.

The third round of GATT was held in Torquay (Great Britain) in 1951. This time the number of participating countries increased to 38 but the negotiations covered only 9% of the value of world trade leading to a 3% rate of tariff reduction. In total, 147 bilateral agreements were signed and 8,700 concessions were granted.

The fourth round of GATT was held in Geneva in 1956 and brought together 26 countries. The tariff reductions covered 11% of world trade with a 3.5% tariff reduction rate.[25] In total, 56 bilateral agreements were signed.

The fifth round of GATT (called the Dillon Round) was held in Geneva in the 1960–1. It was attended by 45 countries, with negotiations covering 14% of world trade. Yet, the obtained rate of customs tariffs reduction was not impressive and amounted to 2.4%. In total, the countries extended to each other 4,400 customs concessions which covered 11% of world trade.

The attention of the round focused primarily on evaluating the economic effects of the creation of the EEC on the growth of international trade. The United States was particularly interested in this evaluation as it feared the external customs tariff common to the EEC as a whole. It was also the United States that put forward the proposal to renegotiate this tariff.

Discussion on this subject was continued with particular intensity during the fifth round of GATT held in Geneva between 1964 and 1967. The negotiations were

---

24 Comp. J. Kaczurba, E. Kawecka-Wyrzykowska (eds), *Od GATT do WTO. Skutki Rundy Urugwajskiej dla Polski* (IKiCHZ, Warsaw, 1995), p. 16 and A. Budnikowski, *Międzynarodowe stosunki gospodarcze*, op. cit., p. 259.

25 Comp. E. Latoszek, M. Proczek, *Organizacje międzynarodowe*, op. cit., p. 259.

attended by 48 countries and covered 64% of the value of world trade, giving a customs tariffs reduction rate of as much as 36%.

The sixth round of negotiations was held on the initiative of the United States and came to be known as the Kennedy Round. In January 1962 President J.F. Kennedy submitted to the US Congress a draft trade act, the so-called Trade Expansion Act on the basis of which he was authorized to conduct trade negotiations and to reduce the value of customs tariffs by 50%, with the power to abolish duties on tropical products if this were to contribute to an increase of US exports to the EEC. The United States wished to acquire facilities of access to the EEC market through relaxing the common customs tariff in exchange for customs concessions on the part of the United States.

The Kennedy Round departed from the character of 'product for product' bilateral negotiations, introducing multilateral negotiations of a linear character, covering whole commodity groups. The expectations concerning this round of negotiations were far-reaching, indeed. It was to cover not only industrial goods but also foodstuffs, on the one hand, as well as para- and non-tariff restrictions, on the other. In practice, the negotiating parties failed to reach these objectives. On their part, the EEC countries did not agree to a 50% reduction of duties on foodstuffs, as a result of which these goods were excluded from the negotiations. Also para- and non-tariff restrictions were not negotiated.

The seventh round of GATT was held in Tokyo in 1973 to 1979 with the participation of 99 countries. It covered 33% of the value of world trade, including also foodstuffs and industrial goods. It also addressed the question of reducing para- and non-tariff barriers.

The round generated six codes regulating the application of para- and non-tariff restrictions so that they would not hamper the growth of international trade. The codes concerned dumping and anti-dumping duties, import licences, valuation of the value of goods for customs purposes, technical obstacles to trade, subsidies and compensatory duties as well as government purchases.

Another code on subsidies and compensatory duties was adopted in 1979. It was accepted by 25 countries and became effective as of 1 January 1980. Its goal was to regulate the use of subsidies and to prevent their use through the application of compensatory duties. The code did not provide, however, for a ban on the use of subsidies but only obligated the signatories not to use subsidies with reference to goods other than raw materials and primary products.

The Tokyo Round also witnessed the adoption of an anti-dumping code containing provisions regulating the ways and scope of dumping. However, the code did not provide for the elimination of the form of restrictions to international trade. Neither did it prevent the use of anti-dumping procedures to eliminate foreign export in situations when this export was not of a dumping character.

During the seventh round of GATT, 27 countries also signed an agreement on import licensing procedures that were designed to neutralize the impact of this instrument on the development of international trade and give it a non-discriminatory character.

The remaining codes concerning the application of para- and non-tariff restrictions, and thus the code on the valuation of the value of goods for customs purposes, code on technical barriers to trade and code on government purchases, also proved to be of such vague precision that they did not prevent discriminatory application of these restrictions in international trade and consequently required further consideration, work and specific supplementation.

The undisputed success of the Tokyo Round was, nevertheless, the fact that it was the first to tackle the question of para- and non-tariff restrictions. Although no significant progress was made in eliminating such barriers to the development of international trade, yet the ground was prepared for future negotiations. In general, the Tokyo Round led to the adoption of a 28% customs reduction rate.

The eighth round of GATT held in Punta del Este between 1986 and 1994 came to be known as the Uruguay Round. It concluded in Marrakech (Morocco) on 15 April 1994 and was attended by 125 countries extending its customs negotiations to approximately 30% of the value of world trade.

The initiative to hold the eighth GATT round came from the United State as early as in 1982. Its most important reason was the growth of neo-protectionism, which came to affect in almost all European and numerous non-European countries at the time of the crude oil crisis (1973–80). Another reason was that, despite numerous attempts foodstuffs, still remained outside the scope of negotiations and the United States was their most important world exporter. The third reason could be found in the need to adjust the GATT to the new problems arising in international trade, since customs duties had been reduced to 4–5%, their place being taken by para- and non-tariff restrictions, the latter remaining outside GATT. Neither did the General Agreement provide for other new phenomena which had emerged in international trade such as services, foreign direct investments, intellectual property, and the like, which required regulation.

The Uruguay Round negotiations brought about a 38% reduction of customs rates. The round also adopted the rules of the so-called tariffication, i.e. conversion of para- and non-tariff restrictions (quantitative restrictions, surcharges, minimum import prices, voluntary export restraints and others) into customs tariffs, in particular in farm products trade. Another outstanding success of the Uruguay Round was the adoption of the General Agreement on Trade in Services (GATS), which consisted of five parts. The first specifies the rules of granting the most favoured nation clause in international trade in services. The second obligates member countries to liberalize international trade in services. The third specifies the principal sectors in trade in services which should be first covered by negotiations on liberalization. The fourth identifies liberalization provisions in the services sector which are already in existence. And finally, the fifth part provides the institutional framework for the functioning of international trade in services.

GATT allows a national monopoly to be uphold for rendering services. Countries can also introduce new regulations in the services sector but are obliged to do so in a non-discriminatory manner. This is allowed in specific cases when the protection of the balance of payments or the protection of citizens against damage caused by foreign service-rendering subjects (e.g. insurance companies) is at stake. In the case of a customs union, the member countries are not obliged to extend liberalization to the remaining GATS members.

Apart from an attempt to regulate the process of liberalizing international trade in services, the Uruguay Round also strove to develop a unified system of international standards with respect to the protection of intellectual property rights. It was one of the most controversial subjects of the round. The greatest controversies arose between the technology exporting countries (TEC) and the technology importing countries (TIC). While the former wanted to unify the regulations concerning the protection of intellectual property, the latter opposed it, fearing monopolization of the ways of transferring intellectual property by a narrow group of countries. These controversies led to the Agreement on Trade Related Aspects of Intellectual Property Rights (TRIPs), which extended the scope of regulations protecting the unification of intellectual property rights. This involved, in particular, extending the patent-protection period up to 20 years and of copyrights to 50 years, giving exclusivity rights to authors of software and films, as well as better protection of trademarks and trade secrets. The countries which accepted the agreement committed themselves to introducing its provisions immediately to internal legislation, of developed countries, less developed countries being obligated to do so within five years, the least developed countries to within 11 years.

The Uruguay Round also resulted in the Agreement on Trade Related Investment Measures (TRIMs). The aim of the agreement was to facilitate foreign investments as well as to eliminate means of investment policy which restrict international trade or can distort it.

The World Trade Organization

The World Trade Organization commenced operations on 1 January 1995. It was established as an agreement reached on 15 April 1994 in Marrakech, in Morocco where the Uruguay Round concluded. The WTO was established to replace GATT, which ceased to be adequate to contemporary international conditions. GATT concentrated on commodity trade while contemporary international relations have acquired a more diversified character. Apart from trade in goods and services, the international flow of factors of production was rapidly growing. Simultaneously, GATT focused on the reduction of customs duties, the role of which in international trade has decreased to a few per cent, primary attention nowadays being given to the removal of para- and non-tariff restrictions.

The World Trade Organization is not merely an extension of GATT activity, but signifies the opening of a new chapter in the history of international relations. To some extent it is the practical implementation of the idea which found expression in the Havana Charter of 1946 and was to be developed in the form of the International Trade Organization. The International Trade Organization was never established, no conditions existing for it directly after the Second World War. The WTO, set up 50 years later, did not encounter the same barriers as the International Trade Organization.

The WTO inherited GATT structures with its well-developed and fairly wide scope of competence. Added to that were the provisions of the Uruguay Round, including the GATS and TRIMs. The main task of the WTO is implementing all these agreements. Unlike GATT, WTO has a legal personality. The majority of decisions are made unanimously, others are made by a majority of votes (different depending on subject matter discussed), The organization is of an international character (each country has one vote).

The Marrakech agreement consists of a preamble, 16 articles and four annexes.[26] From the formal point of view there are major differences between WTO and GATT. GATT was a collection of rules in the form of a multilateral agreement without a permanent institutional structure. WTO is an international organization with a corresponding structure. Despite its 50 years' existence, WTO always was a temporary and, simultaneously, interim institution as it was established only to replace an organization (the International Trade Organization) to be established when the proper conditions arose, in negotiating international trade. The majority of GATT agreements were not of an obligatory character for its participants. On the other hand, WTO members are committed to respecting these agreements. Unlike GATT, WTO has a legal personality and, thus, can be the owner of assets, can conclude international agreements and appear as party in a dispute or litigation.

The superior body of the WTO is the Conference of Ministers held at least every two years. So far, four such conferences have been held (the first in 1996, the second in 1998, the third in December 1999 and the fourth in 2002). The conference decides on such issues as admission of new members, amendments to the articles of agreement, establishment of committees of different type, and such like. Between the conferences, its functions are performed by the General Council – an executive body meeting when the need arises. The decisions of the Conference and the Council are adopted by voting, some requiring three-quarters of the votes and some an ordinary majority. The General Council is divided into the Council for Trade in Goods, Council for Trade in Services and Council for Trade Related Aspects of Intellectual Property. The Councils can also set up committees and working groups. The WTO Secretariat works in Geneva, headed by a general director.

The main goal of WTO is to liberalize economic ties on the global scale. It aims at removing all and any barriers to international trade in goods, services and factors of production. The primary principle leading in this direction is the mutual non-discrimination of countries reflected in the use of the most favoured nation clause and the national clause. It is to be accompanied by the principles of reciprocity, unrestricted access to national markets and fair competition. Governments can intervene (as it was under GATT) only when a need arises to protect the balance of payments, domestic production, the nation's health or a country's security.

At the end of November 2001, the Ministerial Session of the WTO adopted in Doha, the capital of Kuwait, a decision to open another, ninth round of negotiations

---

26 Comp. J. Kaczurba and E. Kawecka-Wyrzykowska (eds), *Od GATT do WTO*, op. cit., p. 28.

to reduce barriers to international trade.[27] The decision was of particular importance in view of the failure of WTO countries' negotiations in Seattle in 1999. The failure resulted from differences in approach to liberalization of international trade. The United States preferred sector-focused negotiations, while others favoured a general approach. A significant role in the development of the situation was performed by the less developed countries which considered the results of the Uruguay Round to be their failure, the settlements of this round not ensuring preferential treatment in applying of para- and non-tariff restrictions to the less developed countries.

The interest of the Doha negotiation round focuses on eliminating subsidies to agriculture and reducing import restrictions on farm products. The less developed countries refer here, in particular, to the European Union market and the market of OECD countries. Suffice it to say that annual subventions to EU agriculture amount to as much as 350 billion dollars, well above the total aid to less developed countries.[28]

Apart from reducing subventions, liberalization of the agricultural market will also require a significant reduction of customs duties. While duties on non-farm products in trade of highly industrialized countries (the European Union, United States and Japan) were reduced to approximately 4–5%, duties on farm products still oscillate around 17–18% in trade of the European Union and Japan and 11% in US trade.[29]

In addition, the Doha Round is to address the question of eliminating certain other para- and non-tariff restrictions under conditions of preferential treatment of less developed countries.

The Organization for Economic Cooperation and Development

The OECD is another important subject of international economic policy. It was established on 14 December 1960 but only initiated activity on 30 September 1961.

The OECD replaced the Organization for European Economic Cooperation established in Paris in 1948. Its members are 18 West European countries, with the United States and Canada participating in the works of the OEEC as associates. The principal aim of the OEEC was to develop international economic cooperation between member countries, to be accomplished through the removal of barriers to mutual trade, in particular customs tariffs and quantitative restrictions. The OEEC also took part in the preparation of plans for the reconstruction of Western Europe from war destruction and subsequently in the reconstruction of the region.

The OECD aimed at long-term targets, in particular the creation of conditions for sustainable economic growth. They included liberalization of international trade, introduction of full convertibility of national currencies (and thus not only the external convertibility introduced in 1959, but also full external convertibility),

---

27 Comp. J. Kaczurba, E. Kawecka-Wyrzykowska, *Polska w WTO*, op, cit., p. 13.

28 J. Kaczurba, 'Wyniki Konferencji Ministerialnej w Doha', in J. Kaczurba, E. Kawecka-Wyrzykowska, *Polska w WTO*, op. cit., p. 62.

29 Ibid., p. 63.

development of new forms of international cooperation, in particular cooperation in production, technological cooperation, cooperation in investment, and the like. Members of the OECD included, apart from the 18 founders of the OEEC, also the United States and Canada. Since 1962 the organization has been subsequently joined by Japan, Finland, Australia, New Zealand, Mexico, Hungary, Poland, South Korea, Slovakia. For years, the OECD used to be called the 'rich club'. However, this name lost justification after the accession of Mexico and other countries with a modest level of economic growth. Nevertheless, it is these countries that are said to gather world leaders and decide on world economic and technological progress. Though they occupy only one-quarter of the Earth's surface and one-fifth of world population, they generate as much as 80% of the world gross national product, are also responsible for two-thirds of world trade and dominate in the financial markets.

The OECD can make decisions, recommendations and adopt resolutions. The decisions are not obligating for countries which abstained from voting, being simultaneously obligating for the others. The recommendations can, but need not be, converted by member countries into decisions. They are, thus, basically of an advisory character. The resolutions perform only an informatory function. All these forms of exerting influence on member countries are instruments of shaping international economic policy. Some aims of this policy are formulated through coordination of foreign economic policy, while another part takes the form of a common policy. Foreign economic policy within the OECD is coordinated among, others, through consultations on the goals, means and instruments of this policy pursued in the past. These are the so-called surveys of the policy of member countries, and serve to analyse the effects of the policy pursued by individual countries on other countries. All and any dangers find their expression in recommendations addressed to the countries which generate them. Apart from consultations, OECD countries also coordinate their policy ex ante, agreeing on goals, means and instruments of future foreign economic policy. To some extent, the OECD countries pursue a common economic policy. This finds its reflection in the uniform stance adopted towards basic economic and social phenomena concerning the contemporary world. The OECD is not authorized, however, to make decisions of a supranational character.

The supreme body of the OECD is the Council composed of representatives of all member countries. The Council meets at ministerial sessions, in the presence of ministers of economy and foreign affairs or at ordinary sessions with the participation of permanent representatives of member countries. The Secretariat is directed by the secretary general, who presents the goals of the activity of the OECD and methods of their achievement at annual ministerial sessions, which result in the publication of communiqués informing on programme settlements. The ordinary sessions of the Council with the participation of permanent representatives are held at least every two weeks.

The executive body of the OECD is the Executive Committee consisting, in half, of seven permanent members (i.e. G7: the United States, Japan, the FRG, France, Great Britain, Canada and Italy) and in half of seven non-permanent members selected from among the remaining countries. The Executive Committee meets weekly to consider statements and reports of sector committees and other OECD bodies. The two sector committees of the OECD that perform a particularly significant role are the economic policy committee and the committee for surveys of economy and development. The former deals with the coordination of foreign economic policy and development of direction of international economic policy.

The principal goals of the OECD have evolved in the course of time. In the 1960s attention was focused on attaining high economic growth rate, in the 1970s it was on ensuring energy-supply security and structural changes in the economy, and in the 1980s it was on transformations in the economic policy of member countries, translating into replacement of state interventionism with liberal monetarism. In the 1990s the activity of the OECD was entirely dominated by questions related to systemic transformations in Central and Eastern Europe.

Throughout the analysed period, the OECD has advocated international trade liberalization, in particular the elimination of tariff, para-tariff and non-tariff restrictions. This followed from the fact that it was the 'rich club' of countries with highly developed economies, competitive, high-quality and technologically advanced production, which was seeking new, ever larger markets. Restrictions to international trade made access to potential markets more difficult and did not allow the principal targets of member countries' foreign economic policy to be accomplished. This policy found its expression in the ideas of a free market and free trade promoting unrestricted access to internal markets for foreign goods, services and factors of production. It was for these reasons that the OECD participated actively in the negotiations of the Uruguay Round and afterwards in the transformation of GATT into WTO.

The OECD got particularly involved in the liberalization of international trade in services, as well as flow of capital. This involvement can be seen in the special codes adopted by the member countries and promoting the elimination of all restrictions in this respect. They are based on the principle of standstill and non-discrimination.

5.2.3. Integration Groupings

Integration groupings occupy a special place among international organizations of a grouping (regional) character. They can be subjects of international law, the scope of their subjectivity being, however, determined by the countries forming such organizations. These countries can also decide on their dissolution.

The specificity of the integration groupings consists of the growing scope of their power in relation to member countries. In the simplest forms of these organizations this scope is relatively small while in advanced integration organizations it can be so large that these organizations are referred to as supranational.

In general, the concept of international economic integration signifies that nations, states, economic potentials, markets and ultimately individuals of different nationalities and states belonging to them unite.[30] The point, however, is not to add but to create new economic organisms which will eventually generate abilities significantly surpassing the total of national abilities. Otherwise integration would not make sense since it is accompanied by costs borne by each member country individually and all the countries together.[31] In its substance, integration signifies coordination of foreign economic policy and development of international economic policy, the scope and forms of this coordination depending on the adopted integration solutions. The most important institutional forms of economic integration include a free trade area, a customs union, a common market, a monetary union, economic union, political union and full economic integration.[32]

A free trade area is the simplest institutional solution. It means liquidation of customs tariffs in trade between specified countries with simultaneous maintenance of independent trade policy towards countries from outside the grouping. The scope of foreign economic policy coordination is in this case extremely limited and concerns exclusively trade policy (as a rule only customs policy) in mutual relations. It can cover mutual trade as a whole or only selected commodity groups (e.g. only industrial goods and sometimes even selected products). When a free trade area is limited, the trade policy pursued by individual countries with respect to the remaining goods is autonomic in character. The foreign economic policy of such countries can also be of an autonomic nature and can be conducted with the help of para- and non-tariff instruments. Finally, also the macroeconomic policy pursued by individual countries aided by instruments also affecting economic relations with other countries (and thus the exchange rate, the interest rate, budget policy, fiscal policy, credit policy and price policy) remains autonomic.

A customs union involves, apart from a free trade zone, also a uniform customs policy towards non-union countries. It constitutes further limitation of the autonomy of foreign economic policy (in particular, foreign trade policy). A country which is a member of a customs union must resign from the autonomic character of its pursued customs policy not only inside but also outside the union. This policy favours the development of trade between member countries and limits the development of trade with countries from outside the union. Thus, there can be talk of a preferential and discriminatory character of the international economic policy conducted within the customs union, i.e. about giving preferences to imports from union countries and discriminating against imports from countries outside the union. In this case, preferential treatment consists of removing customs duties in trade between the union countries and their non-application (such a preferential treatment also had

---

30 Comp. A. Marszałek, *Z historii europejskiej idei integracji międzynarodowej* (Uniwersytet Łódzki, Łódź, 1996), p. 4.

31 P. Bożyk, J. Misala, *Integracja ekonomiczna*, op. cit.

32 Comp. B. Balassa, 'Przyczynek do integracji europejskiej', in *Z problemów integracji gospodarczej* (Warsaw, 1968), p. 78; S. Ładyka, *Z teorii integracji gospodarczej* (Oficyna Wydawnicza SGH, Warsaw), p. 15; and J. Pelkmans, *European Integration, Methods and Economic Analysis* (Longman, New York, 1997), p. 5.

place in the free trade zone), while discriminatory treatment consists of introducing an external customs tariff common to all the countries. Before the introduction of a common customs tariff (and thus under conditions of a free trade area) customs tariffs in relations with non-member countries were differentiated, some lower and some higher. The introduction of a single customs tariff means the introduction of a tariff which is, as a rule, closer to the higher rather than the lower level.

A common market is a form of integration more developed than the customs union. It means not only resignation from the autonomy of the customs policy pursued within the grouping and in relation to countries from outside the grouping, but also resignation from the autonomy of the interest rate and exchange rate, price and wages policy constituting the prerequisite for the free flow of factors of production (capital, labour and technology) within the integration grouping. A common market is simultaneously a free trade area and a customs union. It creates better conditions for the undisturbed functioning of the mechanism of free competition within the integration grouping and, in consequence, adjustment abilities better than in the case of a free trade area, owing to the optimal allocation of capital and labour resources, development of large-scale production, faster introduction of technological progress, and the like. Thus, apart from the effects of the creation and diversion of trade, there are also dynamic effects of integration in the form of an increased level of investment and acceleration of the economic growth rate.

A monetary union (also called currency union) covers, apart from a customs union and a common market, coordination (or unification) of the currency policy pursued by the countries being members of the integration grouping. The autonomy of foreign economic policy is thus restricted even further since the involved countries must coordinate their money-emission policies, introduce rigid relations between exchange rates of their currencies (or replace their national currencies with a supranational currency). A uniform monetary policy limits the ability of member-countries of the integration grouping to shape the structure and size of mutual economic cooperation by manipulating the exchange rate, with the help of emission of money and other monetary policy instruments, the principal role in developing such cooperation being performed by advantages in the production efficiency.

An economic union involves, apart from a free trade area, a customs union, a common market and a monetary union, coordination (or unification) of individual domains of economic policy, both macroeconomic and microeconomic. On the macroeconomic level, coordination should embrace the exchange rate policy, price policy and wages policy. Part of these had to be coordinated already at the level of the creation of the common market, part upon the creation of the monetary union. On the microeconomic level, the scope of the coordination covers, in the first place: industrial and technological policy, agricultural and transport policy, education and natural environment protection, and also foreign economic policy, including notably its para-tariff and non-tariff instruments. Therefore, one can speak of an economic union when all sectors of economic policy within the integrating countries, important from the point of view of the functioning of the grouping, have been covered by the coordinated economic policy, performing the function of international economic policy.

A political union is not only a free trade area, a customs union, a common market, a monetary union and an economic union. It also ensures coordination (or unification) of foreign policy *sensu stricto* and, thus, a uniform policy adopted by the integration grouping towards basic political and military events and world developments, not only in the short term but also in the long perspective. This is an exceptionally difficult stage in the formation of an integration grouping.

Full economic integration is treated as the crowning of the process of economic integration embracing all the forms of this integration, ranging from the free trade area to the political union. It needs, however, more than macro- and microeconomic coordination to be created. A single economic policy must also be pursued. Hence, full economic integration should be, in principle, supranational in nature, and is, at least for the time being, a theoretical construction. In practice, only one grouping has succeeded in introducing a single, supranational policy in selected sectors of the economy. In the remaining sectors, coordination of the economic policy pursued by individual countries and national policies still prevail.

The most important integration groupings now in existence include the EU, NAFTA, EFTA, CEFTA, LAIA, Mercosur and ASEAN.[33]

The European Union
The EU is characterized by a considerable scope of internationalization of foreign economic policy, with international policy giving way to supranational solutions in some domains. Simultaneously, the EU is marked by a significantly wider scope of the power of this organization over the member countries. It is a subject of international law and can, therefore, shape the legislation to be effective in the member countries. However, the process of law-making is still mainly of an intergovernmental rather than supranational character.[34]

The treaty establishing the European Economic Community was signed simultaneously with the treaty establishing Euratom, i.e. on 25 March 1950, in Rome. The founder members of the EEC included Belgium, France, the Netherlands, Luxemburg, the FRG and Italy. In 1973 the EEC was joined by Great Britain, Denmark and Ireland, by Greece in 1981, by Spain and Portugal in 1986 and by Austria, Finland and Sweden in 1995. The Treaty of Rome provided for the establishment of a free trade area, a customs union and a common market as well as the adjustment of foreign economic policy within the integration grouping, in accordance with the requirements of these institutional solutions. The deadline for the completion of this process was to be 1970. In practice, the free trade area and customs union were created earlier than expected while the common market appeared at the set time. It soon turned out, however, that the functioning of the common market without coordination of monetary policy as well as the coordination

---

33 See: P. Bożyk, J. Misala, *Integracja gospodarcza*, op. cit.
34 See: E. Latoszek, M. Proczek, *Organizacje międzynarodowe*, op. cit., p. 37.

of the macro- and microeconomic policy is unsatisfactory. The attempts to create a monetary and an economic union made on the basis of the Treaty of Rome in the 1970s and in the 1980s did not bring satisfactory results. That is why, in February 1986, the EEC countries signed a Uniform Economic Act modernizing the foundations for the integration of member countries. The Act gave new competences to EEC bodies and modified the decision-making process, thus strengthening their supranational character. It emphasized clearly the need to establish a monetary and economic union. Five years later, on 9–10 December 1991, the member countries signed the Maastricht Treaty containing, in addition, provisions to establish a political union and full economic integration. The approval of the Maastricht Treaty by the parliaments of member states and the European Parliament, and its coming into force as of 1 November 1993 should be treated as acceptance of a common programme for the establishment of a monetary union, economic union, political union and full economic integration leading to the introduction of a single currency, establishment of an area free of internal borders and with a single economic policy, foreign policy, defence policy, citizenship and strong supranational authority. These assumptions were to find confirmation in practice by the end of the 1990s. There are, however, strong and numerous signs that this time horizon must be significantly extended. This concerns, in particular, the introduction of a uniform foreign policy and the broadening of the scope of supranational integration decisions.

The hitherto accomplished integration of the European Union (previously EEC) countries has involved almost all the targets concerning replacement of national trade policies with an international policy, which found its reflection in the establishment of a free trade area and a customs union. EU practice has shown, however, that trade policy has not yet acquired an entirely common character. In particular, the member states have not resigned from the right to apply residual national restrictions to trade which they had applied even before the EEC was established.

The replacement of national industrial policies with international policy within the EEC proceeded in two directions: through the establishment of a free trade area and customs union and also directly unifying industrial policy *sensu stricto* in the member states. The former is based on the assumption that the elimination of customs duties within the grouping and introduction of a uniform customs tariff in relations with non-member countries would lead to the establishment of an international free market and would thus unify the parameters of production decision-making in the grouping. However, practice showed that although the customs policy was unified, diversification still persisted as regards technical standards, principles of government purchases, scope of state monopolies which actually proved to have a much more powerful impact on production decisions than customs duties. The method of the direct generation of a transition from national to international industrial policy failed to bring the expected results. The second method, that of coordinating national industrial policies, was consequently applied. 1970 saw the publication of a memorandum on the introduction of a uniform industrial policy on EEC level. The memorandum laid out the major goals and assumptions of the strategy of industrial development of EEC members. They were adopted by all member states in 1973.

In accordance with the memorandum, the principal goal of the EEC was to increase the adaptation ability of industrial enterprises and industries to the fast-changing conditions, in particular through structural changes, more rapid technical progress, prevention of the devastation of the natural environment, and the like. These goals were to be reached through acceleration of the implementation of the provisions of the Treaty of Rome on establishing a common market, the removal of legal, fiscal and other obstacles to the development of cooperation and mergers of enterprises from different countries, increased government assistance in the structural transformation of traditional industries and acceleration of the technological development of modern industries, adjustment of the labour market to the needs of industry, etc.

Achievements of EEC countries in pursuing a common agricultural policy were particularly remarkable. The fundamental principles of this policy were determined in the Treaty of Rome, aimed at increasing agricultural production of the EEC countries, making them independent of food deliveries from outside the EEC and ensuring a level of farm labour income equal to the income in non-farming sectors. The price policy became the principal instrument of the EEC's common agricultural policy. It was used to eliminate income differences between rural and urban population, to create preferential selling conditions on the EEC market for producers in member states, to regulate the volume of production of individual goods and such like. Every product covered by the common agricultural policy had a price set at a level higher than the world price, uniform for all countries. The price was maintained using customs duties and compensatory amounts, which protected the EEC market against cheap imports from outside the EEC. Simultaneously, the EEC countries applied a system of centralized purchases (at guaranteed prices) which countered a decline of price below the guaranteed level (when supply exceeded demand). Exports from the EEC to countries outside this grouping were subsidized due to the differences between prices on the internal EEC market and world prices. Financing of the system was based on the Fund for Orientation and Guarantees in Agriculture (FEOGA). The Fund assisted when surpluses of farm products appeared on the EEC market and when a need arose to subsidize exports. The transformation of the EEC into the European Union was accompanied by a change of its farm policy, though its principles were said to remain constant. Thus, the farm policy still consists of supporting domestic production and maintaining internal market prices higher than world prices, ensuring the parity of rural and urban incomes and basing agriculture on individual land-holdings. What has changed, however, is the scope of agriculture subsidizing. Aid from EU funds does not go to all farmers but only to those who produce most efficiently, in the best ecological conditions, and, thus, those who produce health food. At the same time, the Union strives to reduce expensive and contaminated production.

On the other hand, little progress has been made by EEC countries as regards transition from a foreign to international transport policy. The fundamental principles of the common transport policy were established by the Treaty of Rome. They were to apply in the first place to the overland carriage of cargoes and passengers between EEC countries. At the beginning of the 1970s this policy was extended to embrace air and sea transport as well. The common transport policy was initially designed mainly to unify transport rates and to abolish national transport quotas. It was as late as 1968 that common quotas were introduced. Little progress was also made in the development of uniform transport regulations. In the 1970s the Community focused primarily on financing transport infrastructure although here progress was smaller than expected. That is why, in the mid-1980s the Community adopted a programme to establish a liberal market of transport services, abandon quotas in international vehicle transport and harmonisation of market conditions.

Particular attention was attached in the EEC to the development of a common monetary policy. The Treaty of Rome did not formulate a long-term programme in this field. It provided for the member states to introduce convertible currencies and multilateral settlements in these currencies, which was how the situation actually developed. When the EEC was established, the currencies of its member states were internally convertible. In the 1960s it turned out, however, that more than that was needed to broaden integration and, in particular, to create a common market. As a result, at the beginning of the 1970s the EEC countries had already commenced to develop a monetary union by stiffening exchange rate relations. That was an attempt to limit the government influence on the structure and volume of trade through changes of the exchange rate (a devaluation or a depreciation, a revaluation or an appreciation). The so-called 'snake in the tunnel' which was then introduced limited exchange rates fluctuations to +/- 2.25%. This was by no means a satisfactory solution. Consequently, in the late 1970s the EEC countries already decided to apply new solutions in their monetary policy by introducing a common currency unit, the ECU. The European currency unit was to replace national currencies in mutual trade settlements. The function of circulation units was still to be performed by national currencies. The system existed till 2000, that is till the introduction of the euro – a common currency which replaced the national currencies in all their functions.

Apart from the above-mentioned types of common policy, the EU pursues also a common regional policy, common technological policy, common energy policy, common environment protection policy, and others. All of these constitute elements of the developed economic union. Simultaneously, efforts are being made to increase the share in these policies of uniform solutions, a prerequisite to the evolvement of full economic integration.

The European Free Trade Association
The European Free Trade Area (EFTA) was established in Stockholm on 20 November 1959 by seven countries, namely Austria, Denmark, Norway, Portugal, Switzerland, Sweden and Great Britain. It was to some extent a reply by these countries to the establishment by Belgium, France, the Netherlands, Luxemburg, the FRG and Italy of the EEC. The main goal of the EFTA was to establish a free trade area for industrial goods. The process of lifting customs duties was divided into stages, the final liberalization of trade in industrial goods between member countries becoming finally effective on 1 January 1967. Liberalization of trade in farm and food products was to be achieved on the basis of bilateral agreements between EFTA countries. In

1967 EFTA was joined by Finland, in 1970 by Iceland, in 1991 by Liechtenstein. At the same time other countries left the EFTA, becoming members of the EEC, namely, Denmark and Great Britain in 1973 and Portugal in 1986. The same was done by Austria, Finland and Sweden in 1995. Thus, only Norway, Switzerland, Iceland and Liechtenstein remained in the EFTA. The EFTA agreement does not foresee any forms of integration (like a customs union, a common market, or the like) apart from a free trade area.

The North American Free Trade Agreement

The North American Free Trade Agreement was set up on 1 January 1994. Its precursor was the Canada–United States Free Trade Agreement (CUFTA) established on 2 January 1988. The CUFTA agreement took effect on 1 January 1989, providing for liberalization of trade in goods and services. Apart from abolishing customs duties, it also envisaged the removal of para-tariff and non-tariff restrictions.

NAFTA constituted an extension of the CUFTA provisions covering, apart from the trade between the United States and Canada, also trade between these two countries and Mexico. The assumption was that by 2008 a free trade area in industrial goods will have been created step by step, with customs duties and other restrictions to mutual trade being eliminated. The NAFTA agreement did not, however, include foodstuffs. The United States and Canada and also Mexico decided to reduce restrictions to trade in foodstuffs only gradually in the long term and on the basis of other (bilateral) agreements.

The Central European Free Trade Agreement

The Central European Free Trade Agreement (CEFTA) was signed on 21 December 1992 and came in force on 1 January 1994. It provided for gradual liberalization of trade in industrial goods and selective liberalization of trade in farm and food products. In the long term, the agreement envisages also the abolition of para-tariff and non-tariff barriers. Initially, the CEFTA was composed of Poland, Hungary, the Czech Republic and Slovakia, and was later joined by Slovenia, Romania, Bulgaria and other countries of the region. CEFTA is an extremely institutionally loose form of integration, as the establishment of a free trade area in industrial articles is not accompanied by the establishment of any body responsible for implementing the agreement.[35]

Attempts are also being made to create integration groupings in less developed countries but, as a rule, they are limited to the simplest form of a free trade area.

The Latin American Free Trade Area

One such attempt on the part of the less developed countries made directly after the establishment of the EEC, was the Latin American Free Trade Area (LAFTA). The Latin American Free Trade Area was set up in Montevideo on 18 February 1960 and

35 P. Bożyk (ed.), *CEFTA i integracja gospodarcza w Europie* (Oficyna Wydawnicza SGH, Warsaw, 1996).

comprised Argentina, Brazil, Chile, Mexico, Paraguay, Peru and Uruguay. LAFTA was later joined by Ecuador and Columbia in 1961 and by Venezuela and Bolivia in 1967. It was dissolved 20 years later as it failed to achieve its goal, which was to consist of the maximization of the effect of trade diversion and of trade creation. The reasons for its failure were structural in nature and were, therefore, difficult to eliminate. Trade between member countries constituted but a fraction of their global trade, since their economic structures were competitive and not complementary, with raw materials and semi-finished products prevailing. Each member country was highly protective of its domestic industrial production subsidizing and destining it, primarily, to satisfy the internal market needs. The obstacles to the adjustment of these structures through international specialization were too hard to overcome.

The Latin American Integration Association

The Latin American Integration Association (LAIA) was to replace LAFTA. Its goals were more ambitious than those of its predecessor. Apart from a free trade area, they also included a customs union, a common market and, subsequently, higher institutional forms of integration. The years which have elapsed since the establishment of LAIA, have shown, however, that integration depends to a much lesser extent on the institutional will of member countries than on the conditions necessary to make such integration effective.

The Common Market of South America

Another ambitious venture of South American countries is the Common Market of South American (in Spanish MERCOSUR – Mercado Comun del Sur), set up in 1995 with the participation of Argentina, Brazil, Paraguay and Uruguay. Like LAIA, it was to be not only a free trade area but also a customs union, a common market and an economic union. The aim of Mercosur is thus to ensure both a free flow of goods and that of services and factors of production. Unlike LAIA, Mercosur is composed of a limited number of countries, hence its sub-regional character, with particular attention to the development of integration between Brazil and Argentina, and between Paraguay and Uruguay. So far, the organization has focused its attention on the development of trade. The creation of a common market and the ensuing flow of factors of production encounters obstacles generated by lack of progress in the coordination of economic policy.

The Association of South-East Asian Countries

Asia has also not escaped the temptation to create an integration grouping. On 8 August 1967, five Southeast Asian countries (the Philippines, Indonesia, Malaysia, Thailand and Singapore) signed a declaration establishing the Association of South-East Asian Nations (ASEAN). ASEAN was also joined by other countries of the region – in 1984 by Brunei, in 1995 by Vietnam, in 1997 by Laos and Myanmar and in 1999 by Cambodia. During its first 20 years the association was mainly political in nature. The desire to tighten and broaden economic cooperation was voiced as a target of primary interest only at the third summit meeting in Manila in 1987. The

ASEAN free trade area was established in January 1992 at the fourth meeting in Singapore of heads of governments of the member countries. It was then decided that customs rates on 15 groups of industrial goods would be gradually reduced to circa 0.5%, starting from 1993. In 1995, a decision was taken to commence the creation of a common market. Apart from the development of free trade in industrial goods, ASEAN countries were to initiate industrial cooperation and common investments, among others, through adjustments in the economic policy. Unfortunately, differences in the level of economic growth, in particular as regards industrialization, gave rise to fears on the part of some ASEAN countries that their markets might be flooded with cheaper articles (manufactured, for instance, in Singapore) which would hinder the growth of domestic industry, especially so since industry in the majority of the ASEAN countries was anti-import in nature. In spite of the efforts made, the share of mutual trade in their global trade did not increase while the share of the United States and Japan grew.[36] ASEAN is, in general, a very loose association of member countries. It has, therefore, failed to accomplish any of the goals set. In the first place, they have not managed to create a free trade area of even commodity-limited scope. Neither have they succeeded in establishing a customs area or a common market. Nevertheless, what they have created is an atmosphere which favours the development of international trade even if it is not so much mutual trade as trade with countries from outside ASEAN.

The common denominator of all the above discussed integration organizations is a free trade area signifying the introduction of international trade policy within each of the groupings. Whereas, in the case of the EU, the free trade area was merely an initial institutional form, in the case of the remaining groupings it was the only and final institutional form. Even when declarations were made that higher institutional forms would be established (a common market or an economic union), this was not achieved in practice. Nevertheless, the establishment of a few free trade areas has also contributed to the acceleration of the growth rate in international trade. Hence, they should be treated as a link in the process of transition from foreign economic policy to international economic policy – naturally of a territorially limited scope.

In accordance with the GATT principle,[37] regional integration and the resultant liberalization of international trade should be treated as a 'second best' solution, which means that universal liberalization of international trade would naturally be a better solution but as that is impossible (for various reasons), territorially limited liberalization is also advantageous. WTO upheld these principles.

The United Nations Conference on Trade and Development
A significant role in developing international economic policy was also performed by the United Nations Conference on Trade and Development, first convened in Geneva in 1964 and attended by 120 countries. At the second conference in New

---

36 Comp. *Directions of Trade and Statistics*, IMF Annual Papers 1968–74, 1991, 2000, Washington, DC, 2001..

37 Article XXIV of the General Agreement

Delhi in 1968, UNCTAD was converted into a permanent UN programme with a secretariat in Geneva. UNCTAD is thus not an international organization. From the formal point of view its importance is much smaller than if it were.

The main aim of this body was to defend the interests of less developed countries in international trade. The point was to provide privileged treatment of these countries and create a system of preferences for exports of their industrial goods to economically developed countries. UNCTAD also prepared an integrated raw material programme comprising a common fund for financing international stocks, mutual interdependence between raw material prices and industrial goods prices as well as a system of international commodity agreements. The goal was to increase revenues from raw material and farm products exports from less developed countries, as well as to stabilize these revenues in relation to the incomes from international trade reached by highly developed countries. The UNCTAD also endeavoured to increase gratuitous aid on the part of economically developed countries in favour of less developed countries, to a level of 0.7% of the GDP of the former. UNCTAD also advocated that less developed countries should be given assistance in the form of low-interest credits, scientific and technical assistance, redemption of debts and aid in industrialisation.

All these postulates of less developed countries found hardly any reflection in foreign and international economic policy. Part of the postulates already appeared at the time of the development of the concept of the International Trade Organization, i.e. in the mid-1940s. However, the position of less developed countries was then so weak that the postulates passed unnoticed. Neither did GATT initially envisage any exceptions for less developed countries. Only in the mid-1950s did the member countries supplement the General Agreement with provisions allowing for state interventionism in cases when member countries are at an initial stage of development and represent a low standard of living. Article XVIII of the Agreement provides for possible application by these countries of higher tariffs, quantitative restrictions, foreign exchange restrictions and other solutions of this kind. In order to benefit from Article XVIII less developed countries were, however, obliged to obtain the consent of all GATT member countries and take into account possible retaliation. As a result, Article XVIII did not change the position of less developed countries in international trade. In the 1950s and 1960s, their trade developed much more slowly than the trade of highly industrialized countries.

That was one of the factors that strengthened the bargaining position of less developed countries in the development of international economic policy. This resulted in the adoption in 1964 of Part IV of the General Agreement comprising Articles XXXVI–XXXVIII. The developed countries confirmed in these articles their resignation from the principle of reciprocity of concessions in trade negotiations with less developed countries, under pressure from UNCTAD. Less developed countries benefited from these provisions during the Kennedy Round of GATT negotiations (1964–7). However, even without the obligation of reciprocity, less developed countries had little to say during that round, remaining outside the negotiations and waiting for indirect effects of negotiations between Western Europe and the United States.

In 1968, at the II UNCTAD Conference, less developed countries demanded the introduction of a general system of trade preferences. However, only in 1971 did GATT countries introduce the possibility of not applying the principle of equality in trade negotiations (exemption from the obligation to subordinate to Article I of the General Agreement).

During the Tokyo Round of GATT (1973–9), less developed countries tried to obtain maximum customs preferences. At that time they represented a major political power. In 1974 to 1975 two special UN sessions devoted to the new economic world deal were held under pressure from less developed countries. The pressure resulted in the adoption by GATT of the clause of preferential treatment of less developed countries, with the least developed countries being exempted from any reciprocity obligation. The remaining less developed countries were obliged to increase gradually the reciprocity of concessions as the level of their economic development increased. This concerned, in the first place, newly industrialized countries.

Nevertheless, generally speaking, the benefits reaped by less developed countries from the application of the system of universal customs preferences were insignificant, since the level of customs duties in international trade had been drastically reduced in the meantime (in particular, on industrial goods) and even significant decreases of customs duties applied to less developed countries brought about insignificant effects.

The role of UNCTAD in influencing international economic policy kept decreasing as time passed. This can be seen in the effects of subsequent conferences (Geneva – 1964, New Delhi – 1968, Santiago in Chile – 1972, Nairobi – 1976, Manila – 1979, Belgrade – 1983, Geneva – 1987, Carthagena – 1992, Midrand-RPA – 1996, Thailand – 2000). In the meantime, the role of less developed countries in the world also decreased. The General System of Preferences (GSP) for imports from less developed countries did not concern so-called 'sensitive goods', of enormous importance for these countries. Simultaneously, it covered a considerable part of imports from economically developed countries. Moreover, ceilings were set for the growth of imports of goods enjoying the preferences.

At the beginning of the 1990s, the sense of further existence and operation of the UNCTAD in its original shape, i.e. as a form of exerting pressure on highly developed countries to obtain various preferences, came to be questioned. At a conference in 1992, it was decided that the negotiation form should be replaced with an analytical form supporting the introduction of free market and free trade mechanisms in less developed countries. In cooperation with the IMF and the World Bank, UNCTAD is to assist less developed countries in developing of international trade (e.g. by creating a network of trade information), debt reduction, and the like.

5.2.4. Transnational Corporations

Transnational corporations (also referred to as multinational corporations) are responsible for generating over a half of the world industrial output. These transnational corporations with the largest branches abroad include Royal Dutch Shell, Exxon, IBM, General Motors, General Electric, Toyota, Ford, Hitachi, Sony, Mitsubishi, Nestle, Mobil and Nissan Motor.[38] Almost 90% of these corporations have their headquarters in five countries: the United States, Great Britain, Germany, France and Japan. Branches of these corporations are concentrated in the highly industrialized countries, half of them in Europe and approximately 10% in North America. The remaining branches have their seats in less developed countries (one-quarter), the largest number of branches belonging to American (one-third) and British (one-fifth) corporations. Whereas in the highly developed countries transnational corporations are primarily interested in the processing industry, in the less developed countries they concentrate on the extraction, food-processing, metallurgical, tobacco and chemical industries.[39] The growth of processing industries by transnational corporations in these countries is mainly restricted to the assembly of articles based on sub-assemblies manufactured in their mother countries or in their branches located in highly industrialised countries.

Production, technical and trade links between mother enterprises and their branches are as a rule vertical in nature, as illustrated in Figure 5.1. The principles on which these links operate differ from those between horizontally linked international enterprises, cooperation which is horizontal in nature being affected by the foreign economic policy of the countries in which they are located or also by international economic policy. Vertical cooperation loses its national character, which allows transnational corporations to reach even the most protected local markets, placing there production destined for these markets or developing other forms of economic activity. They can thus overcome not only tariff barriers but also para- and non-tariff barriers. Moreover, production, technological, trade and other links of parent enterprises with their branches are often developed on the basis of economic principles other than those operating in the countries in which the branches are located and often also differing from those generally acceptable on the international market. Transnational corporations may, for instance, use specific forms of financial settlements, with prices differing from those on the world market, part of settlements may be made in kind not in money, and the like. Transnational corporation are, therefore, in the international market subjects, which differ from national enterprises. Frequently, they are not present in this market at all, the links between parent enterprises and their branches, as well as links between branches, being developed as if inside one enterprise.

---

38 *World Investment Report. Transnational Corporations and Competitiveness* (United Nations, New York, Geneva, 1995), pp. 20–21.

39 Comp. L. Ciamaga, *Światowa gospodarka rynkowa* (PWN, Warszawa, 1990), p. 242.

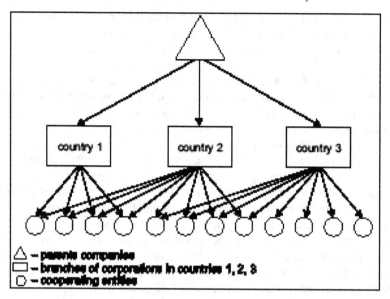

Figure 5.1. Vertical links in transnational corporations

Source: Author's own elaboration.

Four essential types of strategy pursued by transnational corporations can be distinguished which have a different impact on foreign and international economic policy, national, international, transnational and global.[40]

The national strategy is pursued on markets protected against international competition with tariff, para-tariff and non-tariff barriers. Its idea revolves around the development of production, technical and trade cooperation with local enterprises. Branches of transnational corporations receive capital and cooperation procurement from the parent organization and attempt to sell the manufactured goods on the local market. They also strive to obtain from the governments of countries in whose territories they are located, the most favourable conditions for the transfer of capital and procurement elements as well as maximum exemptions from tax and other dues towards the budget. At the same time they are not interested in the preferences obtained being extended to other subjects operating in the international market.

In the case of the international strategy, branches of transnational corporations receive from the parent headquarters capital, technology and know-how which is not used in cooperation with local market entities but to act together with branches located in other countries, as a rule of the same region (e.g. in the EU, CEFTA, EFTA, etc.). The headquarters is in charge of pursuing policy in the whole region,

---

40 Comp. A. Zorska, 'Korporacje transnarodowe w krajach CEFTA', in P. Bożyk (ed.), *Rola CEFTA w integrującej się Europie* (Oficyna Wydawnicza SGH, Warszawa, 1999), p. 123.

dividing the production process between individual branches, using local factors of production in a diversified way and locating sales markets from the point of view of the region as a whole. In this case, regional preferences (for instance, within an integration grouping) are most important for the corporation.

The transnational strategy surpasses the geographical region, manifesting in the location of branches in several regions and the drive to discounting production factors as well as differentiated conditions of production and sales in these regions. In this case, it is not enough to influence the foreign economic policy of one country or the international economic policy of a group of countries (within a sub-region or region); what is also required is to affect the international-transregional policy.

Finally, the global strategy of transnational corporations signifies location of branches in different regions, taking account of the improvement of production efficiency in absolute rather than comparative terms. Thus, those places are selected where production conditions are most favourable, where access to factors of production being in short supply is the easiest and where the results are the best. In this case, transnational corporations are interested in the globalization of the world economy and, hence, in its universal liberalization, complying with the international policy represented by such institutions as the IMF or the WTO.

5.2.5. International Cartels

International cartels are, in principle, agreements (as a rule, between manufacturers) obligating their signatories to pursue a production, export, price policy agreed between them. Frequently, they are informal agreements kept secret from other economic entities, protecting their signatories against retaliatory action by remaining market participants.[41] In many countries, cartels are forms of organization forbidden to economic entities.

Basic forms of cartel activity include the obligation to refrain from exporting to the partner's main markets, to avoid price competition, to operate in assigned market segments, and so on. Participants in such agreements may be not only private enterprises and state-owned enterprises but also governments.

Cartel agreements flourished between the two world wars. After the Second World War many anti-cartel laws appeared that restricted concluding such agreements. Cartels came to be treated as a form of production and market monopolization negatively effecting competition and, consequently, prices, quality and technological level of production. In spite of these limitations, some forms of cartel agreements still exist, among them the Organisation of Petroleum Exporting Countries). Between 1972 and 1980 the OPEC led to an over 15-fold rise of the world crude oil price by limiting output and export. The low price flexibility of the demand for crude oil only facilitated OPEC countries the attainment of their goal.

---

41 Comp. J. Sołdaczuk, Z. Kamecki, P. Bożyk, *Międzynarodowe stosunki gospodarcze. Teoria i polityka*, op. cit., pp. 75–7.

Summing up, subjects of international economic policy do not shape this policy in the same way. Neither do they act in the same direction. This results primarily from contradictory economic interests. The latter concern, in particular, divergences between governments, corporations and cartels but can also be observed among integration groupings and international organizations. In effect, international policy should be treated as some kind of outcome of all these influences.

Chapter 6

The Concept of Global Economic Policy

6.1. Definition of Global Economic Policy

Global economic policy is a policy envisaged through the world economy. It may be comprehensive and cover all countries, all types of economic activity and all issues linked with globalization. It may also be fragmentary and involve specific regions, sectors or issues.

Geographically, global economic policy can be followed by either one country or a group of countries. In both cases, exogenous factors determining this policy take priority over endogenous factors.[1] For example, the United States, while pursing a global economic policy, should subordinate endogenous factors to exogenous ones that are dependent on the world economy. Similarly, the EU should take into account the needs and possibilities of its member states determined by exogenous factors.

In sector terms, global economic policy can be pursued in reference to a specific product, several products or a whole sector. In this case, exogenous factors should also be decisive. This means that the major producers and consumers of a single product or group of products should pursue a policy subordinated to the needs and possibilities of the world economy. For example, a global fuel policy should not be determined by the interests of oil producers and exporters but by the world as a whole. These interests are often contradictory, making such a policy difficult to implement.

As regards the third criterion, global economic policy can deal with a specific problem viewed from a global perspective (for example, environmental protection) or a group of problems (for example, international indebtedness and the economic backwardness of the Third World). It may also embrace all the global problems facing the world.

6.1.1. Global Economic Policy and Foreign Economic Policy

In keeping with the aforementioned definitions, global economic policy is not a sum of foreign economic policies pursued by different countries around the world. Factors determining this policy are approached in different ways. Endogenous factors play a primary role in foreign economic policy, while exogenous factors play a supplementary role. In the case of global economic policy, the reverse is the case:

---

1   See P. Bożyk, J. Misala, M. Puławski, *Międzynarodowe stosunki ekonomiczne*, op. cit., p. 400.

exogenous factors prevail, while endogenous factors play a supplementary role. Furthermore, in foreign economic policy, exogenous factors may be approached selectively, depending on their significance for a given country. In global economic policy, exogenous factors should be approached comprehensively, without differentiation between those of greater and lesser importance.

Similarly, the goals, means and instruments of foreign and global economic policies are formulated in different ways. The greatest differences are between an endogenous foreign economic policy and a global economic policy. In an endogenous policy, the emphasis is on the needs and possibilities of a single country. Exogenous factors are treated as supplementary. The United States continues to pursue such a policy, its economic growth being some 95% based on endogenous factors (including domestic factors of production, the level and structure of production, consumer demand at home, etc.). In this approach, exogenous factors should at best facilitate economic policy goals determined by endogenous factors. When this is not the case, the United States seeks to modify exogenous factors instead of subordinating economic policy goals to the needs and possibilities of the world economy. The problem is that, while following a global economic policy, the United States does the opposite. For example, the Kyoto Protocol, which protects the world from excessive hazardous emissions, should be treated as a fixed system under a global economic policy. Individual countries should adapt their economic policy goals determined by endogenous factors (structure of industrial production, technology used, methods of counteracting pollution, etc.) accordingly. However, the United States, even though it pursues an endogenous economic policy, did not sign the Kyoto Protocol. It continues to pursue its economic policy goals, polluting the environment to the detriment of all other countries.

The differences between a contractual foreign economic policy and a global economic policy are smaller. A contractual policy is a step toward a global economic policy. It involves a partial subordination of foreign economic policy goals to exogenous factors. These goals are formulated by considering the needs and possibilities not only of a specific country but also those of the rest of the world. International agreements that bind a given economy to the world economy are the main institutional form of this dependence. A contractual policy can be treated as a fragment of global economic policy. Focusing on select countries, it is not optimal because it may involve the dependence of the country pursuing a contractual policy on random exogenous factors instead of the most beneficial factors for both this country and the world economy.

6.1.2. Global Economic Policy and International Economic Policy

To a large extent, international policy is free from the deficiencies that foreign economic policy displays in relation to global economic policy. It approaches exogenous factors in a uniform manner, which means that foreign economic policy goals, means and instruments formulated by individual countries are coordinated more strictly than in a situation when each country does that on its own.

International economic policy can be either global in range or limited to a certain number of countries. In the first case, this may be a policy followed by producers of raw materials (copper, zinc, tin, etc.) or food (wheat, coffee, cocoa), for example. In the second case, this applies to policies such as integration policy, commercial policy (pursued as part of the GATT/WTO system), economic development policy (pursued as part of the OECD) and credit policy (followed as part of the IMF and the World Bank).

Understood in this way, international economic policy is a form of coordinating the foreign economic policies of countries interested in such coordination. This is the essence of the difference between an international economic policy and foreign economic policy. In a situation when coordination is conducted on an ex post basis, limited possibilities exist for bringing about a uniform influence of exogenous factors on the foreign economic policy goals, means and instruments of countries participating in the process. Information about exogenous factors is obtained with delay, and countries following a foreign economic policy may (but do not have to) use them when formulating their future policy goals, means and instruments.

Ex ante coordination of foreign economic policy, providing for a uniform influence of exogenous factors on foreign economic policy goals, means and instruments, is free from these drawbacks. This coordination may take various forms, from harmonizing or lifting limitations in the international movement of goods, services and factors of production to introducing uniform pricing, exchange rate and monetary policies. Ex ante coordination of foreign economic policy may thus lead to the introduction of a common economic policy.

A common foreign economic policy (coordinated ex ante) and global economic policy differ chiefly in terms of geography, covered sectors and the range of problems. A common foreign economic policy (coordinated ex ante) may cover a geographically limited group of countries (for example, members of a specific group, members of the WTO or members of the IMF). The principles of this policy are not obligatory for other countries. A common foreign economic policy (coordinated ex ante) may also apply to a specific business sector (such as manufactured goods, textiles, speculative capital, etc.). Other sectors are excluded from this type of coordination. Finally, a common international economic policy (coordinated ex ante) may focus on a uniform approach to solving a specific problem to a limited extent, either geographically or in sector terms. For example, the policy may take the form of a ban on the trade of hazardous materials within the EU. It therefore represents a local approach to solving a global problem.[2]

6.2. Forms of Global Economic Policy

Global economic policy can be either exogenous or endogenous. In an exogenous global economic policy, only foreign economic policy is uniform, while

---

2   N. Acocella, *Zasady polityki gospodarczej*, op. cit., pp. 541–2.

macroeconomic policies are determined on an independent basis by individual countries participating in the globalization process. An exogenous global economic policy focuses on pursuing a common policy in the movement of goods, services and factors of production on a global scale. This policy is referred to as a 'software' policy.

An endogenous global economic policy, on the other hand, is the result of uniform macro- and microeconomic policies pursued by countries participating in the process of globalization. This policy can be termed a 'hardware' policy.

6.2.1. 'Software' Global Economic Policy

A 'software' global economic policy boils down to opening individual markets to the movement of goods, services and factors of production. The policy was initiated after the Second World War along with the liberalization of international trade. The GATT (1947–94) and its successor, the WTO, have played an especially important role in this area. As a result of their operations, import duties and other restrictions have been either removed or seriously reduced worldwide, which has enabled free movement of manufactured goods and initiated liberalization in the movement of services and factors of production.

A 'software' policy may take various institutional forms from loose international affiliations to stricter agreements. 'Software' global economic policy forms include a free trade zone, a customs union and a common market.

The simplest institutional form of a 'software' global economic policy is a free trade zone open to all countries interested in this form of globalization. The scope of a free trade zone could range from select commodity groups to overall trade. Such a zone brings two types of benefits to member countries. First, it facilitates global market access for goods produced by member countries, reducing their prices by the value of import duty lifted. Second, it makes market access difficult for goods from outside the free trade zone, with regard to which duty does not change; these goods are thus more expensive than goods produced within the zone. Therefore a free trade zone primarily expands the export market for member countries; in consequence it contributes to an increased scope of production, reduced costs by unit and increased benefits from trade. In the longer term, it changes the structure of production in member countries as a result of the trade creation and trade diversion effects.

The trade diversion effect is expressed by an increased participation of countries belonging to a free trade zone in their overall trade at the expense of countries outside the zone (as a result of decreased purchases of specific goods from non-zone countries, even those with lower costs). The diversion effect also involves a different scope of difficulties in market access; inside the zone, customs barriers are removed, unlike in zone members' relations with external countries. This leads to a situation in which goods produced more expensively within the zone are cheaper to buy for zone members than goods produced outside the zone. This is because the prices of the latter include the effects of import duty and other barriers.

The trade creation effect is expressed by an increased volume of mutual trade among countries participating in the zone as a result of lifting import duties and other trade barriers. Prior to the establishment of a free trade zone, individual countries meet the market needs with their own production not subject to foreign competition. Imported goods subject to barriers would be more expensive. The establishment of a free trade zone and the related removal of barriers lead to a situation in which domestic production by more expensive manufacturers becomes unprofitable due to the possibility of importing cheaper goods from zone member countries. As a result, comparative benefits grow, as does mutual trade within the zone. The trade creation effect can also be viewed in a wider perspective, assuming that the establishment of a free trade zone influences not only the trade of countries belonging to the zone, but also overall global trade. In such a situation, the trade creation effect reflects the overall increase in demand for imports in zone member countries as well as changes in demand for imports in countries outside the zone.

The trade diversion and creation effects should be treated as key factors stimulating interest in 'software' globalization. Both effects are easy to obtain. The first could result from a relative drop in the prices of goods produced by a new member state (as a result of removing import duties or other limitations that negatively affect the competitiveness of the country's products) in relation to other countries outside the zone. The second effect could stem from an increased competitiveness of goods produced by a new zone member in relation to goods previously produced in the zone. Prior to entry to the zone, this country's goods were more expensive (due to import duty) and consequently uncompetitive on the zone's internal market.

In the short term, the trade diversion and trade creation effects results in an increased volume of trade for a given country within the free trade zone, along with improved terms of trade. In the long term, they lead to favourable structural changes in the economy, based on either abandoning or restructing relatively ineffective production and investment activities, accompanied by an increased importance of specialization. Concessions in the movement of goods and services at the same time enable individual countries to concentrate on the most effective areas in their spending policies.

As a form of software globalization, a free trade zone is created in the absence of a direct movement of factors of production and autonomous micro- and macroeconomic policies. The only exception is the customs policy practised within the zone.

A slightly more complex form of 'software' globalization is a customs union based on introducing a uniform duty in commercial relations between the free trade zone and non-member countries. At the same time, the establishment of a customs union could be accompanied by the removal of some para- and non-tariff limitations (for example, quantitative limitations) within the free trade zone. However, the basic task of a customs union is to prevent imports from outside the zone by those member countries which had the lowest customs duties in relations with non-member countries, prior to the establishment of a customs union.

A customs union, as a form of 'software' global economic policy, would consequently mean further limitations in the scope of the autonomous economic policies of associate countries, compared with the free trade zone. These countries are unable to shape their national customs policies independently either within the customs union or in relations with non-member states. These restrictions could apply to all goods indiscriminately or to a specific group of goods. Countries belonging to the customs union, however, continue to pursue an autonomous policy on the movement of factors of production.

Another step toward a global economic policy is a common market, covering countries interested in such an institutional form of globalization. Common market members would be obligated to meet all the requirements of a free trade zone and customs union and also have to guarantee free movement of labour, capital and technology among member states. In this way, common market members have free access to both goods and factors of production generated as part of this form of globalization. This modifies their commercial and production decisions compared with the situation within the zone and the customs union. The concept of scarce and plentiful factors of production changes. In a free trade zone and customs union, factors of production depend on the capability of an individual country; in a common market, they depend on the capability of all member states, thereby determining the structure of both mutual trade and trade with non-member states. However, an autonomous economic policy continues to be pursued by member countries in those areas which are only indirectly linked with the international movement of goods and factors of production. This primarily applies to monetary, financial, budgetary and credit policies.

'Software' global economic policy is an instrument for a diversified approach to globalization in the world economy, taking into account different economic conditions in individual countries and consequent diversification in globalization possibilities. This approach is based on the assumption that identical global economic policies can produce strongly diversified results in different structural, technological and social conditions. That is why individual countries should choose their own institutional forms of globalization depending on their specific situation. The least developed countries with unbalanced economies and limited development potential should be capable of taking advantage of different economic policy means and instruments to a greater extent than highly developed countries with balanced economies and stable structural and system foundations. In this way, they can prevent pathological practices triggered by insufficient development and the lack of equilibrium in the economy, including foreign debt, budget deficit and public debt.

A shared feature of global economic policy in this approach is a free trade zone, either universal – covering all goods, or selective – covering selected groups of goods (manufactured goods, for example). A move to more developed forms of global economic policy involves a selection of countries. Some are interested in such forms due to the possible economic benefits involved, while others would choose to remain at the free trade zone level without taking advantage of these opportunities for fear of potential pathological developments.

The three forms of 'software' global economic policy discussed above (free trade zone, customs union and common market) create potential possibilities for the more effective use of capital, labour, technology and natural resources than in the case of a single country or a group of countries. This contributes to prosperity and economic growth, but only when countries pursuing this policy meet specific requirements; otherwise, instead of benefits, pathological practices may develop.

Thanks to competition, the movement of goods and services leads to higher labour and fixed asset productivity, along with accelerated technological progress, modern production methods and better product quality. It forces domestic producers to make an effort to reduce production costs; otherwise they will go bankrupt due to demand shifting to better and cheaper foreign goods. Individual countries, enjoying autonomy in their endogenous macroeconomic and microeconomic policies, are in a position to encourage national producers to increase their competitiveness. On the other hand, they cannot hinder market access for foreign producers and suppliers. National economic policy can thus help enterprises reduce production costs through easier access to modern designs, technology, know-how and better management and marketing methods. However, none of these methods can be classified among tariff, para-tariff or non-tariff limitations.

Free movement of capital, labour, technology and natural resources additionally requires national producers to either increase competitiveness or face bankruptcy. The autonomy of individual countries in their endogenous macroeconomic and microeconomic policies positively influences the competitiveness of domestic entities (provided such influence is possible).

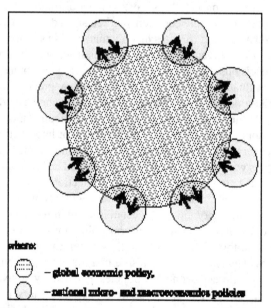

Figure 6.1. 'Software' Global Economic Policy in Graphic Terms

Source: The author's own research.

The effectiveness of a 'software' global economic policy depends on an individual economy's ties with the world economy. When exports account for no more than a few percent of the gross domestic product, these ties are much looser than when the share is 50% and more. Similar differences occur between countries with a marginal share of foreign direct investment and those in which this is much higher.

The influence of a 'software' global economic policy varies. Individual economies which open to the movement of goods, services and factors of production must be aware of growing foreign penetration: indirect – in the form of goods and services, or direct – in the form of investment, know-how, etc. This process leads to the 'maturing' of national economies whereby they succumb to the rules of a 'hardware' global economic policy. This occurs through increased competitiveness of some national entities and bankruptcy of others. The autonomy of endogenous national macroeconomic and microeconomic policies is expressed by their positive effect on those national entities that offer prospects for higher competitiveness in relation to foreign entities. At the same time, attempts are discarded to influence foreign entities to reduce their competitiveness in relation to domestic entities.

6.2.2. 'Hardware' Global Economic Policy

The simplest institutional form of a 'hardware' global economic policy is a global monetary union favouring a uniform monetary policy – a macroeconomic policy instrument. Monetary union members have to meet all the requirements of a free trade zone, customs union and common market and additionally be required to maintain fixed exchange rates (or rates that fluctuate within strictly specified bands). A monetary union then prevents member countries from influencing the production and commercial decisions of enterprises by changing the value of national currencies (through either devaluation/depreciation or revaluation/appreciation). The issue is to make sure that these decisions are made exclusively on the basis of differences in production costs. At the same time, a monetary union requires member countries to harmonize their money issuance policies and methods of intervention on the money market. Global economic policy carried out in the form of a monetary union could only cover countries with balanced economies (balanced budget, balanced payments, no foreign debt) and a competitive structure of production.

An economic union is characterized by a much wider scope of economic policy globalization than a monetary union. An economic union features a uniform policy on the global movement of goods, a uniform policy on the movement of factors of production and uniform financial (as well as fiscal), budgetary, lending, capital and social policies. The issue is to make sure that the actions of businesses are not determined by the different economic policies pursued by individual countries. Enterprises with unlimited global access to goods and factors of production are guided exclusively by different production costs; the global division of labour among countries should consequently be determined by differences in management effectiveness.

In this form, global economic policy countries participating in the process of globalization remain autonomous only in the law-making, respect for the law and preventing violations of free market and free trade rules. However, this autonomy is not complete. Even though individual countries are able to legislate, their legal systems would be unified globally. The issue is to make sure that enterprises conducting business activity did not encounter barriers in the form of different legal rules. Methods to guarantee respect for the law, including the operation of the court system, prosecutors' offices and the police become unified. Finally, methods to counter infringements of free market and free trade rules, including anti-monopoly regulations, become identical.

Legal system unification in all countries participating in the process of globalization primarily guarantees a free movement of goods, services and factors of production and greater benefits than those derived from a social or international division of labour. Unification also guarantees a situation in which enterprises would make their global business decisions exclusively on the basis of different production costs, with no distortions caused by economic policy.

These guarantees should be expressed by uniform micro- and macroeconomic policies that would encourage global market players – including both corporate bodies (enterprises and banks) and individuals (retailers, producers and investors) – to sell their goods and services and make direct and portfolio investments in countries that follow such policies. These policies should promote low inflation, balanced budgets, stable exchange rates and low interest rates. The balance of payments should show a surplus and public debt not exceeding certain limits. If this

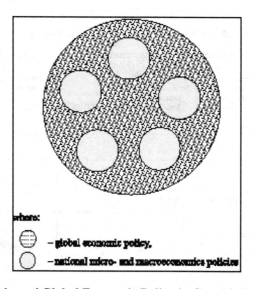

where:

⬤ – global economic policy,

◯ – national micro- and macroeconomic policies

Figure 6.2. 'Hardware' Global Economic Policy in Graphic Terms

Source: The author's own research.

is to be the case, a universal form of ownership must be private ownership based on stable legal foundations, while the role of the state is limited to providing a legal framework and pursuing a macroeconomic policy.

The macroeconomic policy pursued by individual countries and the global economic policy become fully compatible. The global policy would result from national policies; at the same time the policies of individual countries are consistent with the rules governing the global policy.

Countries participate in the global market on a voluntary basis as a result of their own decisions. Countries whose economic policies would not comply with the principles governing global economic policy fail to attract the interest of global market players in direct capital investment, technology transfer and goods and service imports, along with many other negative consequences for economies left out of the globalization process – including a deficit in the balance of payments, growing indebtedness, imbalanced budget, increased public debt, and consequently high inflation, slow GDP growth and a slide to the peripheries of the world economy.

Such countries are deemed to credit assistance from the IMF or other institutions. However, such assistance is impossible without obligating an indebted country to pursue micro- and macroeconomic policies congruent with the global economic policy. The 'Washington consensus' then applies.

The aim of the 'Washington consensus' is to guarantee collision-free operations of the free market and free trade in countries which avoid micro- and macroeconomic policies compatible with global economic policy. At the same time, the 'Washington consensus' is designed to guarantee businesses limited participation in this process.

Table 6.1. Institutional Forms of Global Economic Policy

Institutional form of global policy	Elimination of barriers to the development of mutual commercial ties	External common commercial limitations	Free movement of factors of production	Harmonization of monetary and fiscal policies, fixed exchange rates or single currency	Global unification of economic policy
Free trade zone	'Software' global economic policy				
Customs union					
Common market					
Monetary union				'Hardware' global economic policy	
Economic union					

Source: Compiled on the basis of P. Bożyk, J. Misala, Integracja ekonomiczna, op. cit., p. 38.

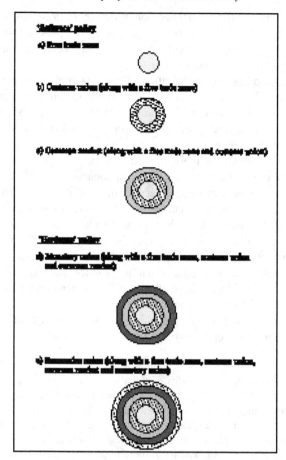

Figure 6.3. Institutional Forms of Global Economic Policy

Source: Author's own elaboration.

6.3. Ways of Introducing Global Economic Policy

Generally, there are two different methods of developing and implementing global economic policy: polycentric and monocentric. The polycentric method is based on many simultaneous decisions taken autonomously by individual countries or groups of countries as part of various international organizations. These decisions can be voluntary or taken under the pressure of external factors. As a result, macro- and microeconomic policies become uniform.

At the core of polycentric decisions is the interest of states and businesses in potential benefits to be derived from participation in globalization. Predominately, this applies to economically developed large and medium-sized countries that enjoy a strong position in the international division of labour. Their decisions to participate actively in the globalization process are taken under the pressure of domestic and foreign transnational enterprises interested in wider export markets, a greater scope of production and longer production runs.

Some decisions on active participation in globalization are made by small and medium-sized, poorly developed countries struggling with economic difficulties. These countries hope to improve their condition through an inflow of external capital, especially in the form of foreign direct investment, an influx of modern technology and highly qualified specialists.

Some countries decide actively to join the globalization process under the pressure of various international organizations such as the IMF, the World Bank and the WTO. Countries with troubled economies are most likely to request these organizations for assistance, or expect that membership in these organizations would earn them preferential treatment (such as access to a larger market, investment loans granted along preferential lines, etc.). Both the IMF and the World Bank require that countries which ask for help to resolve their debt problems act in keeping with the 'Washington consensus', which in practice necessitates a 'hardware' global economic policy. Countries interested in WTO membership are instructed to introduce a 'software' global economic policy.

However, action in line with the 'Washington consensus', as in the case of WTO resolutions, does not produce the expected results, particularly for poorly developed countries.

> If, in too many instances, the benefits of globalization have been less than its advocates claim, the price paid has been greater [...] The crises that have brought in their wake massive unemployment have, in turn, been followed by longer-term problems of social dissolution – from urban violence in Latin America to ethnic conflicts in other parts of the world, such as Indonesia [...] Protestors see globalization in a very different light than the treasury secretary of the United States, or the finance and trade ministers of most of the advanced industrial countries. The differences in views are so great that one wonders, are the protestors and the policy makers talking about the same phenomena? Are they looking at the same data? ...[3]

J.E. Stiglitz blames the three aforementioned international institutions, the IMF, the World Bank and the WTO, for imposing the current model of 'hardware' globalization. He also criticizes regional banks, World Bank sister institutions and various organizations included within the United Nations system such as the United Nations Development Programme (UNDP) and the UNCTAD.[4]

However, this does not mean that all international institutions advocate a 'hardware' global economic policy based on a free market and free trade according to the American model. For example, the Asian Development Bank supports a 'software' solution that enables globalization participants to conduct an exogenous

---

3   See J.E. Stiglitz, *Globalization and its Discontents*, op. cit., pp. 25–6.
4   Ibid., p. 27.

macroeconomic policy and endogenous microeconomic policy, taking into account local conditions. In this approach to global economic policy, the role of the state is not necessarily limited to making and enforcing the law and preventing infringements of free market and free trade rules. The state also plays an active role in creating and managing the market.

A monocentric method makes use of the experiences of the US economy, which operates as part of a federal system.[5] The federal government has the right to influence individual states, which enjoy a certain measure of legal and economic independence. However, the federal government is equipped with superior powers; it makes federal law, safeguards respect for the law (using local courts, prosecutors and the police force) and prevents violations of free market and free trade rules. The federal government, with the help of the central bank, issues legal tenders that are obligatory nationwide and is responsible for the banking system, the stock market and other instruments necessary for the functioning of the federal economy. At the same time, economic decisions are taken on the basis of absolute (not comparative) differences in production costs.

A global federation of countries – in which national markets are treated as local markets and no single currency exists created by one global bank – operates along similar lines. There are no currency exchange rates, no trade or balance of payments deficits, and no national micro- and macroeconomic policies. At the local level, national centres could exist equipped with some governmental powers, but responsible to the federal government in fundamental matters. Economic decisions are taken by businesses on the basis of absolute differences in costs and local parameters (such as wages, prices and pensions). This means that the federation features different standards of living, accompanied by a free movement of goods, services and factors of production.

However, such a vision of globalization does not answer one question: according to what pattern would the federal government be formed? Would each country have the same number of votes regardless of their size and per capita GDP? In what way would decisions be taken: international (on the basic of the principle of majority) or supranational (unanimously)? Nor is it known how the federal government would prevent transnational corporations – whose economic capacity is often greater than that of medium-sized countries – from cornering local markets. Would local markets with adverse economic conditions (an unfavourable climate, scarce national resources and underdeveloped infrastructure) be deserted, or would the federal government be capable of determining production destinations on the basis of non-economic criteria?

As it stands, the monocentric global economic policy method seems to be completely detached from the current political realities and has no chance of practical application.

---

5   See W. Szymański, *Interesy i sprzeczności globalizacji* (Difin, Warsaw, 2004), p. 129.

Chapter 7

Exemplification of Foreign and International Economic Policy

7.1. The Core of Exemplification

The term 'exemplification' is used here to denote practical verification of macro- and microeconomic policy instruments. The aim is to show how these instruments have been applied in practice to solve specific economic problems.

The second half of the 20th century is characterized by essential revaluations of the criteria of the international division of labour followed by profound changes in foreign and international economic policy. These changes find reflection in the differentiation of this policy between individual geographical regions and groups of countries. Simultaneously, tendencies exist towards making this policy more uniform.

Broadly speaking, four geographical regions pursuing different foreign economic policies can be distinguished: the economically developed countries, the newly industrialized countries, the poorly developed countries and the countries transforming their economies. In the second half of the past century all the groups mentioned tended to pursue a similar foreign economic policy. However, a deeper analysis of this policy reveals the existence of a clear differentiation of aims, means and instruments of foreign economic policy also within each of these groups. Therefore, not only each of group but also a number of their subgroups will be subject to a separate analysis.

7.2. Highly Industrialized Countries

After the Second World War, the economically developed countries found themselves in different economic situations.

The United States of America enjoyed the best position. Following the economic expansion during the Second World War, this country became the world's principal industrial and financial power. In 1948 the United States accounted for approximately 60% of world industrial output. At the same time, it outpaced the remaining economically developed countries in terms of technical progress. The latter accelerated significantly during the Second World War, manifested in new product design, new materials and technologies unknown in other countries. Consequently, the United States became the world's main exporter, in 1948 accounting for over

23% of world exports. Moreover, every year the country recorded an enormous current account trade surplus with Western Europe and the rest of the world. In Western Europe this generated the problem of the so-called *dollar gap*, i.e. a long-term shortage of dollar foreign exchange resources which forced the United States to extend to Western Europe credit assistance and provide gratuitous commodity deliveries of the total value of 16.4 billion dollars.[1]

In addition, in 1948 the United States started a special economic aid programme for Europe – *the European Recovery Programme* – known as the Marshall Plan.[2] Apart from Western Europe, Japan, the Middle East and some other countries also benefited from US assistance. Total American government aid between 1946 and 1953 amounted to 42 billion dollars.[3] This, together with the export of private investment capital, gives an amount of 50 billion dollars serving to cover the world's dollar deficit towards the United States at that time.

That solution was advantageous not only for Western Europe and other highly industrialised countries but also for the United States. After the Second World War, the United States became the unquestionable, though lonely, world power. The transformation of part of the armaments industry into civilian production generated a state of commodity surplus which the demand on the American market was too weak to absorb. A solution had to be found in the development of different forms of export, since the demand in Western Europe, Japan and other countries was practically unlimited. But this required credit, as such exports could not be offset by exports to the United States due to commodity shortages.

The United States was, therefore, interested in the fastest possible reconstruction of Western Europe, Japan and other war-destroyed countries to allow them to develop exports and stop suffering from the dollar shortage i.e. from imports exceeding exports.

The position of Western Europe after the Second World War was the exact opposite of the United States'. Its infrastructure and thus roads, towns and social facilities were destroyed. Its industry was ruined, there was a shortage of professional staff, machines, construction materials. The demand for imported goods considerably exceeded the export supply. The trade balance was, consequently, negative and internal currencies inconvertible.

Japan also found itself after the Second World War in a difficult economic situation. Industrial production dropped significantly in comparison with pre-war, unemployment and inflation were running high.[4] This resulted not only from war destruction but also from the discontinuation of armaments-related purposes and

---

1   J. Sołdaczuk, J. Misala, *Historia handlu*, op. cit., p. 160.

2   From the name of the author of the programme, US Secretary of State, G. Marshall.

3   J. Sołdaczuk, J. Misala, *Historia handlu*, op. cit., p. 164.

4   Comp. J. Bossak, *Japonia. Strategia rozwoju w punkcie zwrotnym* (PWN, Warsaw, 1990), p. 23; M. Niesiołowski, *Japonia; źródła i kierunki rozwoju gospodarczego* (PWE, Warsaw, 1974), p. 63.

demobilization of an army of almost 7 million. Simultaneously, a radical reform of industry and agriculture was undertaken.

All this substantially reduced Japan's export potential with a simultaneous upsurge of its import requirements. Japan became an importer not only of raw materials and foodstuffs but also industrial goods. The level of Japan's foreign trade at the same time was significantly lower than pre-war. Japan exceeded its 1935 import level only in 1956, and that of 1935 exports in 1959. Between 1945 and 1951 the United States covered the Japanese negative trade balance in the form of aid.

7.2.1. The United States of America

Traditionally, the United States was dependent on the world economy to a relatively small extent. Prior to the Second World War its share in global exports did not exceed 10% and was three times lower than its share in the global industrial production.

However, the situation changed drastically immediately after the Second World War. The United States' share in global exports increased to 22%, and in global industrial exports to 27%.[5] Simultaneously, the United States came to be the world's principal capital exporter. As a result of all these developments, the country began to pay much more attention than before the Second World War to the world market with the aim of regulating it. In the first place, the United States wanted to prevent any recurrence of the inter-war period when the paper money introduced to replace the gold-based currency system failed to prevent chaos in international settlements, due, among other things to continuous devaluation of national currencies and high inflation. Simultaneously, after the Second World War the United States found itself in the position of a creditor helping others in the form of donations and loans.

The American concept consisted of reforming international economic relations in such a way that every country would bear the burden of maintaining equilibrium in their own balance of payments. Thus, the United States rejected the concept of the British economist J.M. Keynes, who proposed that mainly the United States be burdened with the costs of offsetting the balance of payments deficits of countries whose exports were lower than imports following the Second World War. According to Keynes, this equilibrium could be attained by liberalizing access to the American market with the purpose of accelerating exports from countries with payment difficulties.

The United States did not want, however, to commit itself to liberalizing access exclusively to their internal market for imported goods. Traditionally, this market was shielded by a number of tariff, para-tariff and non-tariff restrictions. Instead, the United States put forward a concept to liberalize international trade as a whole, understood, in the first place, as eliminating restrictions of access for American goods to the European market. It was to this end that the International Trade Organization as well as the IMF were established. The latter was, moreover, to lead

---

5   Comp. P. Bożyk (ed.), *Gospodarka światowa* (PWE, Warsaw, 2003), p. 27.

to the establishment of the convertibility of national currencies and the replacement of bilateral settlements with multilateral settlements.

And so it happened. In spite of the failure to establish the International Trade Organization immediately after the war and to liberalize international trade at a fast rate, the GATT concluded in place of this organization led, in the long term, to a reduction of the level of customs duties on industrial goods while the IMF, with the help of other organizations and institutions, led to the convertibility of national currencies in many countries.

Since its inception, the IMF has become an instrument of consistent implementation of the American concept of international economic relations according to which every country should shape its standard of living to ensure long-term equilibrium in the balance of payments in relations with foreign countries.[6] In the short term, lack of such equilibrium can be financed by the IMF but a long-term solution should be found in a departure from living beyond one's means.

The international economic policy of the United States after the Second World War was marked by a kind of dualism. Externally, the United States advocated liberalism in foreign and international policy but internally propagated Keynesism, which, with all its properties sanctioning extensive state interventionism, remained the dominating doctrine.[7] Access to the American market was protected not only by customs duties but also by para-tariff and non-tariff restrictions. Anti-dumping procedures as well as procedures preventing market disruption were frequently launched. In exports, subventions and other actions increasing the competitiveness of American goods on foreign markets were applied.

The policy of autonomic development of American economy made the United States lag behind the development of Japan and Western Europe, especially in the 1960s and the 1970s. This meant that the United States was gradually losing the advantage it had, especially technologically, over other countries. Also, the GDP growth rate in the USA was lower in comparison with Western Europe and Japan. As a result, the share of the United States in the world product went down (from around 40% in 1950 to 30% in 1970). The share of the United States in world exports also decreased gradually (from 16% in 1950 to 14% in 1970). Moreover, starting from the late 1970s, the United States found itself in an unfavourable payment situation in relation to other countries. The deficit which emerged came to be financed by dollar emission which undermined confidence in this currency and generated an increased demand for gold. As a result, gold reserves in the United States decreased by one-third. The country was, thus, forced to take the steps which it proposed to other countries immediately after the war via the IMF. Taxes were raised, monetary policy tightened and import restrictions increased. This resulted in a weakening of the economic growth rate. However, it did not hamper the growth of negative trends in the balance of payments, which were further aggravated by the outflow of American

6   Comp. J. Sołdaczuk, *Współczesna gospodarka światowa*, op. cit., pp. 46–7.

7   Comp. W. Bieńkowski, *Oddziaływanie rządu U.S.A. na rozwój zdolności konkurencyjnej gospodarki amerykańskiej 1981–1988* (SGH, Warsaw, 1993), p. 123 and following.

capital abroad. As a result, in 1971 confidence in the dollar was shattered to the extent that the United States was forced to devalue its currency and abandon the dollar's convertibility into gold (in relations with central banks). In effect, the system developed in Bretton Woods (sometimes called the dollar-gold system) collapsed.

In the 1970s, the health of the American economy worsened even further compared with the 1960s.[8] Its competitiveness indicators worsened in comparison with Western Europe and Japan. The United States recorded a lower GDP growth rate and the growth of its product per capita dropped to zero. However, while in Western Europe a certain slowdown in the economic growth rate also registered in the second half of the 1970s was due to the world raw material-energy crisis, in the United States it was autonomic development and its consequences in the form of growing unemployment and inflation that were the main reasons. One of the symptoms of autonomic development was, in the 1970s, the worsening balance of trade deficit which reached almost 40 billion dollars at the end of the period. The raw-material-energy crisis had an insignificant impact on the state of America's economy (unlike in Europe), due to the fact that the United States had its own rich raw material base and was dependent on imports much less than Europe.

All that together highlighted a need for a change in the development strategy of the US economy. A new strategy, commonly known as 'Reaganomics', put the stress on liberalizing the American economy, primarily internal economy, to enable a free flow of goods and factors of production within the United States. Simultaneously, a decision was taken to reduce restrictions in foreign economic relations, with respect not only to commodities but also factors of production, in particular, capital.

In US foreign economic policy, the stress was on a feedback between widening the scope of freedom in relations with other countries and the free play of market forces inside the country. In this context, the foreign and international economic policy came to be referred to as 'domesticism'.[9] In practice, this meant treating US foreign economic policy as a derivative of internal economic policy. In this sense, the United States did not depart from the concept of autonomic development of its economy but solely introduced another economic policy to replace the Keynesian pro-supply policy with a liberal-monetary pro-demand policy.

Yet, after a lapse of but a few years, increased liberalism in US foreign economic relations, being the function of liberalism in internal policy, began to be limited under the influence of domestic manufacturers' demands. One expression of this was forcing Japan to introduce voluntary restraints on exports of industrial goods as well as the imposition by the USA of import limits on Japanese steel. High customs duties were also maintained on textiles and other goods imported to the United States. Meanwhile, foreign economic policy still voiced slogans concerning the need to ensure reciprocity in market access. In the sense of this principle, goods imported to

---

8 Comp. W. Bieńkowski, *Reaganomika i jej wpływ na konkurencyjność gospodarki amerykańskiej* (Wydawnictwo Naukowe PWN, Warsaw, 1995), p. 102.

9 Comp. ibid., p. 215.

the United States should be treated in the same way as American goods exported to other countries.

The autonomic character of US foreign economic policy led to a situation in which the reasons for the balance of trade deficit tended to be sought not internally but in the behaviour of America's trade partners. This tendency found its reflection in the Omnibus Trade and Competitiveness Act of 1988, which became effective as of 19 August 1988.[10] The Act sanctioned the existence of a number of restrictions in access to the American market making it easier for the president to conclude agreements on abolishing tariff, para-tariff and non-tariff barriers in foreign trade, in both bilateral and multilateral negotiations. The president was also given powers to extort reciprocity as regards imports from the USA from exporters to the USA. Should such countries refuse to do so, the president was authorized to apply retaliatory measures.

The result of this was to freeze the degree of the opening of the American economy reflected in an unchanged share of the USA in global exports at a mere 12%, almost the same as in the inter-war period. Only the share of imports to the USA in global imports increased (to about 17%) which meant that goods exported to the US market were more competitive than American goods. It was only the depreciation of the US dollar that brought about a reversal of these proportions – the share of the United States in world exports increasing slightly. This did not prevent, however, the emergence of a US deficit in foreign trade which exceeded 100 billion dollars in 1990. Its net foreign indebtedness also rose, exceeding 600 billion dollars in 1990.

On the whole, Reaganomics halted downward trends in the American economy preventing a decline of the US position in the global economy. This manifested itself in the growth of America's economy share in the world economy in the second half of the 1980s and in the first half of the 1990s. It did not, however, bring about the opening of this economy, which still remains developed in an autonomic way, though the degree of protection in access to the American market is smaller than it was in the 1985.[11]

7.2.2. Western Europe

Before the Second World War (1938) West European industrial production was similar to that of the USA, the difference in its share of global industrial output in favour of Western Europe amounting to 1.2% points (Western Europe had 42.4%, the United States 41.2%).[12] On the other hand, the share of Western Europe in the global

---

10 Comp. ibid., p. 228.

11 Comp. J. Bossak, E. Kawecka-Wyrzykowska, M. Tomala, *Stany Zjednoczone-EWG-Japonia. Współpraca i rywalizacja* (PWE, Warsaw, 1988), p. 69 and following.

12 P. Bożyk, *Gospodarka światowa*, op. cit., p. 172.

exports was three times higher than the share of the United States and amounted to 44%.[13]

Departure from Protectionism (1945–53)

After the Second World War (1948) the United States' share in global industrial production increased to 55.4% while that of Western Europe decreased to 25.4%. This was accompanied by a decline in differences in the shares of both parties in global exports (the United States – 23.2%, and Western Europe – 37.2%), the reason being the enormous damages suffered by West European economy. The reconstruction of the latter was connected in the initial period with the government aid of the United States (under the so-called *lend-lease* and later the Marshall Plan). In the late 1940s and in the 1950s, an important role was also played by direct capital investments by American private concerns, their value amounting to 17 billion dollars in 1950 and 27.5 billion dollars in 1970, thus accounting for 15 to 25% of the total investment outlays of Western Europe.

The foreign economic policy of Western Europe in the first post-war years was typically marked by protectionism in the form of high customs rates (averaging some 40%) and drastic quantitative and foreign exchange limitations. On the other hand, exports were widely subsidized. A policy of this kind was the consequence of the severe economic crisis caused by war damages, loss of part of foreign capital deposits and also substantial indebtedness towards the United States by virtue of military, food and other assistance received in the final phase of the war or immediately after the war. The protectionist foreign trade policy was aimed at reducing imports and supporting exports so as to ensure equilibrium in the balance of trade. It was obvious that under the conditions of Western Europe's complex economic situation at that time and the competitive offer of American companies, a liberal foreign trade policy was equivalent to a deepening payment crisis. The remains of the inter-war period characterized by tendencies toward limiting economic liberalism, disturbances in the convertibility of currencies and protectionism in international relations were also of some significance. During the Second World War even the limited liberalism of the late 1930s was suspended in all its forms, this referring also to the suspension of convertibility of currencies in countries which enjoyed it before the war.

Following the Second World War, economically weak Western Europe with its protectionist foreign economic policy and inconvertible domestic currencies was very inconvenient for the United States. From an economic partner, Western Europe changed into an aid-expecting region. So, the United States decided to extend such aid to Western Europe, but at the cost of thorough and deep-reaching reforms which were to lead to the transformation of this region into a sound and resilient economic partner. These reforms were to be based on the American concept of maintaining equilibrium in the balance of payments with the use of the *help yourself* method, by adjusting the standard of living to the economy's possibilities.

---

13 J. Sołdaczuk, *Współczesna gospodarka światowa*, op. cit., p. 35.

The Americans gave special attention to persuading Western Europe to build a strong export sector capable of offsetting the latter's import needs. The point was to develop the production of such articles which would be in demand on the American market.

This target was to be achieved by Western Europe by an industrial policy understood as government actions inducing enterprises and other economic entities to allocate existing production resources in sectors deemed particularly important for future development.[14] The instruments used for this purpose included both instruments of internal economic policy, that is the exchange rate, interest rate, money, finance, budget, prices, taxes, and instruments of foreign economic policy, including tariff, para-tariff and non-tariff ones. With their help, West European governments accelerated the development of certain industries in comparison with the development which would have taken place had the free market mechanism been its only determinant. Simultaneously, the development of other industries which would have developed faster had the free market mechanism been allowed to operate without disruptions (and thus without the industrial policy), was hampered. The first group included, in particular, such industries as electronics, aviation and precision engineering while the second included steel, coal and heavy industry.

At the same time, the United States emphasized the need to introduce convertibility of domestic currencies in Western Europe. It was for this purpose that the European Payment Union, comprising all West European countries, was established. Bilateral clearing introduced after the Second World War as an instrument of balancing exports and imports, was very painful for West European countries. Clearing agreements of bilateral character simultaneously limited mutual trade to the weaker partner's abilities. That is why in 1948 bilateral clearing was replaced with multilateral clearing and in 1950 limited multilateral exchange began to be introduced within the framework of the European Payment Union. This meant that every country made settlements jointly with all the remaining countries. The balances of trade of every country with the remaining countries of the Union were simultaneously offset partly by mutually extended credits and partly by transfers of gold and convertible currencies. In 1958, West European countries introduced external convertibility of their domestic currencies, as a result of which the European Payment Union was dissolved.

At the same time, the United States strove to liberalize the foreign trade of West European countries. It was for this purpose that the GATT, the IMF, the OEEC and later the OECD and other institutions as well as international organizations established after the Second World War were created. Two plains can be distinguished in the liberalization process of West European foreign trade: within integration groupings and in relations with countries from outside these groupings. The former were the Benelux countries, EFTA countries and members of the EEC. The process of removing access barriers to member countries' markets was proceeding much faster than in relations with countries from outside these groupings. The Benelux countries

---

14 See: P.R. Krugman, M. Obstfeld, *Międzynarodowe stosunki*, op. cit., p. 180.

abolished customs duties in mutual trade already on 1 January 1948.[15] A year later a uniform tariff was adopted for non-member countries. EFTA abolished customs duties on industrial goods in mutual trade in 1960. The EEC abolished quantitative restrictions in mutual trade as early as in 1961 and customs duties in 1968. Two years later uniform customs duties were introduced in trade with countries from outside the EEC, a customs union being thus created.

The reduction of barriers in the foreign trade of countries belonging to the above-mentioned integration groupings with countries not being members of the groupings proceeded much more slowly, in general under the auspices of GATT, on the basis of negotiations carried out during subsequent rounds. Customs duties were the first to be tackled. Till the raw-materials-energy crisis the average level of customs duties in international trade was lowered by a half (from 40% to 20%). Between 1974 and 1986 the pace of customs duties reduction slowed down somewhat, while in 1986 to 2002 it accelerated again. In total, the level of customs duties on industrial goods was lowered to a few per cent.

Quantitative restrictions were abolished or reduced primarily within the framework of the OEEC under the so-called liberalization code. Every year this code determined the part of imports to be covered by liberalization, with countries deciding independently about the goods in relation to which quantitative restrictions were to be abolished. In general, however, quantitative restrictions in trade between the OEEC countries and those outside this organization were abolished at a much slower pace than in mutual turnover between the OEEC members.

Foreign exchange restrictions in Western Europe were lifted in 1958 following the introduction of convertibility of domestic currencies. The aim was, however, reached step by step since the European Payment Union was established. This graduation solely concerned turnover within the Union. In relations between West European countries and those outside the region, foreign exchange restrictions were lifted at a much later period.

Liberalization of West European foreign trade also took the form of a reduction of the scope of export subsidizing. An important role in this process was played by GATT, which authorized member countries to counter subventions by using compensatory customs duties in cases where they had an adverse effect on the development of production in countries importing the subsidised goods. This concerned primarily the application of direct subventions.[16] Indirect subventions proved much more difficult to detect. In 1960, the economically developed countries signed a declaration forbidding the use of subventions with respect to industrial goods. However, the declaration left out most indirect subventions which meant that they continued to be applied also by West European countries.

The liberalization of trade of West European countries with countries outside the region between 1945 and 1973 concerned exclusively industrial goods. On the other hand, international food trade was not subject to any liberalization. On the contrary,

---

15 Comp. P. Bożyk, J. Misala, *Integracja ekonomiczna*, op. cit., p. 45.
16 J. Sołdaczuk, Z. Kamecki, P. Bożyk, *Międzynarodowe stosunki*, op. cit., p. 287.

the introduction of the common agricultural policy of the EEC countries intensified protectionism in relations with countries from outside the grouping. This concerned, in particular, para-tariff and non-tariff restrictions (especially quotas, subventions, foreign exchange limitations, and the like).

Neo-Protectionist Period (1974–86)

The increase of the crude oil price by members of OPEC from 1.9 dollars per barrel in 1972 to 12.7 dollars per barrel in 1978 (an almost seven-fold rise) contributed significantly to hampering the liberalization processes in international trade. Notably, trends to reduce customs duties weakened while attempts to introduce para- and non-tariff restrictions in international trade intensified markedly. These phenomena aggravated even further at the turn of the 1960s and the 1980s following another crude oil price hike by the OPEC countries from 12.7 dollars per barrel in 1978 to 30 dollars per barrel in 1980. In effect, between 1972 and 1980 crude oil prices rose over fifteen times.

This adversely affected development trends in Western Europe, which was hit particularly hard by the multi-fold growth of international crude oil prices as well as of other energy carriers. It was the trade and payments balances of energy-importing countries that deteriorated most, with deficits in these balances replacing surpluses. As a result, quantities of imported fuels decreased, exerting a negative impact on supplies to both the consumer market and production. Users of cars as well as other equipment requiring fuel or other energy carriers suffered serious difficulties in their access to fuels. Supplies of energy for production needs also diminished.

In consequence, the growth rate of the gross domestic product declined. Between 1974 and 1975, the GDP growth rate in Western Europe ranged from 1–2% annually to below zero. The second OPEC crude oil price hike slowed the GDP growth rate in Western Europe even further but did not cause an absolute drop (between 1980 and 1983 the GDP of West European countries increased by 0.8% while that of the OECD countries by 1.45% annually). It did, however, have a more adverse effect than the 1974–5 recession on unemployment and inflation; Western Europe as a whole registered a two-digit unemployment rate (10–12%) and a two-digit inflation rate. As a result, personal incomes declined and so did demand. Simultaneously, American banks raised interest rates thrice (from 6.8% in 1977 to 21% in 1981). This exerted a negative impact on investments in Western Europe as American capital investments in Europe decreased while West European capital began to flow to the United States instead of being invested at home.

All this contributed to the growth of the interest of European countries in raising exports and decreasing imports. In both cases para- and non-tariff instruments were employed.

Subventions, in particular indirect subventions, became the principal export-supporting instrument, with tax relief of all sorts, credit preferences, state assistance in advertising and promotion extended to a country's firms operating on foreign markets being common practice. To this end countries availed themselves of industrial or regional policy. Efforts were made to use all these forms of protectionism so that they would remain in compliance with GATT principles or be hard to detect.

In imports, particular attention was given in the analysed period to the maximum widening of the range of so-called 'sensitive' goods. Traditionally, 'sensitive' goods included textiles, steel and steel articles, coal and coal derivatives as well as foodstuffs and farm products. In the neo-protectionist period, the list of 'sensitive' goods was repeatedly enlarged. Apart from the above mentioned four groups, it came to include also footwear and leather articles, glass articles and china, wood and paper articles, cables, transport equipment (including ships), simple machines, electrical and electronic durables, roller bearings, fertilizers and other chemical articles.[17] Once these articles were classified as 'sensitive', governments could apply import restrictions of all sorts without exposing themselves to criticism by GATT.

A significant role in that period was played by so-called voluntary export restraints or agreements on voluntary export restraints to which exporters were forced by importers. In 1974 to 1986 they became such a common instrument of import-restricting that they had to be given special attention by the Uruguay Round which eventually forbade their application.

Other essential neo-protectionist instruments also included a variety of administrative formalities required when importing, as well as quality and technical requirements which imported goods had to satisfy. For instance, with respect to foodstuffs and farm products strict sanitary, veterinary and other similar requirements were imposed. Requirements concerning natural environment protection were also of significance.

Anti-dumping procedures were also common practice having a restrictive influence on imports even when dumping accusations proved unjustified.

In the foreign economic policy pursued by Western Europe in the neo-protectionist period, essential attention was given to accelerating regional integration within the European Economic Community and intensifying mutual trade, with special emphasis accorded to development of international cooperation in production and liberalisation of mutual trade. Simultaneously, West European countries strove to accelerate technological progress focusing on the development of the production of energy and material consuming products. Thus, neo-protectionism was prevalent in West European countries' relations with countries outside the region.

The foreign economic policy pursued by Western Europe in the neo-protectionist period encountered difficulties in the form of an overestimated dollar exchange rate and high interest rate as well as an extended system of investment relief and tax relief for foreign capital in the United States. Western Europe was unable to compete with the United States in interest rates and was, therefore, forced to face the outflow of capital to the United States.

---

17 Comp. J. Sołdaczuk, Z. Kamecki, P. Bożyk, *Międzynarodowe stosunki*, op. cit., p. 292.

Departure from Neo-Protectionism (1987–2004)

In the late 1980s Western Europe, on a par with the United States, witnessed an emergence of intensive trends aimed at replacing the post-Keynesian pro-supply economic policy with a liberal-monetary policy of a pro-supply character. The new policy advocated limitation of the role of the state in economy and concentration on the development and protection of basic private enterprise institutions, i.e. ownership, as well as on ensuring freedom of action for the market mechanism.[18]

The principles first came to dominate British economic policy under Margaret Thatcher and, subsequently, the economic policy of other European countries.

Simultaneously, they came to exert a dominant impact on foreign and international economic policy since when acting in compliance with the liberal-monetary economic policy, West European countries were unable to continue neo-protectionism. The continuation of the latter would create a situation in which a liberal economic policy would be accompanied by a non-liberal foreign trade policy.

To eliminate this discord, the Uruguay Round of GATT was convened. It continued the endeavours of the Tokyo Round to reduce para- and non-tariff barriers. The point was that, in practice, before the Uruguay Round came into being all attempts to elaborate solutions which would eliminate neo-protectionism satisfactorily, had failed. The codes adopted by the Tokyo Round had proved imprecise. Instead of preventing para- and non-tariff restrictions, they only opened additional possibilities for their intensification (in particular, as regards the application of so-called anti-dumping and anti-subvention procedures).

The Uruguay Round reversed these trends, focusing its attention on direct as well as indirect elimination of para- and non-tariff restrictions from international trade. It produced so-called *tariffication*, a replacement of part of para- and non-tariff restrictions with customs duties, a ban on applying certain restrictions (in particular, involving voluntary export restraints), limiting of the export-subsidizing possibilities and stricter specifying dumping and subventions to countering procedures. All this gave rise to the birth of the process of departure from neo-protectionism and initiated renewed acceleration in the pace of the elimination of tariffs.

Differences still were in place concerning the scope of neo-protectionism in mutual trade between West European countries and in West Europe's relations with countries from outside the region. As regards the former (trade within the European Union) para- and non-tariff restrictions have already been abolished (at least nominally). In Western Europe's relations with countries from outside the region the process of lifting para- and non-tariff barriers has only been commenced and its end is still far ahead.

---

18 Comp. M. Friedman, *A Program for Monetary Stability* (Fordham University Press, New York, 1960) and A. Laffer, G. Perry, 'The New Economics. A Debate', *Economic Impact*, no. 3, 1981.

7.2.3. Japan

After the Second World War Japan was among the most severely destroyed countries. Large towns lay in ruins, razed by American air raids. National assets decreased by one-quarter. There was a food shortage. Unemployment was rife as labour resources increased by over 6 billion people (demobilized troops, administrative staff returning from the captured territories), while possibilities of providing them with jobs were limited.

From the formal point of view, American occupation terminated in Japan on 8 September 1951 but in fact it was only on 28 April 1952 that the Japanese government took over rule of the country. Simultaneously, the United States ceased to extend economic aid to Japan, in particular as regards maintenance of balance of trade equilibrium. Thus, the process of post-war reconstruction of the Japanese economy got off to a start.

Autonomic Development of Japanese Economy (1951–73)
The growth of the Japanese economy between 1951 and 1973 exhibited many features of autonomic development, which meant that foreign trade performed functions subordinated to internal economy.

This stemmed, first and foremost from the policy of radical transformations in the Japanese economy which found reflection in the rapid growth of the share of industry in national income and deep changes in the structure of industrial production. Imports, being the source of providing the economy with energy, raw materials, foodstuffs and licences played a major role in this policy. The task of exports was to offset imports.

The share of exports in the national income did not undergo any major changes in the discussed period, running at a level of 10–15% (similar to that of the United States).[19] It was thus much lower than in the Netherlands (55%), the FRG (29%), Canada (28%) and Great Britain (22%). The value of per capita exports in Japan was even less favourable and much lower than in the economically developed countries.

However, it was not the slow growth of exports that was responsible for its low share in Japan's national income but the high growth rate of the national income. In the period under discussion, national income increased over six-fold which was a world record. At the same time, Japanese exports remained lower than imports till the end of the 1960s, a surplus in the balance of trade first being recorded in 1971.

This meant that in those days foreign trade was not the main driving force of the growth of the Japanese economy. Though the national income to be divided at the end of the 1960s was larger than the national generated income, this surplus was not significant. In 1951–73, it was internal accumulation and investment financed from this accumulation that played a leading role in the development process of the Japanese economy. The share of accumulation in the national income in Japan increased from

---

19 Comp. M. Niesiołowski, *Japonia: źródła i kierunki rozwoju gospodarczego*, op. cit., pp. 63–5.

about 30% in the 1960s to over 40% in 1970–73, while the share of investments rose from about 30% to 35%. At the same time, the share of foreign capital in financing Japan's economic growth at that time was marginal, the share of American capital ranging from 2–3% and that of other countries being insignificant.

The high share of accumulation and accumulation-related investments in Japan's national income made it possible for the country to develop modern export-oriented industries and contributed to a marked acceleration of technological progress in industry. The fastest developing industries included machine-building, electric and electronic, oil-processing, iron, steel and non-ferrous metals, chemicals, precision industry and others.

The state had basic role to play in this process, with instruments of direct state influence on economic growth prevailing between 1951 and 1973. Notably, it was the state that drew up plans for economic development and encouraged economic entities to become involved in the implementation of these plans. The influence of the state was partly of directive and partly of indicative character. The directive action was targeted mainly at state enterprises. On the other hand, private enterprises which wanted to enjoy state credits were obliged to obtain consent from the Ministry of International Trade and Industry (MITI) to get them. In addition, whole sectors of the economy (power engineering, communication, railways) were administered directly by the state.

Foreign economic policy in the period under discussion was a derivative of overall economic policy, which meant that the state exerted a largely direct influence on both exports and imports. This was possible due to the foreign exchange and foreign trade control law of 1949,[20] which gave the Council of Ministers and the MITI the right to shape exports, both in terms of objects and geography, with economic entities being obliged to obtain licences. First and foremost, obtaining of a licence conditioned extension of export subventions. Subventions remained an important instrument of supporting Japanese exports throughout the analysed period, in spite of a completely different situation in terms of the exchange rate.

The yen exchange rate had a varying influence on the profitability of exports. In the 1950s it was an overestimated rate introduced to combat inflation and make imports less expensive. Thus, it had an adverse effect on competitiveness of exports. On the other hand, in the 1960s, despite the exchange rate of the yen still being fixed, faster growth of labour productivity in Japan than elsewhere made the yen exchange rate under- rather than overvalued, which contributed to enhancing the competitiveness of Japanese goods. This enabled Japan to adopt an active position in GATT negotiations (in particular, in the Kennedy Round) as it could meet half-way the restrictions in export subventions proposed by the Round without fearing their negative impact on the competitiveness of Japanese goods.

---

20 'Foreign Exchange and Foreign Trade Control Law, no. 288, 1 December 1949', in *Japan Laws, Ordinances and Other Regulations Concerning Foreign Exchange and Foreign Trade*, (Ohuo Shuppan Kikaku Co., Tokyo, 1982).

In general, however, the Japanese system of export-subsidizing was still among the most extensive. It involved, among others, extension of preferential investment credits to export-oriented enterprises, facilitation of access to foreign exchange for export development, insurance relief, tax relief and state support for promotion (and advertising) activities abroad.

Simultaneously, Japan exerted a direct and indirect impact on imports by applying tariff, para-tariff and non-tariff restrictions. The latter included, in particular, quantitative restrictions, increased quality, sanitary and veterinary requirements, import quotas, voluntary export restraints and others. The accession of Japan to GATT and OECD was accompanied by some reduction of restrictions required of all the candidates. Nevertheless, the Japanese system of export and import control still remained one of the most restrictive.

At the same time, Japan pursued an active policy of facilitating access of their goods to foreign markets, which was reflected in the country's participation in negotiations within GATT and other international organizations.

Neo-Protectionism (1975–86)

Japan's economic policy and, in particular, its foreign economic policy proved particularly effective at the time of the raw-materials-energy crisis, in 1973–4 and 1978–80. This allowed the country to benefit from its economic advantage over others and record benefits in the balance of payments as well as in other domains. This gave Japan an advantage over the United States, which remained passive during the raw-materials-energy crisis (its own rich fuel and raw materials resources and their relatively low imports caused the American economy to be affected to only a lesser extent by the hike of world prices). However, the US economic policy was passive to the extent that it did not allow the United States to benefit from its economic advantage. This was soon reflected in the mounting balance of trade difficulties and a labour productivity growth slower than in Japan, which generated fast-growing inflation and unemployment.

Japan could not remain indifferent to the growth of fuel and other raw material prices on world markets, this country's entire raw material and energy procurement proceeded from imports. A solution had to be sought in offsetting the ever more expensive imports of fuels and raw materials with an attractive export offer.

Japan focused its export expansion at the time of the raw-materials-energy crisis on modern industrial goods, energy and raw-materials-saving advanced technologies, being simultaneously price competitive. To this end, when the raw materials and energy crisis first appeared Japan revalued the yen so as to bring down domestic prices of imported fuels and raw materials used in its export-oriented production. The government also continued to subsidize export-oriented production, primarily through direct subventions, tax and credit relief for exporters, credit guarantees and other forms of state aid.

However, the principal efforts at countering the crisis focused on raising labour productivity, both by automation and better work organization. Also, the state began to reduce its share in the economy, especially through the privatization of state enterprises, resignation from planning (especially directive planning), limitation of direct MITI intervention in shaping the structure of production, and the like.

At the end of the 1970s (at the time of the so-called fuel and raw materials crisis) Japan took advantage of the depreciation of the yen from 180 yens to the dollar to 250 yens to the dollar to further enhance export effectiveness.

All this contributed to Japan's economic success. The growth of the gross domestic product in 1974 to 1986 was running within 6% annually and was double that of Western Europe and the United States. Japan's trade balance was also positive. The country became a world creditor exporting capital in the form of credits, direct investments and portfolio investments. Direct investments in Japan were, on the other hand, insignificant, amounting in 1985 to a mere 80 billion dollars, though as early as in 1973 Japan had liberalized access to its market for foreign capital. The need to obtain government permission for investing in Japan was limited to agriculture, forestry, fisheries, mining, petrochemical industry and leather industry as well as to industries connected with the country's security or being in collision with preferences of individual supervisory boards.[21]

The opening of the Japanese economy could also be seen on the domestic market. Though at the previous stage of development it was mainly foodstuffs which Japan's agriculture could not produce (about one-quarter of the total) which reached the domestic consumer, at the second stage, especially towards its end, imported industrial consumer goods (clothes, textiles, cosmetics and others) began to flow into the Japanese market. Japan did not fear the competition of those goods because of their higher prices, lower technical standard and poorer quality.

Being in relatively better economic health than Western Europe and the United States, Japan presented initiatives liberalizing access to its market, especially in terms of tariffs, thus replying to the recommendations of the Tokyo Round. The expansion of Japan on the forum of international organizations (GATT, OECD and others) was an important export promotion instrument for Japanese enterprises.

In general, however, Japan's share of world exports was still insignificant and oscillated around 10%. In industrial goods its presence in total imports was also low (around 25%). The remainder was made up of energy, raw materials, foodstuffs and farm products. The share of imported industrial goods in the gross domestic product did not exceed 3%, being thus almost one-tenth of that in the remaining developed countries.

Liberalization of the Japanese Economy (1987–2004)

At the third stage of the evolution of its foreign and international economic policy, Japan, following the United States, Britain and other economically developed West European countries, considerably liberalized its economic policy. The state resigned, in the first place, from the method of exerting direct influence on the economy. The role of the MITI was restricted to the minimum, banks gained independence in crediting economic entities. Macroeconomic instruments became the main economic policy

---

21 *Profit and Grew. Overseas Investment in Japan* (IRDC, 1982), p. 1.

instruments, with the Ministry of Finance acting as the principal state institution responsible for economic policy.

These revaluations in economic policy resulted primarily from Japan's good economic position in the world in the mid-1980s and not only from its desire to follow other countries. In particular, Japanese export surpluses kept growing steadily owing to the high competitiveness of Japan's industry. This process was not hampered by the appreciation of the yen from 240 yens to the dollar in 1985 to 160 yens to the dollar in 1986. After a short recession, the Japanese economy returned to its road to recovery, since an almost 50% drop of oil and energy prices on the world market appeared at the same time.

A long-lasting recession in Japan's economy commenced only at the beginning of the 1990s. It was directly precipitated by a crash on the stock, real estate and land markets and the resultant substantial slump of their prices. However, it was the revaluations in the Japanese economy in the second half of the 1980s which were indirectly responsible for the recession. Restricting the role of the MITI and a significant growth of banks' independence in financing economic ventures started the mechanism of practically uncontrolled money creation. Previously, large enterprises, recommended by the MITI (for which the state was responsible) were the major customers of banks. In the second half of the 1980s, MITI recommendations were no longer required and the bank customers came to include a large number of medium and small enterprises applying for loans against pledges of their property or land. Banks were interested in extending the range of borrowers, expecting higher profits in virtue of the large number of extended loans. Simultaneously, they refused to take into account any possible collapse of the credit market due to expected government and central bank intervention should economic difficulties appear. In this respect, in spite of having been transformed into independent economic entities, banks still acted upon the previous assumptions, when the government and its institution, the MITI, were burdened with the same responsibility.

The collapse of the credit market placed thousands of enterprises in a very painful situation as banks encumbered with so-called 'bad' loans stopped financing them. This entailed a decline in the investment rate, an increase in the rate of unemployment and a slump in personal incomes. As a result, demand dropped and inventories increased.

Enterprises began to seek rescue in exports. Consequently, since 1990 the balance of trade surplus began to rise, reaching almost 120 billion dollars in 1992. Direct capital investments abroad also grew.

Simultaneously, Japan substantially increased and liberalized imports of industrial goods, resigning also from direct intervention methods. This was caused by the strong Japan's competitive position on international markets and also pressure on the part of the United States and West European countries. Japan signed numerous obligations resulting from the Tokyo Round and the Uruguay Round, demanding the abolition of restrictions to foreign trade, including para-tariff and non-tariff restrictions.

In terms of the average level of customs duties, Japan found itself among countries with the lowest tariffs. At the end of the 1990s, tariffs on industrial goods in Japan ranged within 4%. By comparison, in the United States the average customs duty on industrial goods amounted at that time to 4.6%, while in the EU countries to 5.7% and in Canada to 9%. A mere 4% of Japanese goods carried a duty of 20–30% while only 2% carried duty exceeding 30%. The value of the customs rate was made dependent on the degree of processing. Raw materials were free from customs duty or enjoyed very low duties. Semi-finished products faced a slightly higher level of duties while highly processed goods carried the highest duties.

On the other hand, para- and non-tariff restrictions are still of much greater significance in Japan than customs duties. The most important include: tariff quotas allowing goods to be imported duty-free or at lower duties, import restrictions, an extended customs procedure, norms and standards concerning notably such issues as security, sanitary regulations (particularly stringent), after-sale service obligations, state monopoly, import licences, import bans (concerning especially animals and plants), government procurement orders and others.

In the second half of the 1980s and in the 1990s Japan significantly liberalized access to its market for foreign capital investments, as a result of which major transnational corporations as well as smaller American and West European companies established branches in the country. Despite that, Japan, accounting for one-sixth of the world gross domestic product, has less than 1% of the world's foreign direct capital investments within its borders. The reason for this can be sought in the traditional closing of Japanese borders to foreign capital investments as well as barriers still encountered by foreign investments in Japan.

7.3. Newly Industrialized Countries

7.3.1. The Concept of Newly Industrialized Countries

The term 'newly industrialized countries' is used herein to denote traditionally less developed countries which have made profound structural changes in their economies under conditions of a fast growth rate. There is a number of such.[22]

These countries have been classified into several generations. The first includes South Korea, Taiwan, Hong Kong, Singapore, Brazil and Mexico. The second includes Thailand, Indonesia, Malaysia, the Philippines, Cyprus and Jordan. The third one India, Egypt, Argentina and Chile. The first generation of these countries accelerated their growth rate and commenced the process of economic restructuring in the mid-1960s, the second generation in the mid-1980s.

The majority of these countries were former colonies of highly industrialized countries, completely politically and economically dependent on them. Though the disintegration of the colonial system brought them independence, it also placed

---

22 See: L. Ciamaga, *Światowa gospodarka rynkowa. Zmiany struktury*, op. cit., pp. 140–41; P. Bożyk, *Gospodarka światowa*, op. cit., pp. 289–390; J. Kulig, *Dylematy polityki dostosowawczej w Trzecim Świecie. Wyzwania dla Polski* (Polski Instytut Spraw Międzynarodowych, Warsaw, 1990), p. 38.

them in the group of poor, raw-materials and agricultural countries, producing and exporting foodstuffs, farm products, condiments (especially coffee and tea), textiles, leather articles, shoes, and the like.[23] This specialization did not guarantee success and the majority of these countries suffered a permanent balance of trade and balance of payments deficit. Market fluctuations in conditions of a high price flexibility of demand on the international market led simultaneously to profound changes in export incomes, which complicated the economic situation even further.

In accordance with the doctrine of autonomic development prevailing after the Second World War, the less developed countries, also including the later newly industrialized countries, adopted the orientation known as *import substitution*, seeking a solution in anti-import development, that is domestic market needs-oriented development geared to making the countries involved independent from purchases of machines and equipment as well as industrial consumer goods from highly developed countries. This strategy was implemented in the Third World as a whole till the first half of the 1980s.

Unlike the whole Third World, the newly industrialized countries withdrew from the *import substitution* strategy earlier, some of them already in the mid-1960s.

7.3.2. The First Generation of Newly Industrialized Countries

South Korea, Taiwan, Hong Kong, Singapore, Brazil and Mexico (drawing primarily on Japanese experience) based their development strategy on four pillars: development open to the world economy, adjustment of the structure of production to export needs, aggressive pro-export policy and protection of the domestic market.

In terms of the *open development strategy* the first generation of newly industrialized countries became a precursor in the Third World as a whole, this strategy being commonly introduced there only in the 1980s. It was based on careful and thorough observation of the directions of development of the world economy and adjustment to it of the industrial production of individual countries. First-generation newly industrialized countries started from filling market niches in the world economy, omnipresent in the 1960s.

Structural changes in industry were subordinated to this target, introduced with export development uppermost in mind. First steps were taken in the direction of the heavy and machine industry, followed by the development of the processing industry, including the electric-machinery and electronic industry, automobile industry, shipbuilding, textile, chemicals and others. Technological assistance to Asian countries came from Japan, and to Brazil and Mexico from the United States. Markets were sought in West European countries but also in the United States and Canada. The opening of the economy let those countries avoid developing production unadjusted to the needs of foreign markets, sales opportunities being the main criterion. The state played a major role in shaping that development. The

---

23 See: J. Sołdaczuk, J. Misala, *Historia handlu międzynarodowego*, op. cit, p. 235.

state sector comprising major enterprises and even whole sectors of the economy dominated in the majority of those countries.

The state also pursued an aggressive pro-export policy, striving to ensure competitiveness on foreign markets to producers of export-oriented articles and directly to exporters. Export promotion instruments applied by first-generation countries included methods of both indirect and direct influence. As for the latter, the state purchased modern technologies abroad and passed them on to domestic producers on easy terms or free of charge, extending to domestic producers foreign exchange credits to import raw materials as well as machines and equipment for export-oriented production. The state also provided other export subventions, eliminated or limited competition by foreign producers as well as facilitated access of domestic goods to foreign markets by negotiating, bilaterally and multilaterally, reductions of customs duties as well as para- and non-tariff restrictions to international trade within the framework of the GATT and other international organizations.

The fourth pillar of the economic policy of newly of the first-generation industrialized countries – protection of the domestic market – performed several functions in the process of their development. Firstly, this strategy guaranteed sales of domestic products, both foodstuffs and industrial goods. Secondly, it protected domestic producers, simultaneously increasing employment. And thirdly, it regulated domestic market procurement with goods either not produced in the country at all or produced in quantities insufficient to satisfy the domestic needs. The latter concerned notably fuels, raw materials and materials for production, cooperation elements, and the like.

7.3.3. The Second Generation of Newly Industrialized Countries

Thailand, Indonesia, Malaysia, Philippines, Cyprus and Jordan commenced the process of deep structural transformations in conditions of accelerated economic growth in the mid-1970s. In broad terms, these countries based their development on the same four pillars of the strategy which the first-generation newly industrialized countries applied in the mid-1960s.

However, the conditions for the development of international trade had changed significantly by that time. Following GATT negotiations, customs duties were almost halved. Simultaneously, competition on the world market increased both on the part of highly industrialized countries and the first-generation newly industrialized countries. Filling market niches had lost sense. It was, therefore, necessary to find new ways of winning markets. These included price competition, that is offering products similar to the products offered by highly industrialized countries but at lower prices. The mid-1970s also witnessed the outbreak of the second raw-material-energy crisis manifested in a multi-fold growth of crude oil prices. The world responded to this crisis with neo-protectionism and technological revolution.

Neo-protectionism meant, first of all, imposing para- and non-tariff restrictions as well as enlarging the group of sensitive goods, which came to include, apart from the traditionally sensitive goods such as steel and steel articles, coal and coal derivatives, foodstuffs, farm products and textiles, also several other commodity groups, thus limiting access to a prevailing part of imported goods. New methods of export-oriented production development and more effective solutions in export promotion had to be applied to overcome barriers in access to foreign markets.

The technical and technological changes initiated by West European countries at the time of the raw-material-energy crisis constituted another significant factor inducing second-generation newly industrialized countries to make certain adjustments to their growth strategy. Search for material- and energy-saving constructions which would reduce the demand for raw materials and fuels was a priority target. The task was made easier by the experience of Japan, which had considerably outpaced Western Europe in this respect.

Given the changed external environment, the second-generation newly industrialized countries made adjustments in all four pillars of the development strategy, though the overall sense of the strategy did not change. The changes concerned primarily the first pillar, that is open development. Adjustment to the needs and possibilities of the world economy lost it exclusively quantitative character acquiring an ever more evident qualitative character.

The second pillar also had to be adjusted, reflected in a change in the structure of pro-export production, the share of heavy and machine industry products decreasing and that of processing industry products increasing. The latter concerned especially products of the electric-machinery, electronic, precision and chemical industries. Cooperation links were established and developed with Japan and other newly industrialized countries.

Significant changes took place also in the third pillar, that is in export-support methods, connected, in the first place, with the evolution of the state's role in the economy of newly industrialized countries. In comparison with the 1950s and the 1960s, that role came to be more restricted in the 1970s and at the beginning of the 1980s. Public property was partly privatized. Forms of direct export support by the state, which prevailed when the countries of the first generation initiated transformations, gave way to indirect forms of influence (mainly indirect subventions).

Some transformations were also evident in the fourth pillar, that is in the opening of the domestic market to imported goods. In second-generation newly industrialized countries this market was partly open to consumer industrial goods manufactured by highly industrialized countries.

At the time when the second-generation newly industrialized countries started transforming their economies under a development strategy adjusted to the new conditions, a similar direction of change was also adopted by the first-generation countries.

7.3.4. The Third Generation of Newly Industrialized Countries

India, Egypt, Argentina and Chile began the process of structural transformations and acceleration of economic growth in the mid-1980s, in conditions differing completely from those faced by the first two generations of newly industrialized countries. The downward trends in the economic development of Western Europe were over, the United States began a period of major acceleration of growth and liberal monetarism replaced Keynesism in economic policy. These phenomena were accompanied by a departure from state control of the economy, privatization of public assets and domination of the free market principles. In international relations, protectionism began to give way to a free flow of goods, services and production factors. The Tokyo Round followed by the Uruguay Round commenced the process of lifting para- and non-tariff restrictions in international trade.

In such an environment, third-generation newly industrialized countries, under the development strategy applied by the two first generations, faced the need to adjust the basic pillars of this strategy to the new conditions.

This concerned, first of all, the first pillar, that is the strategy of open development. In the new conditions it could not just fill commodity niches on the world market or base its market on price competition. The only solution was to compete in terms of quality and technology, with price competition only in third place.

The second pillar was also adjusted to the logics of this solution. The structure of industry in the third-generation countries came with qualitative competition in mind. The industries then developed included in the first place most advanced technology sectors determining capital productivity. The textile industry began to be replaced with electronics, computing equipment, media-visual equipment, and so on.[24] Development was partly financed from the countries' own resources and partly by foreign direct investments attracted by low wages. This concerned, primarily, American and Japanese capital, both of which also provided the third-generation countries with advanced technologies and both being the main recipients of exported goods.

Significant changes took place also in the third pillar, that is in export-support methods. Direct and indirect forms of protectionism were replaced with macroeconomic policy instruments influencing exports. These instruments included countering inflation, improvement of finances, creating conditions favouring the growth of private savings and investments, adjusting the financial and credit system to the needs of export growth.[25] Other important instruments of export promotion included facilities to give private firms access to information held by the government and concerning export opportunities, assistance in marketing abroad, supporting scientific research to upgrade export-oriented production, creation of free zones of all sorts favouring the development of export-oriented production.

Changes in the fourth pillar found their reflection, first and foremost, in expanding the scope of liberalization of imports of goods and services as well as the influx of production factors, in particular capital. Direct capital investments in the newly industrialized countries increased significantly. So did the role of imported

---

24 Comp. J. Kulig, 'Strategia proeksportowa a restrukturyzacja gospodarki', *Ekonomista*, no. 1,1996, pp. 80–81.

25 Ibid., p. 75.

industrial consumer goods in supplies delivered to the domestic market. In some newly industrialized countries (for instance South Korea) the share of liberalized imports increased to 95%. 2) In addition, customs duties were reduced and the scope of application of para - and non-tariff restrictions limited.

Table 7.1. Evolution of Development Strategies of Newly Industrialized Countries

Generations of newly industrialized countries	Pillars of development strategy			
	First pillar (forms of opening to world economy)	Second pillar (sectors of industrial expansion)	Third pillar (methods of export promotion)	Fourth pillar (scope of domestic market opening)
First generation	Filling niches in the world market	Heavy, machine, electro-machinery textile industry	Microeconomic, direct, indirect	Import of raw materials, foodstuffs, technology
Second generation	Price competition	Electro-technical, chemical industry	Microeconomic, indirect	Import of selected industrial goods
Third generation	Quality competition	Electronics, informatics, telecommunication technology	Macroeconomic	Import of goods, services and production factors

Source: Author's own elaboration.

7.3.5. Factors in the Development of Newly Industrialized Countries

The possibilities of applying the strategy of economic development discussed above and the outstanding effects of this strategy in the newly industrialized countries were determined by a number of factors which can be roughly divided into endogenous and exogenous.

Endogenous Factors
The endogenous factors can be divided into economic and non-economic. In the group of endogenous economic factors, primary attention should be given to accumulation and investments. Both these parameters did not, however, proceed at the same level in all newly industrialized countries. In Asian countries, they were one-third higher than in the remaining newly industrialized countries, in particular in South America, Europe and Middle East.

In the countries of East Asia and Southeast Asia the accumulation rate of private and public savings doubled in the analysed period (1961–90), rising to over 35%. So did the investment rate, which rose to over 30%.[26] By contrast, in the second group of newly industrialized countries (i.e. in South America, Europe and Middle East) the investment rate throughout the analysed period ran within 20% and, thus, not differed little from the average world level. The countries of the first generation registered the fastest growth of capital outlays, with the growth rate in the Asian countries being twice that than in the newly industrialized countries from other continents. However, in the course of time, the growth rate of investments declined, reaching in the third-generation countries in Asia – 8% and on the other continents – minus 8%.

The high investment rate in the Asian countries allowed these countries to adjust the structure of export production to changing demands on the world market. This concerned in the first place Singapore and Taiwan, which changed the structure of their manufacturing apparatus at double the speed of the remaining newly industrialized countries in the second half of the 1960s and in the first half of the 1970s.[27] In the second half of the 1970s the second-generation countries (Malaysia, Indonesia, Thailand) gained an advantage over others as regards the pace of changes in the production apparatus. Finally, in the second half of the 1980s and in the first half of the 1990s, Egypt, a third-generation country, moved to first place in terms of the pace of these changes.[28]

All newly industrialized countries witnessed rapid growth of employment exceeding the demographic growth rate, which meant population movements from rural to urban areas. This process was accompanied by the development of education of all levels, in particular vocational and university education, resulting in a growth of labour productivity. Thus, in total, the acceleration of the economic growth rate of the newly industrialized countries through increasing accumulation led concurrently to the growth of fixed capital productivity (by way of changing the structure of production and its modernization) as well as by raising the labour productivity. In other words, the significant acceleration of the growth rate of newly industrialized countries (in particular in Asia) had its roots in long-term trends of accumulation growth (and consumption restriction), a significant acceleration of the growth rate of investments and the modernization of the production apparatus connected with it, as well as profound qualitative changes in labour resources resulting from changes in the structure of employment and upgraded qualifications.

Particular attention among non-economic endogenous factors should be given to expanded state interventionism, the scale of this expansion being the largest in the first-generation countries when they initiated their transformations and the

---

26 Comp. J. Kulig, *Gospodarka Azji Wschodniej i Południowo-Wschodniej; konkurent czy partner dla Polski?* (Instytut Rozwoju Studiów Strategicznych, Warsaw, 1997), p. 21.

27 Comp. ibid., p. 23.

28 Comp. *Industry and Development – Global Report*, (UNIDO, Vienna and New York, 1985 and 1991/2), p. 39.

smallest in third-generation countries. In particular, state interventionism in those countries was marked by favouring instead of restricting the development of private enterprise. The state attached particular importance to directing private enterprises toward implementation of strategic targets, reflected in increasing accumulation capacities, encouraging investments to be made in the development of export-oriented production, technological modernization to be undertaken, and the like.

Another form of state interventionism was selective industrial policy aimed at directing private enterprises towards implementation of strategic targets of economic policy, in particular foreign economic policy. It was the market that verified the effectiveness of this policy (in the case of exports – the foreign market). In the first place, industrial policy was to induce private enterprises to make savings and invest.[29] Naturally, methods to substantiate this policy varied, different when the first generation of the newly industrialized countries appeared from when the third generation developed. Simultaneously, industrial policy contributed to raising the interest of enterprises toward developing exports, reflected in the rate of protection – high in the case of infant industry and minimal (or zero) in the case of mature production. This entailed the need to revise investment decisions by the international market, from the point of view of their effectiveness.

Summing up, the industrial policy pursued in relation to the first generation of newly industrialized countries was very close to the planning and management methods in the former socialist countries, while in relation to the third-generation countries, it corresponded to the policy pursued in the highly industrialized countries. In both cases, however, its results were better than in the original.[30] The reasons could be sought in both the modification of the original solutions and in the historical, cultural and religious specificity of the Southeast Asian region. That specificity was an essential endogenous factor, lying at the foundation of the economic success registered by the newly industrialized countries.

It concerned, in particular, the proneness to make renouncements (especially consumer ones) which played an important role in the process of accumulation of private and public savings. The traditionally low standard of living made domestic demand for industrial consumer goods manufactured by those countries for export, of lesser importance.

Also, Buddhism, the dominant religion in Asian countries, with its calls for modesty and renouncements in worldly life in return for graces in eternal life and examples of this modesty given daily by Buddhist monks, was not without importance, creating a favourable climate for economies and internal accumulation.

Finally, national discipline, its subordination to management centres on all levels of management and good work organisation, favoured the success of the newly industrialized countries in implementing the program of profound economic transformations.

---

29 Comp. J. Kulig, 'Znaczenie wzorca uprzemysłowienia krajów Azji Wschodniej dla krajów postsocjalistycznych', *Ekonomista*, no. 1, 1997, p. 16.

30 Comp. ibid., p. 20.

Exogenous factors

Like endogenous factors, exogenous factors can also be divided into economic and non-economic. In the group of exogenous economic factors attention should be given to all kinds of non-repayable assistance received from abroad, credits and direct capital investments. Non-repayable assistance was not common and concerned selected countries and assumed various forms. Thus, South Korea received donations from the US government connected with the stationing of American troops in its territory. On the other hand, Japan gave non-repayable (or very advantageous) technological assistance to selected Asian countries.

In the 1970s and in the first half of the 1980s, credits extended by the highly industrialized countries also constituted an important factor in the development of the newly industrialized countries. At that time, there was a surplus of supply over demand on the credit market, which resulted in interest rates advantageous for borrowers. A factor responsible for such a situation was the growing amount of so-called petrodollars on the financial market.[31]

In the second half of the 1980s and in the 1990s, foreign direct capital investments made in the newly industrialized countries took pride of place among the external factors. This concerned, in particular, Hong Kong, Taiwan, Singapore but also Indonesia, Malaysia and Thailand. Those investments transferred capital, know-how and technology, contributing to the modernization of industry in those countries. Transnational corporations, notably American and Japanese, played the main role among foreign investors in the newly industrialised countries.

Another exogenous factor contributing especially to the development of the first generation of newly industrialized countries was good market conditions on international markets, facilitating sales of processed industrial goods.

Among non-economic exogenous factors, mention should be made, first of all, of the favourable world economic climate, which made access to foreign markets easier for the countries in question, treating them as a positive example of rapid development in market economy conditions. This concerned, in particular, the first-generation countries, to a lesser extent the second-generation countries and to the least extent those of the third generation. The newly industrialized first-generation countries constituted a good argument in the discussion on the development possibilities of countries with different political and social systems.[32]

The newly industrialized countries did not pursue their own international economic policy, did not create international organizations recruiting countries of a similar development strategy, did not develop regional integration covering only newly industrialized countries. Their international policy is identical to the policy of less developed countries. This refers, in particular, to the period commencing dynamic economic transformation in these countries. In the course of time, they

---

31 The term 'petrodollars' refers to that part of the incomes of oil-exporting countries which was deposited in American and West European banks.

32 Comp. J. Kulig, *Dylematy polityki dostosowawczej w Trzecim Świecie*, op. cit., pp. 53–60.

would evolve increasingly toward the international economic policy pursued by the economically developed countries. This involves, in particular, support for the liberalization of international trade, introduction of new principles for the flow of goods and services within the framework of the WTO, reforms of the world currency system, and the like.

7.4. Less Developed Countries

7.4.1. The Concept of Less Developed Countries

The concept of less developed countries has not been unequivocally defined in literature.[33] It has numerous synonyms such as 'developing countries', 'Third World', 'economically backward countries', and the like. All these terms refer to a numerically very large group of countries characterized by similar features, treated in an aggregated or disaggregated form. In the first approach, attention is focused on the low level per capita national income, raw material-agricultural structure of national income generation and an insignificant scope of labour-productivity enhancing equipment. In the second approach, a larger number of features typical of these countries is taken into account, among others, the low per capita income and the resultant standard of living close to the social minimum, concentration on development of so-called primary industries, that is agriculture, wood industry and mining, hidden unemployment, domination of expenses on foodstuffs and staple goods consumed by the population, poor living conditions, high birth and death rate,

---

33 Hundreds of books and articles have been published on this subject. The following are some which deserve special attention: M. Dobb, 'O niektórych problemach uprzemysłowienia krajów rolniczych', in *Problemy wzrostu ekonomicznego krajów słabo rozwiniętych* (PWG, Warsaw, 1958); M. Kalecki, 'Zagadnienia finansowania rozwoju ekonomicznego', in ibid.; O. Lange, *Kierunki wyboru dróg rozwoju gospodarczego*, in *Teoria wzrostu ekonomicznego a współczesny kapitalizm* (PWE, Warsaw, 1962); G. Myrdal, *The Challenge of World Poverty. A World Antipoverty Programme in Outline. A Summary and Continuation of Asian Drama*, (Penguin, New York, 1970); W.R. Chine, 'Can the East Asian Model of Development be Generalised?', *World Development*, vol. 10, no. 2, 1962; C. Crockett, 'Stabilisation Policies in Developing Countries: Some Policy Conclusions', IMF Staff Papers, no. 1, 1981; P. Drucker, 'The Changed World Economy', *Foreign Affairs*, , no. 1, 1986; M.S. Khan, Macroeconomic Adjustment in Developing Countries. A Policy Perspective, *World Bank Research Observer*, no. 1, 1987; A.O. Krueger, 'Import Substitution versus Export Promotion', *Finance and Development*, vol. 22, no. 2, 1982; J. Kulig, *Dylematy polityki dostosowawczej w Trzecim Świecie*, op. cit.; L. Ciamaga, *Czy trzecia droga dla Trzeciego Świata?* (Książka I Wiedza, Warsaw, 1986); M. Perczyński, 'Globalne wyzwania rozwojowe we współczesnej gospodarce kapitalistycznej', in *Nowe zjawiska w gospodarce światowej, Studia I Materiał no. 15* (INE PAN, Warsaw, 1989).

undernourishment, low level of education, primitive means of transport, discrimination of women, concentration on exports of raw materials and foodstuffs.[34]

In spite of many common features, the group of economically less developed countries is highly heterogeneous, particularly when an attempt is made to classify them from the viewpoint of certain indicators. As a rule, four groups tend to be distinguished among them: the economically least developed countries, oil countries I and oil countries II and the remaining economically less developed countries. There are significant differences between these groups in terms of economic policy as well as targets, means and instruments of applying foreign economic policy.[35]

7.4.2. The Economically Least Developed Countries

Unfortunately, the group of the least developed Third World countries keeps increasing. In the late 1980s it still comprised 36 countries but over the following ten years the number increased by one-third. At present it numbers 47 countries: Afghanistan, Bangladesh, Benin, Bhutan, Botswana, Burkina Faso, Burundi, Cambodia, Green Cape, Central African Republic, Chad, Comoro Islands, Djibouti, Equatorial Guinea, Ethiopia, Gambia, Guinea, Guinea-Bissau, Haiti, Kiribati, Laos, Lesotho, Liberia, Madagascar, Malawi, Maldive Islands, Mali, Mauritania, Mozambique, Myanmar, Nepal, Niger, Rwanda, Samoa, St Thomas and Prince Islands, Sierra Leone, Solomon Islands, Somalia, Sudan, Togo, Tuvalu, Uganda, Tanzania, Vanuatu, Yemen, Zaire and Zambia. All are characterized by near-zero economic growth, foodstuffs consumption lower than the existential minimum, high birth rate exceeding the average rate for less developed countries and a life expectancy much shorter than the world average. The share of industry in the generation of the national income in these countries does not exceed a few per cent, this industry being usually the extraction of raw materials. The accumulation rate is running at below 15% and the investment rate does not even suffice to regenerate the capital engaged in the extraction of raw materials. The share of these countries in global industrial production ranges from 0.1% to 0.2%. Exports are made up in 90 % of farm products and in 10% of handicrafts. In imports industrial goods account for two-thirds and foodstuffs for one-third.

The countries in question owe their poverty to a variety of factors, partly the highly unfavourable tropical climate and also being situated in territories unfavourable to economic development (deserts, swamps). Many of these countries lack elementary economic infrastructure (roads, postal and telecommunication connections, ports). Some have no mineral fossils and some do not even have elementary natural resources (forests, rivers). However, some of them boast economies well provided with raw materials but which owe their lack of growth prospects to improper economic policies

---

34 See: A. Muller, *Perspektywy rozwoju*, op. cit., p. 22; T. Szentes, *Ekonomia polityczna zacofania gospodarczego*, (PWE, Warsaw, 1974), pp. 36–7.

35 Comp. P. Bożyk, *Gospodarka światowa*, op. cit., p. 304 and *The Least Developed Countries. 1995 Report* (United Nations, New York, Geneva), Annex.

pursued in the past, devastating internal power struggles (especially between tribes) or cession of the right to exploit natural mineral resources to foreign companies.

In such circumstances the least developed countries cannot pursue a rational economic policy as they have no grounds or assumptions to do so. With existing limitations, these countries do not even have a concept of an economic policy which would push them onto the path of development. The point is that they do not have the means necessary to do so, the instruments typical of foreign economic policy in other groups of countries being completely useless in this case.

Thus, the least developed countries remain in stagnation, which means relative backward movement in comparison with countries which advance in the development of their economies. Various development concepts proposed to them by international institutions and organizations have either not been put in practice or failed to bring positive effects. In such a situation the majority of the least developed countries base their existence on foreign aid or foreign direct investments located, however, solely in countries rich in natural resources. All the countries in question are heavily indebted without any chance to repay their debts.

7.4.3. Oil Countries I and II

The term oil countries is used herein to denote a number of countries which derive their main incomes from the production and export of crude oil.[36]

From the viewpoint of pursued economic policy, and also foreign economic policy, the oil countries are divided into two subgroups: oil countries I, whose revenues from the crude oil exports exceed their investment and consumption possibilities in the domestic economy, and oil countries II, with investment and consumption needs markedly exceeding their revenues from the export of crude oil.

Oil Countries I
This group of countries comprises Saudi Arabia, Qatar, United Arab Emirates, Kuwait and Libya. These countries set aside a major part of their revenues from oil exports to finance investments, notably in the development of agriculture, processing industry (crude oil, gas and their derivatives), power engineering, economic infrastructure (roads, hotels, telecommunication) as well as other sectors of the economy importing advanced technologies, cooperation elements, raw materials and materials as well as specialists – engineers, technicians, managers.

The second part of revenues from crude oil exports is earmarked to finance the import of consumer goods, especially industrial goods (luxury cars, utility electronics, means of communication) as well as foodstuffs. Funds are also spent to furnish homes, hotels, public utility buildings.

---

36 The majority of these countries is associated in OPEC (Saudi Arabia, Kuwait, Quatar, United Arab Emirates, Iran, Iraq, Indonesia, Ecuador, Venezuela, Libya, Algeria and Gabon).

The remaining part of revenues from crude oil exports are re-exported by these oil countries as bank deposits, portfolio investments and, more rarely, in the form of direct capital investments.

The foreign economic policy of oil countries I is conditioned, on the one hand, by exogenous factors and, on the other hand, by endogenous factors. The former include factors affecting world oil prices and consequently foreign exchange revenues from its export. The fact that the OPEC countries try to influence oil prices by controlling and regulating the supply of crude oil and, thus, its output is of major importance in this respect. Among endogenous factors of primary significance are the aims of the overall economic policy, both investment and consumption. To be more precise, it is a question of the volume and structure of investments as well as the size and structure of consumption. These are not identical in all oil countries I, an example of which being the differences in this respect between Libya, on the one hand, and Saudi Arabia or Kuwait, on the other.

The size of capital export by oil countries I depends on the difference between oil export revenues and expenditure on investments and consumption, this difference varying among the individual countries of the group.

Living standards in oil countries I are the function of the social and economic policy they pursue. On the other hand, the overall level of economic and civilization development is only of slight importance. In this domain oil countries I are completely import-dependent.

The foreign economic policy of this group of countries has simple and clearly defined goals and uses simple means and instruments. The basic goal of their foreign economic policy is to maximize revenues from crude oil export as well as interest and dividends from the export of capital. The import targets of oil countries I are diversified, their common denominator being, however, adjustment of the structure of imports to the needs defined by the overall economic policy.

The economic success of oil countries I will last as long as crude oil remains the principal source of energy. The emergence of a price-competitive source of energy will mean the dusk of the hitherto pursued economic policy concepts of oil countries I.

Oil Countries II

Oil countries II embrace all the remaining OPEC members as well as countries from outside the organization. Their common feature is that their oil export revenues are lower than their import needs, the balance of trade in these countries being, in general, negative.

This situation can be attributed to two main reasons, namely, a larger population and a different structure of imports resulting from different internal economic policy.

Unlike oil countries I with their small population and significant export potential, oil countries II are characterized by a much lower value of crude oil per capita exports (Algeria, Iran, Iraq). Since the eruption of the fuel crisis they have also been following an economic development strategy other than oil countries I. It has been a concept of autonomic development oriented at becoming import independent. Thus, while oil countries I were import-oriented, oil countries II adopted an anti-import orientation. It had several features in common with the development strategy pursued in the former socialist countries.

The anti-import development of oil countries II manifested itself in the expansion of basic industries, including heavy and machine industry, processing industry and, in particular, electro-engineering industry. Articles delivered by these industries were to satisfy the needs of the domestic market and also constitute the basis for exports to foreign markets. The development of domestic agriculture was to make these countries independent of the import of foodstuffs.

In the initial period of implementing of this strategy, revenues from the export of crude oil were destined to import technology for the needs of the developed industry. It was assumed that in the course of time the export potential would be expanded significantly so as to include not only crude oil but also domestic industry products.

Apart from the development of industry and agriculture, these countries also commenced expansion and modernization of the economic infrastructure, residential housing (but of standards lower than in oil countries I due to its mass character), the development of education and universities, and the like).

Import needs significantly exceeding revenues guaranteed by crude oil exports forced the countries of this group to draw foreign credits, which gradually became an increasingly important source of financing economic development.

The rate of internal accumulation in oil countries II was lower than their development needs which resulted from a low level of industrial development and its insignificant share in the national income as well as from non-economic development conditions differing, for instance, from those in the newly industrialized Asian countries.

The hopes of oil countries II to raise export revenues as a result of an increased share of exports of industrial articles in total exports never materialized in practice. The demand for industrial articles exported by less developed countries, including oil countries II, in the highly industrialized countries was very small and did not display an upward trend. This was due to their low qualitative and technical level which became a major barrier to the development of exports from oil countries II, under conditions of quality competition.

It was for such reasons that oil countries II were compelled to reduce the programme to industrialize their economies as well as the programme to raise consumption. This generated social discontent which, in Iran, brought about the collapse of the government implementing such a strategy, in Algeria initiated long-lasting resistance on the part of forces opposing economic and social transformations while in Iraq, led to the strengthening of authoritarian power. Difficulties connected with the repayment of steadily increasing indebtedness were also mounting in other oil countries.[37] They were similar to those which appeared in all the remaining less developed countries.

The foreign economic policy of oil countries II was subordinated to their overall industrialization-related economic policy. In spite of their oil resources, these countries, like the remaining less developed countries which implemented less ambitious programmes to transform their economic and social structure, were, however, unable to achieve the set economic and social goals.

7.4.4. Other Economically Less Developed Countries

The group of other economically less developed countries (apart from the newly industrialized countries, least developed countries as well as oil countries I and II) is the most numerous. They are not in such a hopeless situation as the least developed countries but the health of their economies is worse than that of the newly industrialized countries and also oil countries, especially oil countries I.

The factors which affect positively the economic health of the group of the other less developed countries include their relative wealth of natural resources. The majority of these countries are rich in deposits of cobalt, chrome, copper, bauxite, uranium, gold and diamonds, as well as in forests, water, fertile soil and other natural resources. They are also rich in human resources. However, these countries suffer from a shortage of capital and technology, few highly qualified personnel, poorly developed economic infrastructure, substantial deficit of foodstuffs and heavy indebtedness. In all these countries internal accumulation and investments are too low, the processing industry is too poorly developed, the structure of foreign trade is unfavourable, being based on exports of foodstuffs, raw materials and less processed industrial goods and on imports of highly processed industrial consumer goods and foodstuffs. The foreign trade structure in most of these countries is the heritage of the colonial subordination to the highly industrialized countries which used to treat them as sources of raw materials and farm goods. Efforts made so far to change the status of less developed countries (with the exception of the newly industrialized countries and oil countries I) have failed.

7.4.5. Concepts of Foreign Economic Policy of Other Less Developed Countries

The foreign economic policy of less developed countries has undergone several transformations since regaining independence, generated by the changing external as well as internal environment of these countries.

The first concept of foreign economic policy applied in less developed countries was the policy of import substitution, also referred to as the policy of developing internal market-oriented production. It was an attempt to become independent of disadvantageous price trends on the world market. The point was that, in the long-

---

37 Comp. J. Kulig, *Strukturalne i systemowe dostosowania krajów silnie zadłużonych* (Poltext, PANINE, Warsaw, 1994), pp. 13–20.

term, prices of raw materials and foodstuffs, basic export items for less developed countries, rose much slower than prices of industrial products imported by these countries. Terms of trade in prices were thus unfavourable for the less developed countries. The conclusion drawn from this situation meant they had to become independent from imports of industrial goods by developing their domestic production with the use of own raw materials and materials.

The policy of import substitution was part of the strategy of autonomic development resembling in many aspects the development strategy applied by centrally planned economies. Yet, it was implemented under market economy conditions and with much lesser state involvement.

The policy of import substitution had a few variants. In some countries it consisted of the development of the heavy and extraction industries while in others it included the development of the processing industry, in particular, the light and leather industries. There were also a few countries which attempted to copy the concept of a comprehensive development of the economy, following the centrally planned economy countries.

The obvious drawback of the import substitution policy was, however, the insufficient development of pro-export production, which resulted in the indebtedness of less developed countries and their inability to meet their repayment commitments. Both the import of technology in connection with the development of industrial production for the internal market and the import of a substantial part of raw materials, materials and cooperation elements required for this production were on credit conditions. As it was, articles produced by the domestic industry did not find a market abroad, despite competitive prices (offered under conditions of export subsidies proceeding from the state budget). Lack of competition on the domestic market by foreign producers did not stimulate producers to improve the quality or upgrade the technology of production.

In total, protectionism and orientation of production on the internal market were the main causes of the failure of the import substitution policy in less developed countries. Protectionism found its reflection not only in customs tariffs being higher than in other countries and more radical para-and non-tariff restrictions, but also in the autonomic macroeconomic policy. This led to the deformation of the principal instruments of this policy in relation to the free market. Notably, this referred to the interest rate, the exchange rate, the monetary policy and the budget policy.[38]

The interest rate policy was guided by the need to facilitate investment. Its level, therefore, was below that justified by the relation between the supply of capital and the demand for this capital. In this way the demand for capital was artificially increased. At the same time, low incomes and low interest on deposits contributed to low internal savings. This gave rise to a long-term domestic capital deficit and increased the demand for foreign capital.

Exchange rates were also shaped in an autonomic way. In particular, this concerned the level of the exchange rate and foreign trade. Citizens of countries in which foreign

---

38 See: P.R. Krugman, M. Obstfeld, *Międzynarodowe stosunki*, op. cit., pp. 258–9.

exchange limitations were applied were obliged to sell back foreign exchange earned abroad to the central bank, at a specified (low) exchange rate. Simultaneously any export of foreign exchange abroad was also controlled. In addition, foreign holders of internal currencies of countries subject to such restrictions did not have the right to exchange them into foreign currencies or to take them abroad. In this way, exchange rates and foreign exchange turnover performed the functions desired by the government in the foreign economic policy. The government gave its consent to some kinds of imports, allowing foreign exchange to be purchased at a low exchange rate or vice versa. In the first case, it meant subsidizing investments (or consumption) and, in the second, their limitation or ban.

A policy of this kind could only result in a long-term deficit of the state budget and high inflation. The budget deficit made governments of less developed countries try to offset it with the emission of money or by drawing foreign credits. High inflation led to a drop of the real value of money, artificially increasing expenses on consumption as well as the demand for foreign currencies in unofficial circulation.

Being a peculiar, distorted form of Keynesism, this economic policy was pursued as long as

... the external environment was relatively favourable, there was no drastic need to adjust to world market requirements and a relatively high economic growth rate allowed internal contradictions to be eased and inflationary tendencies tolerated. Inflation and imbalance were treated as an inevitable cost of the rapid growth required by the structural transformation of internal market-oriented industry.[39]

Such a situation persisted almost till the beginning of the 1980s. Easily accessible and cheap foreign credits at that eased time difficulties resulting from the strategy of autonomic development of less developed countries. It changed drastically in the mid-1980s when credits became suddenly much more difficult to obtain and their rate of interest surged. Less developed countries were then faced with the necessity of adjusting the volume of imports to their own export abilities as well as to reschedule the repayment of past credits and interest. The first part of this operation proved extremely painful as it meant the need radically to reduce imports as well as reduce investment or consumer expenditure, and in some cases both of these. The second part of the operation required the consent of creditors and was not possible without the intervention of the IMF.

The IMF and the World Bank agreed to take the indebted less developed countries under their wings, but on certain conditions. The first was that the less developed countries adopt an adjustment programme elaborated by the IMF, and the second that their foreign economic policy be subordinated to the repayment of the less developed countries' indebtedness.

The core of all the adjustment programmes of the IMF, including that proposed to less developed countries, was the need to change the criteria for the allocation of factors of production and, thus, capital, labour force, technology and raw materials.

---

39 See: J. Kulig, *Strukturalne I systemowe dostosowania*, op. cit., pp. 26–7.

In this case, the point was to resign from the strategy of autonomic development and the related policy of import substitution in favour of an open development strategy, a policy of export promotion and, consequently, orientation of production not exclusively on the internal market but, first of all, on foreign markets.

The adoption of the open development strategy, signifying the need to shape the directions of the development of industry and other sectors of the economy with the world market in view, prevents inefficient utilization of production resources since the world market verifies the decisions made. When they are correct, the goods sell well on foreign markets and when they are erroneous, there is no demand for the goods made.

The export promotion policy is connected with focusing on the production of articles with a positive long-term comparative advantage in relation to foreign articles. In the case of less developed countries, it signified a return to the development of production with a traditional comparative advantage, mainly raw material and agriculture-related, as well as resignation from the export of industrial goods.

Such a development strategy of less developed countries introduced by the IMF also meant the necessity to change their goals, means and instruments in both internal and foreign economic policy. In terms of internal economic policy this change signified a transition from a pro-supply to a pro-demand policy. It was accompanied by a maximum possible reduction of the role of the state as the owner of means of production and privatization of the economy. Also, the regulatory role of the state declined significantly. Instead of developing a microeconomic policy (among others, industrial policy) the state had to concentrate on macroeconomic policy.

The parameters of macroeconomic policy also changed. In accordance with the new strategy all of these should be shaped by the market on a balanced level – the interest rate on the level of balanced capital supply and demand, the exchange rate on the level of the balanced supply of foreign currencies and the demand for them. The budget should be balanced and inflation the lowest possible. The changes were to guarantee the balance of current accounts and the equilibrium of the balance of payments.

The period of application of the export promotion policy under conditions of implementation of the adjustment programmes of the IMF can be divided into three stages[40]: 1982–5, 1985–9 and after 1989.

The first stage was characterized by implementation of IMF's classical adjustment programmes. It did not provide for the redemption of the then existing indebtedness of less developed countries, assuming the transfer of net financial resources from the indebted countries to the creditor countries, which was to signify the commencement of a long-term process of debt repayment. At the same time, less developed countries were to initiate a process of structural transformation in their economies on the basis of the IMF adjustment programmes. By their nature, these transformations could not produce any positive effects immediately after commencement. Consequently, the 1982–5 period was characterized primarily by reduction of imports followed by

---

40 See: J. Kulig, *Dylematy polityki dostosowawczej*, op. cit., pp. 107–11.

a decline of industrial production, gross national product and consumption, growth of unemployment and social stratification. It is for these reasons that the first stage of the export promotion policy has been called the period of recessive adjustments. Despite the repayment of foreign indebtedness being recognized as the main goal of foreign economic policy in that period, the countries concerned failed to reduce it. On the contrary, indebtedness increased even further against the guidelines of the adjustment programme, which did not provide for any new credits to be given to the countries which did not commence the process of net debt reduction.

The second stage was a period of more profound transformations in the economy of less developed countries when compared with the first stage. Its beginning coincided with the announcement of the so-called Baker's Plan, of the then American Treasury Secretary. In 1985, in Seoul, Baker drew attention to the necessity to ensure further flow of loan capital to the indebted countries. That attitude differed from the IMF concept underlying the export promotion policy pursued by the less developed countries during the first stage. Baker's proposal also eased other limitations of the IMF adjustment programme, putting the emphasis on the development of export-oriented production. Unfortunately, also in the 1986–9 period, the adjustment programmes in the version corrected by Baker's Plan did not reverse the long-term, negative trends in the development of less developed countries, reflected in the growth of their indebtedness, stagnation or downward trends in GDP growth, significant rise of unemployment and a rapid spread of the poverty sector.

The third stage covering the post-1989 period was initiated by the so-called Brady's Plan, drawn up by another US Treasury Secretary, N. Brady, who assumed it would be impossible to improve the economic situation of less developed countries without creditors bearing part of the debt reduction costs. He thus confirmed the opinions of economists who had been arguing since the mid-1980s that less developed countries by themselves would not be able to cope with the reduction of their debt (those economists also included American IMF-related economists such as S. Fisher and B. Bradley).[41]

According to Brady's Plan, approximately 30%[42] of the less developed countries' indebtedness was to be written off. In this way creditors were to be encumbered with part of the cost of debt reduction. Another solution admitted a conversion of the debt consisting of the sale or conversion on the international financial market of debtors' liabilities held by banks. In addition, debt reduction was to be accompanied by relief in the interest on the remainder of the debt to be repaid. Finally, Brady's Plan assumed the need to fuel the indebted countries with new financial resources in the form of credits, foreign direct investments or portfolio investments, aimed at stimulating economic growth accompanied by far-reaching structural changes.

---

41 Comp. J. Kulig, *Dylematy polityki*, op. cit., pp. 139–43.

42 Comp. A. Budnikowski, *Zadłużenie jako problem globalny* (PWE, Warszawa, 1991) and A. Budnikowski, *Międzynarodowe stosunki gospodarcze*, op. cit., p. 395.

The directions of that restructuring were to be defined by international financial institutions including, in particular, the IMF and the World Bank.[43]

In Brady's opinion, the implementation of adjustment programmes under strict control of international financial institutions should result in far-reaching market-oriented and efficiency-oriented reforms, open the economies of these countries to external signals and, thus, answer clearly, what they should manufacture and export, bring back to these countries the capital which escaped from them in the past. To make it possible, according to Brady, macroeconomic policy and its parameters, i.e. the interest rate and the exchange rate, had to acquire a market character, the budget should become balanced, inflation should be reduced to a minimum and the monetary policy should abandon the practice of printing money.

In Brady's view, to ensure this it was absolutely necessary to create an adequate institutional and financial infrastructure. Banks were to play a particularly significant role in this system, writing off part of the old debts, facilitating the debt for equity conversion and encouraging debtors to buy them up at market prices (lower than actual prices).

Brady also assumed a substantial capital strengthening of the IMF and World Bank so that these institutions would be able to increase the scope of crediting for less developed countries, manifesting 'sound' economic processes and prospects for fast growth.

The strategy of open development and the export promotion policy did not lead to a change of the position of less developed countries in the world economy but they did hamper the growth rate of their indebtedness. This was true, notably, of the 1990s when not only the debt rate but also the debt service rate decreased.[44] In absolute terms, the volume of indebtedness kept growing but its growth rate declined. The less developed countries needed ten years to record the first ten-fold rise of indebtedness (1970–80), the second rise took as much as 20 years (1981–2000).

Simultaneously, the recession of the 1980s was followed by a certain growth of gross domestic product resulting from the flow of foreign investments as well as macroeconomic stabilization in part of the group's countries. It was accompanied by a rise of exports from less developed countries. Literature on the subject does not provide, however, an unequivocal answer to the question of what extent this was the effect of implementation of the IMF and World Bank adjustment programmes and, in particular, recovery in the United States and other economically developed countries, or reduction of interest rates as well as better terms of trade in less developed countries. IMF and World Bank related economists attribute these effects to the advantages

---

43 Comp. 'US Proposals for Relief of the Debt Problems. Remarks by the Secretary of the Treasury Nicholas F. Brady to the Brookings Institution and the Bretton Woods Committee Conference on the Third World Debt' (Washington DC, 13 March 1989).

44 Comp. J. Kulig, *Strukturalne I systemowe*, op. cit., p. 40. According to the author the debt rate is the ratio of the volume of indebtedness to the GDP while the debt service rate is the ratio of debt service to export revenues.

brought by the adjustment programmes, though others have doubts.[45] One thing is certain: the IMF and the World Bank are institutions representing creditors and hence the emphasis in the adjustment programmes implemented so far has been on the growth of exports and repayment of indebtedness.

The programmes supported repayment of indebtedness by increasing economies and investments while reducing consumption.

No wonder then, that the least developed countries witnessed a simultaneous drop of per capita consumption, growth of unemployment and spreading poverty. This made some economists pose the question of whether the determination of the adjustment programmes in less developed countries exclusively by free market principles was indeed a solution which would ensure them real growth prospects, or whether it was merely an instrument allowing the creditor countries to recover at least part of the loaned capital.[46] The less developed countries do not, after all, have a capital market, a labour market and a technology market. The parameters of these markets used in the adjustment programmes (for instance, the interest rate) are erroneous. Also, the group of entrepreneurs who bear particular responsibility for economic growth in free market conditions is very weak there. The question then is whether the role of the state in directing economic processes should not be increased in such circumstances.

Economists representing this point of view believe that the indebtedness of less developed countries was not exclusively due to implementation of the strategy of autonomic development and the policy of import substitution, but rather the result of a convergence of a number of unfavourable circumstances in the world economy, including the multifold growth of prices of energy carriers (in particular, liquid fuels). Placing all the blame on developed state control and shifting the role of the state to the margin of the economy can, in their opinion, generate a number of problems, especially social problems, in the less developed countries in the long term.

A compromise solution should rather be sought, placing emphasis on rationalization of economic processes, growth of exports and opening of the economy, while aiming at the same time at a symbiosis between an active role of the state and free market growth mechanisms. This path seems to be indicated by the practice and experience of a number of less developed countries which endeavour to seek compromise solutions irrespective of the main trend of free market views.

---

45 Comp. M.S. Khan, 'Macro-Economic Effects of Fund-Supported Adjustment Programs: An Empirical Assessment', *IMF Staff Papers*, vol. 37, no. 2, 1990, pp. 195–231; J. Kulig, *Strukturalne i systemowe*, op. cit., p. 48–104.

46 Comp. R. Prebisch, 'International Monetary Indiscipline and the Debt Problem', *Journal of Development Planning*, no. 16, 1985, p. 173.

Chapter 8

Foreign Economic Policy in Central and East European Countries

8.1. The Periods of Radical Transformations of Foreign and International Economic Policy in Central and East European Countries

It is hard to speak about the evolution of foreign and international economic policy in the countries transforming their economic and political systems, since changes of this policy are made rapidly, usually in response to exogenous factors. Moreover, changes in foreign and international economic policy were much more radical in these countries than in the hitherto analysed groups of countries (economically developed, newly industrialized or less developed), since they accompanied profound systemic political and social transformations.

This group of countries includes the countries of Central and Eastern Europe which made two radical changes in their policy in the second half of the 20th century, at the time when the remaining groups of countries were transforming their foreign and international policy in an evolutionary way.

8.1.1. The First Radical Transformation of Foreign and International Economic Policy of Central and East European Countries

The countries of Central and Eastern Europe underwent a radical systemic transformation for the first time at the turn of the 1940s and the 1950s when for political reasons a market economy was replaced with a centrally planned economy. This meant adoption of entirely different goals, means and instruments of economic policy, alien to the market economy.

The centrally planned economy, introduced first in Russia and next in the countries of Central and Eastern Europe, was governed by structural principles different from those at work in the market economy, namely, the domination of public (especially state) ownership, superiority of macroeconomic over microeconomic goals and planned development of the economy.[1] Following nationalization of the means of production and deprivation of private ownership of any real significance, the state assumed responsibility for overall economic development. It was the state which set economic goals and methods of achieving them. The superiority of economic

---

1 Comp. P. Bożyk, *Polityka gospodarcza Polski 1985–2000* (Wyższa Szkoła Handlowa, Warsaw, 1995), p. 9.

goals was understood as the subordination of individual preferences to general needs which meant, for instance, increased investments in raw materials extraction instead of increasing foodstuffs consumption. Finally, the planned development of the economy meant that long-term goals of a longer time horizon determined current goals.

Till the end of the 1980s, all the above-mentioned functions in Central and East European countries (CEECs) were performed by political centres, state centres and economic centres. The political centre included the supreme authorities of the communist party, which remained in power throughout the period following the Second World War, including the Political Bureau, Central Committee and Party Congresses. The state centre embraced Parliament and the Council of State (or president). The economic centre covered the government, ministries and other central offices of branch or functional character as well as banks.

The system of the functioning of CEECs economies introduced then can be defined as monocentric. The managing role in this system was performed by the political centre. It was there that major decisions concerning the directions of the economy development, changes in the mechanism of its functioning, and the like, were made. The remaining centres dealt with implementation of the political centre's decisions. The absolute majority of the governing party members in the legislative body and in the government meant that decisions of the political centre were always approved and next implemented by the state. The principle of party discipline obliged the governing party members to vote in accordance with the decisions of the political centre. In consequence, the state centre approved the proposals of the political centre, giving them the form of effective laws and bills. As the executive body, the government put them into practice immediately.

The information passed by the centre in the monocentric system had the form of a command, expressed as a rule in physical units, excluding any freedom of choice. Those commands determined the goals and means of activity for the executive levels. They were of an obligatory character, i.e. they had to be implemented by enterprises irrespective of their own preferences, the degree of the implementation of those commands being the criterion of evaluation of enterprises. In that system the selection of partners was also centrally determined. The import and export of individual groups of goods was assigned ex ante to a specific foreign trade enterprise. The same principle concerned domestic procurement enterprises, at least with reference to goods of essential importance for the economy, as well as production enterprises, which were organized into central, subject-related managements, associations or combines.

The role of the market mechanism was also subordinated to the functions of commands. In practice, in an ultimately centralized monocentric model, it was reduced to zero. As years went by and the decentralization of the management system appeared, attempts were made to activate the market mechanism.

In this system, domestic prices did not reflect the conditions of production and trade. Instead they were determined on the market by the administrative centre. They were used, primarily, to aggregate a variety of different natural values in the course of the elaboration and implementation of production and trade plans as well as to square economic settlements between enterprises and the state budget. Moreover, domestic enterprises settled their accounts at prices independent of foreign prices. The financial results of economic activity with foreign countries, covering the difference between the value of goods at foreign trade prices, converted into the domestic currency at the exchange rate in force, did not inform enterprises about the benefits drawn from the international division of labour. It was a natural consequence of the fact that prices, in principle, did not reflect conditions of production and trade and, therefore, the obtained result was solely of a balance-sheet importance. When it was negative, the difference was made up by the state budget. In such circumstances, an enterprise recording positive financial results had no advantage over an enterprise recording negative results. That was because positive financial results did not actually testify to the benefits derived by that enterprise, for instance, from foreign trade. Consequently, they did not contribute to an increased allocation of financial and material resources for enterprises to develop foreign needs-oriented production. Simultaneously, the negative results registered by enterprises did not contribute to the restriction of their activity, either. For the centre, it was implementation by the enterprise of the material production plan that was of primary importance.

Not only were prices void of an active character for enterprises, other elements of the economic mechanism also performed passive functions when decisions were taken by enterprises. This concerned, in particular, the domestic currency which also was not a parameter in making economic decisions. As a rule, it performed settlements-related functions, necessary to compare outlays on production and production results. It was not, however, a measure of value, a means of payment or a means of gathering reserves by enterprises. In much the same way, exchange rates in this model did not affect the creation of prices and the shaping of the structure of production. Instead, they were used to make internal settlements between the enterprise and banks. Functions of import duties, import and export charges and surcharges, as well as other para- and non-tariff restrictions were also harmonised with thus defined functions of prices, currency and exchange rate. In a situation when internal prices bore no relation to foreign trade prices, while imports and exports of individual goods were determined by a plan, import tariffs did not perform an active function in shaping the development of foreign economic relations. The same was true of para- and non-tariff instruments. In the monocentric model they stemmed from the existence of a separate structure of internal prices unrelated to world prices. Inherently, the internal price of an imported article could not result from an ordinary product of the exchange rate and price at which the good was purchased abroad at that time. In the same way, the price at which the domestic producer supplied articles for export to a foreign trade enterprise could not be a conversion of the price at which the articles were sold abroad. Internal prices of imported and exported articles were set on a level similar to prices of comparable domestic articles. In this situation, a difference often existed between the value expressed in the domestic currency which the enterprise paid to the domestic bank for the foreign currency appropriated by the bank to the enterprise to finance the import of given goods, and the value which the enterprise obtained from the sale of the goods to the domestic buyer. Similar differences appeared in exports between the domestic value of articles sent abroad and the amount which the bank paid to the exporting enterprise as a product of the price obtained abroad and the exchange rate. When the exchange rate was set at a relatively high level, the foreign price of the imported article converted into the domestic currency always had to be lower than the price at which the article was sold to the domestic buyer, while the price at which the domestic producer supplied domestic goods for exports always had to be higher than the foreign selling price of the goods converted into the domestic currency. That difference was channelled by importing enterprises to the state budget, imports thus being encumbered with the full charge. On the other hand, an exporting enterprise had to receive from the state adequate financial compensation, a sort of an export subsidy.

Although from the formal point of view there seemed to exist a resemblance in the system of import charges and export subventions between the market economy and the centrally planned economy, in reality they played entirely different economic functions in the two systems. In the market economy, export subventions make it possible to reduce the foreign price of exported goods. In the centrally planned economy, on the other hand, they had no influence on the level of the foreign export price, since the price was set on the basis of world market prices. Consequently, export subventions did not affect the size of exports.

Import charges in the market economy determine (next to the foreign price and customs duties) the level of the domestic price of imported goods. In the centrally planned economy, on the other hand, they had no influence on the level of domestic prices of imported goods, since the internal prices of these goods were set on the basis of other principles, in accordance with which it is not internal prices that are the function of import charges but the other way round. With a given purchase price of foreign imported goods and with a given exchange rate, the charges were the function of the internal price. This produced a situation in which import charges had no influence on the size of imports specified in the plan on the basis of domestic needs, on the one hand, and on the basis of import-financing abilities, on the other. The latter was, as a rule, of primary significance as in the countries of centrally planned economy import needs generally exceeded export abilities.

Although weaknesses prevailed in the centrally planned economy system, it also had some strengths. The latter included, first of all, its ability to focus means on selected social and economic issues of major importance from the point of view of the state as a whole. It allowed for fast and effective implementation of large-scale targets exceeding the competences of even the largest enterprises. This concerned, in particular, strategic targets. On the other hand, a major weakness of the centrally planned economy was its failure to favour the improvement of economic management efficiency and technological progress in enterprises, as well as its negative impact on overall economic equilibrium. As a result, the system generated economic disproportions having a hampering effect on the growth rate and standards of living. In addition, the centrally planned economy tended to produce red tape and restrain the initiative of enterprises, thus creating reserves which the centre was unable to mobilize through commands. Neither did the system ensure compliance of the structure of supply and demand, as a result of which buyers sought goods other than those manufactured by enterprises. The inability of enterprises to make the majority of decisions on their own led to substantial economic losses. At the same time, the system required extensive control of labour-consuming central information systems, and the like, but even their existence could not prevent enterprises from consciously misinforming superior bodies in order to be given the easiest possible planned targets to implement.

The fact that weaknesses definitely prevailed over strengths caused the centrally planned economy to evolve in the course of time. Significant changes in the system took place in this domain, especially in the 1980s. Literature defines their core as the distribution (repartition) of centre-concentrated decisions and the delegation of part of them to enterprises as well as other economic organisations. The so-called strategic decisions, including development assumptions as well as goals, means and instruments to apply the economic policy still remained solely in the hands of the centre. Thus, the centre still set the economic growth rate, the structure of the division of the national income, including notably the rate of consumption and the rate of investment, the level of employment and other economic calculus parameters (the interest rate, exchange rate, and so on) Simultaneously, enterprises were given the right to make current decisions and, in particular, to shape the size of production, employment and certain prices. This model of the functioning of the centrally planned economy is referred to as the repartition model. The difference between this model and the monocentric model is presented inn Figures 8.1 and 8.2.

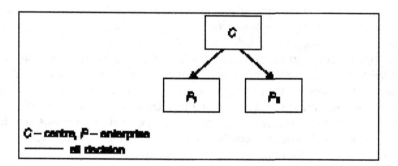

Figure 8.1. Scheme of the Monocentric Model in a Centrally Planned Economy

Source: Author's own elaboration.

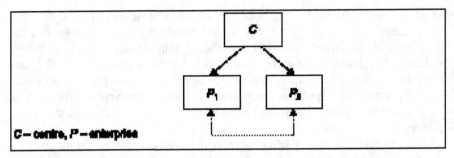

C – centre, P – enterprise

Figure 8.2. Scheme of the Repartition Model in a Centrally Planned Economy

Source: Author's own elaboration.

In the repartition model, enterprises were linked (on the subordination principle) to the centre and mutually (on the principles of equivalence) to one another. They could, consequently, take independent decisions as regards shaping their mutual links. Thus, the repartition model limited significantly the detailed character of the central plan, which became a synthetic plan, given in aggregate values, determining the scope of independence of the executors. Yet, the obligatory character of the plan was upheld.

Changes also occurred in the form in which the centre passed its decisions to enterprises, quantitative commands being replaced with parameters. In the repartition approach, the centre focused on formulating solely general development assumptions, leaving the task of setting detailed targets to enterprises. Generally speaking, to ensure implementation of the plan, the centre had at its disposal two types of instruments. Firstly, it determined the parameters of the macroeconomic policy (the economic growth rate, the structure of the national income distribution, the level of the exchange rate, the principles of the economic policy, and such things). Secondly, it decided on the principles of the actual policy of enterprises (shaping the principles of the distribution of profit in enterprises, the bonus system for employees dependent on registered economic results, financial sanctions to be faced by enterprises for failing to meet their agreed commitments, export subventions, imposition of customs duties, etc.).

Concurrently, the repartition variant of the centrally planned economy attempted to start the market mechanism by broadening the function of prices, exchange rate and currency. The so-called staple goods (most important from the point of view of economic growth or complying with systemic principles) still remained under direct state control. Their prices were stable and production subsidized (in case of need). In contrast, all the remaining goods were subjected to the action of market mechanisms. Their prices depended on the relation between supply and demand while their production was deprived of subventions. In foreign trade, a need appeared for a closer link between internal and world market prices. For the importer, it meant the appearance of a possibility to calculate the selling price of imported goods in the country with the help of the exchange rate and, as a result, to determine the volume of sales and profit. The exporter also came to be directly interested in the price obtained on the foreign market.

In total, the repartition variant of the centrally planned economy was an attempt to apply in practice the so-called mixed economic system, combining planning and market mechanism. The share of these two components varied between particular countries of Central and Eastern Europe and kept evolving throughout the 1980s.

The primary goal of the economic policy in the centrally planned economy (both in the monocentric and in the repartition variant) was to maximize the national income in the macroeconomic and long-term aspects.

This was to be ensured, in the first place, by a radical change of the economic structure connected with industrialization. The model of that industrialization was to be found in the economically developed countries, unfortunately with their historical, 19th-century model of industrialization. Contrary to the newly industrialized countries, which simply outpaced the highly industrialized countries with their growth strategy, subordinating the development of industry to exports, the countries of Central and Eastern Europe subordinated industrialization exclusively to the needs of the domestic market when transforming their industry for the first time.

Obsession with industrialization understood in autonomic terms was the main reason underlying the proneness of the countries of Central and Eastern Europe to become indebted in highly industrialized countries.[2] It found its reflection in the rapid rise of demand for goods manufactured by economically developed countries and, on the other hand, insufficient development of export abilities of CEECs. This generated long-term trends towards a markedly faster growth of imports to the CEECs as compared with exports from the said countries. This phenomenon aggravated in the course of time as the industrial structure of the CEECs was expanded universally from the point of view of self-sufficiency and not from the point of view of export specialization. Exports, being of an indispensable character (and thus expected to serve solely and exclusively the financing of indispensable imports) comprised, in principle, only surpluses of goods left after satisfying the domestic demand.

The third feature, apart from accelerated industrialization and autarchic tendencies, of the economic policy of the CEECs was an attempt to make consumption uniform. This was to be achieved, in the first place, through an egalitarian approach to incomes. Differences in wages and other incomes of the population in the CEECs were much smaller than in any other group of countries. The structure of domestic production, which left no room for luxury goods, favoured giving consumption a uniform character. Also, the structure of imports of consumer goods was subordinated to this aim.

An additional factor which was to contribute to making consumption uniform was an attempt of the superior authorities to shape the model of consumption

---

2 Comp. P. Bożyk, *Droga donikąd? Polska i jej sąsiedzi na rozdrożu* (Polska Oficyna Wydawnicza BGW, Warsaw, 1991), p. 38.

reflected in mass propaganda emphasizing the superior character of basic needs and fundamental human rights, especially the right to work, the right to education, the right to satisfy the existential minimum, covering nourishment, clothing, housing, medical and social care, and such like.

All the three goals of the CEECs' economic policy (that is comprehensive industrialization, autonomic economic growth and making consumption uniform) were implemented consistently till the end of the 1960s though weaknesses of that approach had become obvious already in the mid-1960s.

The weaknesses notably included the investment barrier. The universal growth of industry gave rise to the demand for ever new kinds of investments, which could not be increased endlessly due to the consumption barrier, as living low standards produced the danger of a social crisis. The barrier of foreign trade, in the form of imports exceeding exports, was another significant obstacle.

In these circumstances, the primary goal of the CEECs' foreign economic policy was to adjust the volume of imports to export possibilities. This goal was implemented consistently till 1970. In result, the net indebtedness of the CEECs in convertible currencies amounted to a mere 4.7 billion dollars and, thus, was practically nonexistent. This was caused by the fact that mutual relations were running at a very low level. The CEECs exported raw materials and foodstuffs to the economically developed countries while importing goods required to offset the needs shaped in an autonomic way with investment, production and consumption opportunities.

The Council for Mutual Economic Assistance (CMEA) played the main role in the foreign economic relations of the CEECs.[3] The organization was established in 1949 to facilitate adjustment of the sizes and structures of foreign trade pursued by its member countries to the needs and opportunities of their economies. The second goal pursued by the CMEA was to re-orientate the geographical structure of foreign trade and, namely, to replace economically developed countries with CMEA member countries in trade.

The first of the organization's two goals was achieved, adopting in its functioning such principles as harmonized with the principles of the centrally planned economy. Interstate agreements concluded at government level and specifying in detail the size and commodity structure of trade in bilateral terms were the primary instrument in the development of economic relations within the CMEA On the part of imports, priority was given to goods needed to implement investment and production targets, and only then followed by consumption targets. On the part of exports, the list included own surplus goods starting with those most desired by partners and followed by others in the order of decreasing attractiveness. In such agreements goods were frequently 'linked' horizontally in imports and exports according to the degree of importance.

---

3   Comp. P. Bożyk, *Współpraca gospodarcza krajów RWPG*, 2nd edn (PWE, Warsaw, 1977) and P. Bożyk, M. Guzek, *Teoria integracji socjalistycznej*, 2nd edn (PWE, Warsaw, 1980).

The agreements determined at central level did not offer enterprises opportunities to negotiate delivery conditions, quality of goods, their prices, etc. Consequently, they were executed passively, on the basis of contractual quotas and settled in roubles (first Soviet and then so-called transfer roubles). The settlements were always of a formal character, anyway, and did not play an active role, with concrete products being of primary importance. The cooperating countries, thus, tried to negotiate the agreements so that they would balance.

While the above-discussed goal of the CMEA was mainly of a technical character, the second of its goals, in the form a reoriented geographical structure of trade among the CEECs, was political. Traditionally, all the countries of this region assigned 80% of their exports to the countries of Western Europe and overseas. Thus, as in the first case when the CMEA was to help ensure an autonomic development of individual economies, in the second case the organization was to become an instrument to implement the autonomic development of the region as a whole. The place of traditional economic links with economically developed countries was to be taken over by establishing close links between the countries of Central and Eastern Europe and the Soviet Union. The latter was to supply CEECs with energy, raw materials and materials as well as technologies for the production of industrial goods to be subsequently exported to the Soviet Union. In the first place, those were to be the articles for the armaments industry.

In the 1950s and in the first half of the 1960s implementation of both these CMEA targets proceeded in compliance with the adopted assumptions. At the turn of the 1960s and the 1970s, however, all the three barriers mentioned earlier (the investment, consumption and foreign trade barriers) came to be painfully felt. The autonomic development of the economy led, first of all, to a fast growth of import needs which had to entail increasing indebtedness in conditions of limited export opportunities. Since in trade between CMEA countries turnover had to be balanced, the growth of imports faster than exports had to be in trade with the highly industrialized countries of Western Europe and the United States as well as Japan. Thus, by 1971, the net debt of Central and Eastern Europe had risen to 6.6 billion dollars, in 1975 it was 31 billion dollars, in 1980 74.8 billion dollars and in 1989 114.2 billion dollars.[4] This resulted in a fast growth of the share of the economically developed countries in the global trade of the CMEA countries.

Acceleration of that process was also due to restrictions in fuels and raw materials export introduced by the Soviet Union. The latter was the outcome of its shrinking investment abilities as well as the exhaustion of the raw material resources in the European part of the USSR. In addition, the extraction of these raw materials in Siberia was much more capital-consuming than in the European part of the Soviet Union. The countries of Central and Eastern Europe were thus forced to import not only machines and equipment, technologies and industrial consumer goods from economically developed countries but also energy carriers (mainly crude oil) as well

---

4 *Economic Survey of Europe in 1989–1990*, (United Nations, New York, 1990), p. 416.

as some kinds of foodstuffs (for instance, meat). Contrary to the rapidly growing imports, the export opportunities of Central and Eastern Europe were extremely limited, which resulted from the pursued concept of autonomic development. This explains why the indebtedness of CEECs in trade with the economically developed countries began to increase at such a fast rate.

As years went by, the role of CMEA countries in their global trade began to decline rapidly instead of growing, as the adopted model of cooperation ceased to suit the CEECs as well as the Soviet Union.

One of the more important reasons of the dissolution of CMEA (at the beginning of the 1990s) was the conviction of both parties that trade among them was no longer profitable. An important role here was played, in particular, by the Soviet Union, which followed the doctrine of unilaterally preferential conditions in trade within the CMEA for the CEECs and, thus, of these countries being subsidized by the USSR.[5] In accordance with this doctrine, the Soviet Union sold raw materials to these countries at prices lower than world prices and bought from them industrial goods at prices higher than world prices. All that was done in the name of the mentioned doctrine and, thus, exclusively for political reasons.

This conviction made the CMEA countries replace the clearing system of settlements towards the final moments of this organization with settlements based on free foreign trade and quota agreements, with independence in concluding transactions by enterprises. These changes resulted in the collapse of trade between the CMEA countries and, in particular, trade between CEECs and the Soviet Union.

To Russia, the heir of the Soviet Union, the effect of this re-orientation brought about a significant drop of both exports and imports as well as deterioration of terms of trade.[6] For the countries of Central and Eastern Europe, the re-orientation of Russia's foreign trade from the CMEA countries to world markets signified the need to bear the costs of a radical change in the geographical as well as commodity structure of their trade. This was reflected in the collapse of whole industries which had been originally oriented to exporting to the former Soviet Union.

8.1.2. The Second Radical Transformation of Foreign and International Economic Policy of Central and East European Countries

The second radical transformation of the foreign economic policy of CEECs was initiated at the turn of the 1980s and the 1990s, that is 40 years after the first transformation. It turned out to be a complete reversal of the direction of changes made at the time of the first radical transformation and consisted of replacing the centrally planned economy with a free market economy. As practice showed, this was to prove impossible without profound systemic transformations.

---

5   Comp. M. Guzek, *Międzynarodowe stosunki gospodarcze*, op. cit., p. 278 and following and M. Marrese, J. Vanous, 'Unconventional Gains from Trade', *Journal of Comparative Economies*, December, 1983, p. 383.

6   Comp. M. Guzek, *Międzynarodowe stosunki gospodarcze*, op. cit., p. 290–91.

The systemic transformations consisted, in the first place, of replacing the repartition model of making political and economic decisions with a polycentric model.[7]

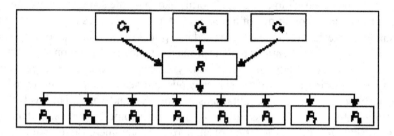

Figure 8.3. Scheme of the Polycentric Model

Source: Author's own elaboration.

The emergence of numerous political parties apart from the ruling parties, caused an opposition to appear, the conduct of the centre becoming determined by Parliament. Owing to the multipartite composition of Parliament as well as (in general) the coalition character of the government, under the conditions of the polycentric system tendencies appeared towards elaborating and implementing economic programmes shaped by compromise, taking account the preferences of individual political parties currently in power.

While the change of the political system which consisted of transition from the repartition model to the polycentric model in the CEECs was rapid (formally speaking), the change of economic policy was impossible without a thorough and profound restructuring of the principles of the functioning of the economy, including the commodity market, service market, capital market, financial market and foreign currency market, as well as without changing the systemic infrastructure and required a longer time.

This concerned, primarily, the function of the state, the principal economic subject under the conditions of a centrally planned economy. In a free market situation, priority had to be given to the numerous enterprises which enjoyed the right to decide on their activities by themselves (on the basis of valid legal regulations). In trade, production and investments, the state as an economic subject acquired the same rights and duties as enterprises.

Secondly, the balances of production and trade, being of decisive importance in a centrally planned economy, had to give way to sovereign decisions of thousands of independent producers and traders, with the needs and tastes of consumers uppermost in mind.

Thirdly, the forms of state influence on enterprises also had to change in an essential way. Command instruments had to be replaced by indicative instruments, the most

---

7   Comp. P. Bożyk, *Polityka gospodarcza Polski*, op. cit., pp. 28–9.

important of which included creating laws, ensuring their observance, countering free market and free trade disruptions. Whereas the directive feature of the state's influence on enterprises was the unequal treatment of different economic subjects, under free market conditions the legal norms had to be the same for everyone.

Fourthly, under conditions of a free market, prices of goods and services on the consumer market had to being transformed into prices of equilibrium between supply and demand, while subventions to their production had to be abandoned. Apart from a few exceptions, this could be effected solely through a multifold rise of prices. The principles of setting prices of consumer goods and services in a centrally planned economy were determined by egalitarianism in incomes and wages. The level of prices was, thus, adjusted to the possibilities of average-income buyers. Simultaneously, the state subsidized the production of numerous goods, the costs of production of which exceeded prices. The consumption of numerous groups, especially those with relatively low incomes, also used to be subsidized. In consequence, the demand for a number of consumer goods and services significantly exceeded demand, since low prices increased consumption, encouraging wastefulness as well as enlarging the circle of buyers who would be unable to pay for them under conditions of market equilibrium prices. At the same time, the possibilities of expanding the production of scarce goods were restricted by investment limits. This gave rise to difficulties in balancing demand and supply on the consumer market. Purchases of goods in short supply required, therefore, long queuing, using personal connections, bribing, and the like.

The introduction of free prices and the simultaneous abandonment of subsidizing eliminated low-income buyers and created incentives to save. This suggested a visual abundance of goods on the market. Queuing was replaced by marketing and advertising to attract buyers. On the other hand, limitations were posed by people's incomes.

Fifthly, under market economy conditions, prices of factors of production also underwent essential change. A free market requires that prices of factors of production be set at the level of equilibrium between demand and supply. This signifies, in the first place, an essential change in the principles of setting prices of raw materials and materials. Under the conditions of a centrally planned economy there was no market in this domain, this function being performed by distribution carried out by the bodies of the central state administration, with the production of raw materials and materials being simultaneously largely subsidized by the state budget. Under free market conditions, prices of raw materials and materials must be set at the level of equilibrium between production demand and investment demand, on the one hand, and production, on the other. The abandonment of subventions to production must lead to a multifold rise of production costs and, thus, to a rise of market prices, which eliminates weaker buyers with lower purchasing potential.

Similar changes were seen taking place in the market of machines and equipment for production. In a centrally planned economy, their manufacture was also largely subsidized, while prices were set below the equilibrium level. This encouraged production to expand in compliance with the strategy of industrialization. However, it simultaneously led to wastefulness in the form of poorly utilized production equipment, facilities, etc. In free market conditions, prices of machines and equipment for production must be set at the level of equilibrium between demand and supply. When state subsidies are abandoned, a multifold increase is inevitably generated. This in turn must lead to restricted demand due to the elimination of buyers who cannot afford purchases at equilibrium prices.

Therefore, a transition from a centrally planned to a market economy had to signify also deep transformations in the labour market. Under free market conditions, the central distribution of the labour force is replaced with its free flow between different economic sectors. In formal terms, the distribution of the labour force in a centrally planned economy practically eliminated unemployment. In fact, however, the situation was far from ideal. While some enterprises had to cope with excessive employment, others suffered a shortage of labour. Hidden unemployment generated lower labour productivity and resultant wastefulness. Liberalization of the labour market makes the price of labour dependent on the demand–supply relation. A differentiation of wages in comparison with a centrally planned economy followed. While some professions and qualifications became highly paid, no demand existed for others, which brought about unemployment and progressive differentiation of incomes.

Also liberalization of the capital market, indispensable in the market economy, gave rise to equally deep changes compared with a centrally planned economy. The central management of capital flows had to be replaced with its free turnover. In such circumstances, the adoption of a uniform interest rate on the level of the equilibrium between supply and demand led, inevitably, to its significant growth which, in turn, limited the demand for capital on the part of buyers who used to have access to it in a centrally planned economy owing to the preferential and frequently differentiated interest rate on capital. The uniform interest rate gave equal rights to the 'better' and 'worse' capital users of a centrally planned economy.

Sixthly, the transformation of a centrally planned economy into a free market economy meant an essential change to the situation on the money market. After being only an instrument of making settlements in a centrally planned economy, money regained its previously lost properties as a measure of value, means of payment, instrument of accumulating reserves and means of circulation, also in the sphere of production and investment. In the sphere of consumption, money also became the only regulator in the market after abandonment of rations, vouchers, allowances, etc. Simultaneously, the domestic currency eliminated all other currencies from circulation, a phenomenon typical of a centrally planned economy, especially in the later period of its existence. The emission of money came to be controlled and its supply came to be adjusted to the needs resulting from the economic situation.

Seventhly, transformation of the mechanism of a centrally planned economy into a free market economy had to signify essential changes in the foreign currency market. The central distribution of foreign exchange was replaced with a free market on which relations between demand and the supply came to decide about prices of foreign currencies. The system of differentiated exchange rates was replaced with a uniform exchange rate which was simultaneously realistic and began to serve to shape prices of exported and imported goods, as well as to make decisions in trade, production and investments.

Eighthly, transformation of a centrally planned economy into a free market economy had to result in opening to foreign markets. That opening proceeded on many planes, covering the market of goods and services, the capital market, the foreign exchange market and others. Opening the commodity market consisted of the same treatment being given to foreign and domestic goods. Barriers to imports were reduced to a minimum, this applying not only to complementary imports but to competitive imports as well which signified that profit became the principal evaluation criterion. Due to the changed principles of shaping prices, exchange rates, money, etc., profit could be determined in real, not calculation, terms (as it was typical in a centrally planned economy). When imported goods proved better and less expensive, they replaced domestic goods. Limitation of access to the domestic market (by means of tariff, para-tariff and non-tariff restrictions) was thus treated as an exception and not a rule. Opening the capital market found its reflection in equal treatment given to domestic and foreign capital, with the price (and not the source of origin) assuming the function of the main criterion of its valuation. The principles and forms of the international transfer of profit were simultaneously liberalized, enabling foreign capital owners to adopt a flexible approach to the place of its location.

The transformation of a centrally planned economy into a free market economy required not only the above-described changes in the mechanism of its functioning but also the transformation of the systemic infrastructure covering, notably, the institutional basis of the economy, its organization, forms of ownership and forms of enterprise management. Unlike the economic mechanisms, which can be changed within a short time, the systemic infrastructure is characterized by significant rigidity. Its transformation thus requires more time and is connected with both economic and also social costs. These costs are particularly high when the change has been far-reaching.

The change of the systemic infrastructure could be seen, first of all, in the restructuring of the economic centre. Some institutions typical of the centrally planned economy proved useless and had to be dissolved. Some of the old institutions had to change their functions. Finally, a need existed to set up a large number of completely new institutions characteristic of a free market economy (commercial banks, stock exchange, fiscal offices, and the like).

The ownership structure also had to undergo a radical transformation. In a centrally planned economy, almost the entire industry belonged to the state, while in agriculture collective ownership prevailed. A change of this state of affairs required, primarily, adequate capital resources of both private and natural persons interested in the purchase of state enterprises.

Another element in the change of the systemic infrastructure was also the transformation of the production structure. While a centrally planned economy led to expansion of the raw-material-related industries: heavy industry, engineering industry and other sectors of the economy oriented to overall industrialization, with the share of consumption-oriented industry being relatively insignificant, a free market economy, by its nature open to foreign institutions, required a completely different structure, shaped bearing in mind international specialization and a much more significant share of imports than before. The restructuring of industry requires, however, rapid growth of investment outlays destined notably for advanced technology. Neither can it be effected within a short time.

The systemic transformation also required a change of the organizational structure of the economy as well as enterprises. In a centrally planned economy, a decisive role was performed by large enterprises with a monopolistic position. This resulted from the centralized system of economic management, giving preference to simple organizational structures facilitating the passage of decisions from the centre to enterprises. The so-called associations, combines and other similar forms of enterprise organization served this purpose. In a free market economy, organizational structure existing in the previous system has no justification as it does not create conditions for the proper play of market forces. On the contrary, it could give rise to pathological phenomena reducing the benefits of the solution. It was, therefore, necessary to increase substantially the share of small and medium-sized enterprises. To some limited extent this could be done by splitting large enterprises into smaller ones. Yet, the main way of reaching this end was to develop a new structure of enterprises from scratch. This, however, required both time and substantial capital.

The transformation of a centrally planned economy into a free market economy must be simultaneously accompanied by a change of the infrastructure of social benefits. This refers, notably, to a change in the function of institutions responsible for health protection, education, university education, social welfare, rest, and the like. In a centrally planned economy, these institutions rendered their services free of charge or for a symbolic charge. The principles of rendering the services resembled the principles in force on the consumer goods market. There were simultaneously more people eager to take advantage of the benefits than the institutions in charge could potentially provide.

In a free market economy, the scope of partly or fully non-gratuitous services increases significantly. Consequently, the number of people benefiting from them decreases. Apart from state institutions rendering these services, private ones also exist. Simultaneously, the state focuses its attention on extending social assistance (gratuitous or largely gratuitous) to the poorest people with the lowest incomes. The transformations referred to are extremely complex and require much time, primarily due to the resistance of the part of the population which were enjoying free of charge benefits in a centrally planned economy.

Finally, another element of the systemic infrastructure which requires essential re-orientation upon transformation from a centrally planned to a free market economy is the system of how state-owned enterprises are managed. In a centrally planned economy, they were run by managements subordinated to the state administration, with workers' councils or employees' self-managements acting as advisory bodies of co-decision-making and frequently the decision-making character in that system. It was the state that decided whether enterprises were established or liquidated, shaped their production structure, whether to cover losses and channel profits to the budget. The self-management system partly adjusted those principles but did not change them in principle. Under free market conditions, the functioning of state-owned enterprises must change primarily because the economy of enterprises becomes subjected the rules of the market. The state ceases to direct its enterprises by means of commands. It no longer nominates their managers. A need exists to commercialise these enterprises and privatise their management. The supervisory board, composed of the managers running the enterprise, a representative of the owner (the State Treasury) and representatives of employees becomes the central management body of the state-owned enterprise.

The systemic changes referred to above initiated in the CEECs at the beginning of the 1990s were introduced with differing intensity and at a different pace. The rapid and far-reaching changes came to be known as the shock transformation, while gradual changes spread in time were called the evolutionary transformation.[8] The differentiation concerned mainly changes in the economic mechanism. The systemic infrastructure was also developed in CEECs at a differentiated pace, the latter being slower, however.

The first group of countries which applied the shock method to transform the mechanism of their functioning, included the former GDR, Poland, Lithuania, Latvia, Estonia, Croatia and, since the mid-1990s also Russia, Bulgaria and Romania. The radical character of the changes introduced in this group of countries consisted of a simultaneous rise of the macro- and microeconomic parameters (and thus prices, interest rate, exchange rate, etc.) to the market equilibrium level. The power of the shock depended, consequently, on the degree of these parameters' deviation from the market equilibrium level in the previous system. When market prices did not differ excessively from the demand–supply equilibrium level, the shock was minor. However, when the difference was significant, a need arose to raise prices repeatedly until they could be set at the equilibrium level. The same concerned all the other parameters. Literature on the subject refers to this phenomenon as stabilization of the economy.[9] The one-off change of the economic policy parameters to the market equilibrium level was to prevent the growth of inflation and to eliminate inflation-related pathologies.

In general, the stabilization of the economy in the countries of Central and Eastern Europe which consisted of introducing prices of goods and services which would balance their demand and supply on the market, an exchange rate which would balance the demand for and supply of foreign exchange and an interest rate which

---

8   Comp. P. Bożyk, *24 kraje Europy Środkowej I Wschodniej. Transformacja*, 2nd edn (Oficyna Wydawnicza SGH, Warsaw, 2002), pp. 31–9.

9   Comp. M. Nasiłowski, 'Czy terapia szkowa w Polsce była uzasadniona?', in W. Jakóbik (ed.), *Transformacja gospodarki, spojrzenie retrospektywne* (ISP PAN, Warsaw, 1997), p. 35; A. Wojtyna, 'Strategia gospodarcza a ekonomia polityczna reform', in M. Belka, W. Trzeciakowski (eds), *Dynamika transformacji polskiej gospodarki*, vol. 1 (INE PAN, Warsaw, 1997), pp. 135–54.

would balance the demand and supply on the capital market, etc., had to translate into a significant revolution in the economy irrespective of how radical it was. In the previous system, both production and consumption were largely subsidized and hence prices of the prevailing part of goods and services were lower than equilibrium prices. The interest rate was also below the equilibrium level for the supply of and demand for capital, which meant that the state subsidized investments. Labour was also subsidized. Subventions to labour were industry-related, with wages in some industries being relatively undervalued in comparison with the free market value of labour, while in others they were higher than their free market value. The foreign exchange market was also run in an entirely different way from in the market economy, with differentiated prices of foreign exchange instead of uniform ones. The official exchange rate of foreign currencies was set at a level close to the average for the economy as a whole. Thus, the official exchange rate did not differ significantly from the unofficial rate (the so-called black market rate) which was a reflection of marginal volumes. In addition, the state applied a differentiated exchange rate also with respect to the operations of enterprises, with foreign exchange being cheaper for some import enterprises and more expensive for others.

The radical stabilization of the economy involved, moreover, not only a rapid and deep-reaching change (rise) of the economic policy parameters but also liberalization of all markets (the commodity market, capital market, labour market and foreign exchange market) as well as the withdrawal of the state from subsidizing economic activity on these markets. The aim of this was to eliminate inefficient production of goods and services, inefficient investments and inefficient labour, thus giving the economy a good starting point for sound, inflation-free growth.

However, in many countries, practice did not live up to these expectations, which translated into persistent inflationary phenomena. Although a consistently applied stabilization policy eliminated demand-related inflation, and, thus, inflation resulting from an unfounded growth of the production of goods and services, rise of incomes and consequently demand, it failed to eliminate cost-related inflation. Another thing was that in almost all CEECs radical stabilization was not fully carried out, with prices of some goods not being liberalized and not being set at the equilibrium demand and supply level, with the subsidizing of the production of part of goods not being fully abandoned. Moreover, the practice of raising employees' incomes above the level justified by the growth of labour efficiency was still widely practised.

The second group of countries, including the Czech Republic, Slovakia, Hungary and Slovenia, adopted the gentle stabilization method, which implied gradual replacement of non-equilibrium prices spread over time (of goods, services, capital and labour force) with equilibrium prices. The same principle of gradual elimination applied to the subsidizing of production and consumption, including the social sphere (social benefits, education, culture, and others). Also, the exchange rate and the interest rate were brought gradually to realistic levels.

The direction of the transformation of the systemic infrastructure in all CEECs is largely similar, though its effects vary. The reason for these differences can be attributed to different historical traditions connected with the market economy, different preparation of the societies to function under free market conditions, as well as diversified political, social and economic situation.

Some CEECs, Poland, Hungary, Slovenia, the Czech Republic and Croatia included, found themselves in a more advantageous situation than the rest of the region at the very beginning of systemic transformation, the divergences between the newly developed systemic infrastructure and the state of the economy in these countries being smaller than in the remaining countries. Whether consciously or unconsciously, the countries in question prepared for the new role while the rules of a centrally planned economy were still in operation. Changes towards a free market appeared relatively earliest in the economies of Slovenia and Croatia, parts of the former Yugoslavia. As early as towards the end of the 1950s, the scope of directive state influence was limited, decentralization was introduced and large monopolies were replaced with thousands of small enterprises. Alongside other similar changes, some (limited) convertibility of the domestic currency was introduced and customs duties were given active functions. Consequently, the process of systemic transformation could proceed more smoothly at the turn of the 1980s and the 1990s without generating such a social shock as in the remaining countries of Central and Eastern Europe.

Also in Hungary, the economy was relatively well prepared for the introduction of the systemic market infrastructure. The reform of the Hungarian economy actually began in 1968, when the independence of enterprises was gradually increased, and prices liberalized. This was accompanied by restricting of the scope of the command management of the economy and banks being given the function of active economic entities.

In Poland, some elements characteristic of a market economy came to be introduced as early as the mid-1950s but significant changes in this domain were made only in the mid-1980s. Generally speaking, the Polish economy proved well prepared for the introduction of the systemic infrastructure typical of a free market. Polish agriculture was predominantly in private hands. Also, in sectors of industry, trade and services the private sector was better developed and more active than in the other countries of the region. Apart from the official currency market, there was an efficient grey market based on the actual exchange rate of the zloty.

The Czech Republic and Slovakia, belonging traditionally to the group of countries with a developed market economy, succeeded in reducing the scope of pathologies natural for the transformation process (unemployment, inflation). Some traditions and customs typical of the market economy (good work and discipline, cultivation of good traditions, and the like) which the central planning system had failed to destroy also proved helpful. As a result, the introduction in those countries of this group of systemic infrastructure following West European solutions did not encounter the obstacle of an economy totally unprepared for the new needs.

The second group of countries, including Albania, Bulgaria, Romania as well as Russia and other former member countries of the Soviet Union, met much more serious difficulties (than the first group) in developing the new systemic infrastructure.

The reason was their lack of experience in this domain as well as the gap between the new infrastructure and the state of the economy.

Practically all these countries had never before had a well-functioning market, the only exception being, perhaps, the European part of Russia where the market mechanism became the principal regulator of economic life in the second half of the 19th and the early 20th century. All the remaining countries had, prior to the introduction of a centrally planned economy, a semi-feudal economy with poorly developed market mechanisms and its pathological effects in the form of high unemployment, low-efficiency agriculture and small, technologically and organizationally backward industrial sector (mainly extraction industry).

In all the CEECs transforming their economies (with better or worse effects), the change of the overall economic policy was accompanied by a change of foreign economic policy.

Maximization of immediate benefits, based on the comparative advantage in the relation between the domestic and foreign market, was the main goal of foreign trade policy. The advantage stemmed from differences in the costs of domestic production and foreign exchange prices of exported and imported goods.

The transformation of the economic system caused the foreign-trade conducting subjects to change, state-owned enterprises to be replaced by private enterprises as the monopoly in foreign trade which gave the state exclusive rights with respect to export and import was abolished. In conditions of a centrally planned economy the state not only set export and import targets but also implemented those targets with the help of its enterprises, while the systemic transformation reduced the role of the state in foreign economic policy to setting targets and encouraging private enterprises to implement them with the help of various means and instruments. Profit became the principal criterion in evaluating foreign trade performance. No wonder, then, that with this criterion in mind private enterprises export and import only those products which generate the highest profit. If the state wants these enterprises to change their priorities and export or import goods of greater importance for the implementation of the foreign economic policy than those which bring the highest profit, then the state is forced to resort to the means of the foreign economic policy and compensate lost profit to private enterprises.

Almost throughout the whole period when the principles of a centrally planned economy were in operation, the state gave pride of place to investment and production-oriented imports over consumer-oriented imports. Needless to say, the structure of foreign trade was dominated by machinery and equipment as well as raw materials and materials for production. Under free market economy conditions, priority shifted to consumer goods and it was consumer goods that came to prevail in the preferences of private importers. At the same time, more expensive credit resulting from the introduction of a positive interest rate significantly restricted interest in investments and import's of capital goods.

The commodity structure of imports was further affected by a change in the structure of consumer demand. Under the conditions of a centrally planned economy this demand was only slightly diversified, since income differences were also relatively small. The introduction of a free market economy, markedly diversifying incomes, gave rise to an enormous diversification of demand. On the one hand, demand emerged in prosperous sections of society, mainly for luxury goods (apartments, cars, household furnishings, clothes, shoes, etc.). On the other hand, a significant poorer group existed which could afford to purchase only the cheapest articles. At the same time, in all CEECs the demand for goods imported from the economically developed countries exceeded the demand for products of the domestic industry, as well as for products proceeding from other countries of the region. The reason for this phenomenon can be attributed not so much to their lower prices or higher quality as to exceptional fascination with goods and services coming from highly industrialized countries; this resulted from the fact that they had been rarely available at the time of a centrally planned economy.

The dissolution of the CMEA also had a significant impact on the change of foreign economic policy targets, following the introduction of a free market economy in the Central and Eastern Europe countries. It signified the need to find new markets for goods manufactured in CEECs and previously exported to CMEA markets. Simultaneously, a transition to free currency settlements on the basis of current world prices in mutual settlements between the former CMEA countries made this export much less attractive. The former buyers, in particular of industrial goods manufactured by CEECs, shifted their demand towards West European countries, the United States and Japan. All this caused the share of the trade between CEECs to drop by several per cent.

The change of the conditions of trade with Western Europe and other economically developed countries was of no lesser importance for the re-orientation of foreign economic policy targets. Following the systemic and political transformations in CEECs, the principal reasons for the developed countries to apply different kinds of restrictions in trade ceased to exist. The scope of the embargo on deliveries of industrial and advanced technology goods to CEECs under the Coordinating Committee (COCOM) which had been imposed during the cold war, was significantly reduced. At the same time, a political climate appeared favouring this trade as well as the development of other forms of economic cooperation. All that had a positive impact on the development of economic relations between CEECs and West European countries, the United States and Japan. Nevertheless, these relations witnessed the emergence of trends towards a return to the traditional structure of trade and, thus, to the prevalence of fuels, raw materials and foodstuffs in exports to and of processed industrial goods in imports from CEECs.[10]

Finally, other factors which affected the transformation of the external links of the CEECs can be found in the association agreements with the EU signed in 1991 by Poland, Hungary and the Czech Republic and later by the other countries of the region. They had a two-fold influence – firstly, psychological, encouraging thousands of enterprises to increase their interest in developing of mutual relations and, secondly, institutional, in the form of initially extended mutual preferences,

---

10 P. Bożyk, *Którędy do Europy?*, op. cit., p. 77.

connected with the establishment of institutions responsible for promoting the development of mutual relations.[11]

8.2. Diversified Effects of Economic Policy Transformation in Central and East European Countries

System transformation has created varied opportunities for economic growth in CEECs, even though an economic policy compatible with the 'Washington consensus' was applied across the region.[12] Several causes lay behind these differences. First, the governments of individual countries adopted different approaches when implementing the rules of transformation proposed to them. This especially applied to different parameters of transformation, including the scope of state intervention in the economy, privatization and liberalization. Second, the economic and social conditions at the start of transformation in 1989 varied from one country to another. This was especially true of inflation, foreign debt, trade deficit, trade union role and pay demands. Finally, the preparedness of individual countries varied considerably in the system infrastructure necessary to introduce free-market mechanisms. While some countries, such as Hungary, Slovenia and Poland, for many years had tried to include elements of the market mechanism in central planning, in the remaining countries, particularly Romania, Bulgaria, Russia and other former Soviet republics, a free market was a purely theoretical idea, completely unknown in practice.

Generally, Central European countries, characterized by the highest level of development and the most favourable structures of production from the perspective of a free market, found themselves in the best situation in the CEEC region. Their system infrastructure was best adapted to free market needs. Despite this, these countries took almost 10 years to recover their GDP levels from before the start of transition in 1989. In the initial period of transformation, in 1991–5, these countries' growth was based on fragile foundations. Small businesses were forced to tap into the reserves that they created under the previous system. This primarily involved the need to reduce employment and boost labour productivity. Only in the second stage of transformation, covering the 1996–2000 period and the start of the 21st century, was the development of Central European countries partly based on investments linked with internal accumulation. In part, foreign investors also played a role through loans and direct capital investments.

The highest rate of economic growth was noted in countries with the most developed small business sectors, including small industry and services. This chiefly applied to Poland and Slovenia, which created relatively favourable conditions for the development of this sector of the economy under the previous system. In the course of transition, these countries transformed their small businesses into the single most important sector of the economy (in terms of GDP share), developing key

---

11 Comp. *The Study on Japanese Cooperation in Industrial Policy for Developing Economies. Poland* (Institute of Developing Economies, Tokyo, March 1995), pp. 39–47.

12 See P. Bożyk, *24 kraje Europy Środkowej i Wschodniej*, op. cit., p. 103.

market economy parameters. This primarily applied to the introduction of realistic exchange rates, internal convertibility and equilibrium prices on the consumer and investment markets. The economy was privatized, and state intervention limited more substantially than in other countries. Foreign trade monopolies were abolished and replaced by thousands of private businesses. Retail trade and services were completely denationalized, becoming the driving force behind economic growth in Poland and Slovenia.

At the same time, this policy put large state-owned enterprises (SOEs) in an unusually difficult position. Deprived of subsidies and other forms of state assistance, these enterprises were unable to meet the requirements of a free market and free trade. By nature inflexible in their reactions to frequent changes in current market parameters (market prices, exchange rates and interest rates), they were crowded out by small businesses, which reported much better financial results. From the very beginning, SOEs were doomed to bankruptcy. Some of them terminated their operations in the first few months after the start of transition. Some others were privatized, and the rest continued to operate for many years. In practice, this group of Central European countries did not have efficient large enterprises that could manufacture long runs of products competitive with goods offered by their counterparts in Western Europe, Japan, newly industrialized countries, the United States and Canada. The wide economic opening in this group of Central European countries led to products previously manufactured by large enterprises being replaced by foreign goods.

Another group of Central European countries, comprising the Czech Republic, Slovakia and Hungary, were more cautious in their approach to privatization and liberalization, leaving the state a broad range of active influence on the economy. In the Czech Republic and Slovakia, so-called mass privatization was introduced that only formally changed the status of SOEs. This policy saved large enterprises in these two countries from the treatment applied to their counterparts in Poland and Slovenia. Hungary, on the other hand, sold its large enterprises to foreign investors. Overall, the small business sector was far less developed in these three countries, which led to a slower rate of economic growth at an initial stage of transformation. The Czech Republic, Slovakia and Hungary were also more cautious than Poland and Slovenia in 'opening' their economies to foreign competition. This protected them from high unemployment and income disparities – problems notoriously noted in the first group of Central European countries.

In Southern European countries, including Bulgaria, Romania and Croatia, system transformation produced less spectacular results. These countries traditionally represented a lower level of economic development than Central Europe, the structure of their economies only marginally meeting the requirements of a free market and free trade. At the start of transformation, these countries did not have small industry and service sectors. Large SOEs dominated. As in Central Europe, they were unable to adapt to free market requirements. At the same time, there was no private capital interested in their privatization. Most of these enterprises represented sectors such as heavy industry, machinery and chemicals. Only a few manufactured consumer goods.

Another reason behind the inferior results of system transformation in Southern Europe – compared with Central Europe – was the greater imbalance of these economies at the start of transition. This chiefly applied to differences between demand and supply on the consumer market, budget deficits and trade deficits. Economic liberalization triggered spiralling inflation and produced drastic reductions in standards of living, in addition to major income differences and a poverty sector larger than Central Europe's.

A third factor that determined transformation in Southern Europe was a complete absence of system infrastructure needed for the development of a free market and free trade. No commercial banks, customs services or stock exchanges were available, and a fiscal/financial administration was nonexistent. Furthermore, there were no specialists capable of developing and managing the necessary infrastructure.

A fourth factor that negatively affected transformation in Southern Europe was a low rate of accumulation. Savings were small due to low standards of living. Consequently, independent sources of financing investments were unavailable. There was also little foreign capital interested in investing in this part of Europe.

The least favourable conditions for system transformation existed in former Soviet republics in Eastern Europe. First of all, countries in this group did not have free market systems and infrastructure. Large enterprises dominated, unfit for privatization due to a shortage of capital. This was accompanied by the absence of small industry, developed service sectors and private farms.

Nor was a full-fledged free-market infrastructure available in these countries, be it in the form of relevant institutions or free trade mechanisms. A commercial bank network and customs and tax infrastructure had to be constructed from scratch. The consumer market in these countries was completely unbalanced, and the investment market was nonexistent (replaced by state administrative decisions). The labour market was characterized by huge covert unemployment.

Moreover, there was a lack of public support for market reforms in these countries. Prior to transition, official propaganda presented a free market as a negative trend that bred economic crises, unemployment and social inequalities. This was confirmed by the first years of building market economies in these countries on the basis of the 'Washington consensus'. The consumer market had to be balanced under conditions of multiple price growth and a decline of real incomes. The number of people without work or only formally working in enterprises began to grow rapidly. The poverty sector burgeoned. Enterprises encountered a lack of demand on both the consumer and investment markets. Growing interest rates led to a major drop in the rate of investing and made enterprises uninterested in increasing production, which could contribute to technological advancement and reduce production costs.

As a result, an unprecedented collapse was noted in industrial and agricultural production, construction and investments, exports and imports on a scale not noted in other groups of Central European countries. Inflation spiralled out of control to mind-boggling levels. In the first five years of transformation alone (1992–7), prices in Turkmenistan grew 1.83 million times, and the average annual inflation rate was 1,000–1,500%. Further down the list in terms of inflation were: Belarus (with about 157,000-fold growth), Uzbekistan (130,000), Tajikistan (108,000) and Ukraine (96,000). The lowest rate of inflation in this group of countries was noted in Russia (3,300) and in Moldova (4,300). In Russia inflation was lower than in Croatia, and in Moldova it ran at the same level as in Croatia.[13] In all the analysed countries in this group, the greatest increases in consumer goods prices were in the first three years of transformation, approaching 1,000% annually. Ukraine set a record in 1993 with a more than 10,000% increase in relation to the previous year.

In the second period of transformation (1998–2005), inflation fell and in some countries even disappeared, yet this had a negative effect on the rate of economic growth, leading to high unemployment and major social diversification. These unsettling trends were the result of using anti-inflation methods compatible with the 'Washington consensus', including efforts to balance the budget, revalue national currency and reduce real wages. For example, in the first five years of transformation, real wages fell the most dramatically in Armenia, by 92.1%. Turkmenistan was second with 88.7%, and Moldova reported 88.3%. The smallest drop was in Kazakhstan, by 30.7%, Kyrgyzstan recording 42.7%.[14]

In all the countries of this group, the first five years of transformation (1992–7) saw a huge drop in gross domestic product and industrial production. Moldova's GDP shrank by 65.1%, Tajikistan's by 64%, Georgia's by 63.5%, Russia's by 40.8%, Kazakhstan's by 34.4%, Belarus's by 31.5% and Uzbekistan's by 14.1%. The slump in industrial production was even greater. Georgia recorded a decrease of 82.5%; Tajikistan noted 67.4% and Russia reported 52%.[15] In the second period of transformation, from 1998 onward, industrial production and GDP gradually increased. However, most of these countries had not managed to make up for their arrears by 2005.

Drastic declines were also noted in foreign trade. Georgia's trade in 1997, for example, accounted for only 10% of the pre-transformation figure. In the remaining countries, the decreases were smaller but nonetheless substantial. They were almost entirely due to a decline in trade among these countries, chiefly commerce with Russia. From the very beginning of transformation, trade among them began to be replaced by commercial relations with Western Europe, Japan, newly industrialized countries and other economically developed countries. If, prior to transition, trade within this group of countries accounted for 80% of total trade, in 1997 more than half of their exports on average were directed to countries outside the group. For Russia, the share of such countries in exports exceeded 80%. In Uzbekistan the figure was 70%, and Tajikistan reported 60%. The smallest share in exports of countries

---

13 The author's own estimates on the basis of *Rocznik Statystyczny 1997* (GUS, Warsaw, 1998) and *Review and Outlook for the Former Soviet Republics* (PlanEcon, Washington, September 1997).

14 P. Bożyk, *24 kraje Europy Środkowej i Wschodniej*, op. cit., p. 97.

15 Ibid., p. 90, Table 41.

other than former Soviet republics was noted in Kyrgyzstan (20%), followed by Turkmenistan with 31%, Moldova with 32%, and Belarus with 35%. The figures for imports were similar.

Trends atypical of former Soviet republics occurred in the Baltic states: Lithuania, Latvia and Estonia. In the past, prior to their incorporation in the USSR, these three countries had different economic structures and a different level of development from Russia and other republics. The Latvian and Estonian economies were based on small industry and services, while Lithuania relied on agriculture and the food industry. After these countries became part of the Soviet Union, their economic structures changed radically. Large industrial enterprises began to dominate, while most small manufacturing plants and services declined. Agriculture in Lithuania was collectivized in the form of *kolkhozes*. All three countries became suppliers of manufactured goods for the needs of other Soviet republics. On the other hand, other republics provided the Baltic states with natural resources and materials for the needs of industry. Trade with the rest of the world was marginal.

System transformation enabled Lithuania, Latvia and Estonia to return to their original economic structures, before their incorporation into the Soviet Union. As a result, Latvia and Estonia became oriented toward the development of small industry and services, while Lithuania focused on the development of agriculture, farm produce and food processing. Large enterprises faced bankruptcy, the Baltic GDP in 1997 being lower than before transformation. Lithuania recorded a 58% drop in GDP. Latvia's GDP went down by 55.7% and Estonia's slumped by 32.7%. The drop in industrial production was even greater.

The Baltic republics began to recover their original pre-transformation GDP levels faster than other former Soviet republics, largely thanks to privatization. Faced with an acute shortage of capital at home, these countries were forced to orient their privatization programmes toward foreign capital. Latvia and Estonia especially sold most of their banks and large chunks of their wholesale and retail sectors to Scandinavian and German investors. The rapid development of production and services in the Baltic states was the key factor behind GDP growth. Since the service sector could develop with little investment, it absorbed a large number of people of working age who previously had lost their jobs in industry and agriculture.

A characteristic feature of Baltic economic growth in the first few years of transformation was a shortage of funds for investing. In 1996, investing accounted for 16.8% of the GDP in Latvia, with Lithuania and Estonia reporting 18.9% and 24% respectively.[16] The inflow of foreign capital was also small in absolute figures in the initial period of transformation. In 1997, foreign direct investments (FDI) in Estonia totalled $964 million. In Lithuania it stood at $403 million and Latvia attracted $896 million. However, in per capita terms, these investments were greater than in other CEECs.

---

16 See *Economic Survey of Europe in 1996–1997* (Economic Commission for Europe, UN, Geneva, 1997), p. 100.

The Baltic states constituted a group of orthodox followers of the 'Washington consensus'. They had surprisingly low budget deficits. In 1991, on the eve of transition, all three countries reported a budget surplus. In 1992–7, the most difficult period, their deficits ranged from 1% to 2%. The Baltic states quickly introduced relatively low interest rates as well. Inflation in the Baltic states was lower than in other former Soviet republics. In 1992–7, consumer goods retail prices increased 118-fold in Latvia, 212-fold in Estonia and 659-fold in Lithuania, the main cause, especially in Lithuania, being market imbalance. However, this problem was quickly brought under control, primarily by reducing the growth of nominal wages, along with a decrease in real wages. At the same time, Baltic currencies depreciated in step with inflation. The only exception was Lithuania, which reduced the value of its currency at a rate slower than inflation. However, overall, in the first five years of transition, real wages grew by 27% in Estonia, 19% in Lithuania and 10% in Latvia. Notably, other former Soviet republics recorded a dramatic decline in real wages during that time.

The Baltic republics also made deeper changes in their foreign trade than other former Soviet republics. From the start, they substantially increased their share of trade with countries other than post-Soviet states. This chiefly applied to imports on credit. Exports grew at a much slower rate, primarily due to the lack of goods marketable in the West. This led to an increase in Lithuania's foreign debt to $2.8 billion, while Latvia and Estonia each reported increases to $800 million. Prior to transition, all three countries were practically free of foreign debt.

In the second period of transformation, in 1998–2005, the Baltic states accelerated their GDP growth, gradually making up for whatever they lost in the initial stage of reforms. However, this process has been accompanied by an increase in foreign debt, resulting from the absence of a well-developed pro-export sector.

8.3. Internationalization of Economic Policy in Central and East European Countries

System transformation in Central and Eastern Europe initiated a process of globalization involving economic policy. The IMF and the World Bank played an important role in this process, making credit assistance to these countries conditional on their subordination to the rules of the 'Washington consensus'. All CEECs complied, even though the scope of this subordination varied.

Some countries unconditionally brought their economic policies in line with the principles of the 'Washington consensus'. In particular, this included Poland, Latvia, Georgia and Estonia, which made their markets readily accessible to foreign goods, services, technology, capital, and, to an extent, also labour, focusing their policy mainly on the fight against inflation. The interest rate, exchange rate, monetary, pricing, remuneration and budgetary policies were all subordinated to this goal. As a result, these countries managed to overcome inflation and reorient their economies toward growth, though its rate was uncertain, and the side effects – in the form of a budget deficit, foreign debt, social diversification and a rapidly growing poverty zone – substantial.

Another group of countries, comprising most of the remaining CEECs, approached the IMF's recommendations with greater reserve. They adopted milder parameters of the 'Washington consensus' with regard to the devaluation of their national currencies, interest rates, privatization, methods for balancing the budget and market access for foreign goods. If the first group of countries actually radicalized these parameters (for example, Poland devalued its internal currency more considerably than recommended by the IMF), the second group softened them. These countries included the Czech Republic, Slovakia, Hungary, Slovenia, Croatia as well as Russia, Lithuania, Bulgaria and Romania. Some of these countries – specifically the Czech Republic, Slovakia, Hungary and Slovenia – managed to steer clear of problems that generally plagued the first group, though their GDP growth was moderate, and they took a long time to overcome the consequences of the recession recorded at the start of transition. In other countries within this group – specifically Russia, Lithuania, Bulgaria, Romania and Croatia –economic policy parameters were largely selected at random. Some of these countries closely followed the 'Washington consensus', while others ignored it. Overall, their economic results were far from satisfactory and their GDP growth moderate and unstable, accompanied by aggravating problems in the form of unemployment, impoverishment of the population and foreign debt.

A third group of Central and Eastern European countries – comprising Albania, Serbia and Montenegro as well as the remaining former Soviet republics, among them Moldova, Kazakhstan, Kyrgyzstan, Tajikistan, Turkmenistan, Uzbekistan, Armenia and Azerbaijan – applied 'the Washington consensus' selectively, choosing those of its recommendations that were designed to implement further specific economic goals (such as stifling inflation, limiting the budget deficit and balancing trade). In the case of these countries, it would be difficult to attribute directly the economic results obtained to the 'Washington consensus' as a system solution. In most of these countries, free market infrastructure is still at a formative stage, and the functioning of the economy has more to do with administration rather than the market mechanism. The growth of GDP and industrial and agricultural production depend on factors other than those related to these countries' economic systems – such as changes in oil prices, crops and foreign financial assistance.

Efforts to develop a 'hardware' global economic policy based on IMF and World Bank recommendations produced unsatisfactory results in Central and Eastern Europe. This was due to various reasons. In the first group of countries, free market fundamentalists became the reformers, introducing the recommended solutions at any price, regardless of the consequences. Other countries applied the principles of the 'Washington consensus' in a milder form when it came to liberalizing and privatizing the economy, monetary policy and interest rates. Moreover, these countries maintained greater autonomy in their economic policies than the first group. The remaining CEECs approached the 'Washington consensus' selectively, using only some of its recommendations. Consequently, it would be difficult to argue that CEEC reforms involved a consistent application of a 'hardware' global economic policy.

By contrast, during their 15 years of system transformation, CEECs have made visible progress in introducing a 'software' global economic policy, subordinating their foreign economic policy to international policies pursued by such organizations as GATT/WTO, OECD and the United Nations Economic Commission for Europe. Regional organizations have played a particularly important role in this process.

In particular, an international economic policy vis-à-vis manufactured goods was followed in the form of a free trade zone as part of the Central European Free Trade Agreement (CEFTA). In the food sector, only selective liberalization of trade was envisaged. Ultimately, the agreement provided for liberalized para- and non-tariff barriers.[17]

International economic policy in the region expanded considerably after eight CEECs – Poland, the Czech Republic, Slovakia, Hungary, Lithuania, Latvia, Estonia and Slovenia – joined the EU on 1 May 2004. Prospectively, this meant that CEEC foreign economic policies would be subordinated to the rules of EU international policy, especially with regard to common commercial, industrial, agricultural, transport, regional, technological, energy and environmental policies. Such a wide scope of internationalization of the EU's foreign economic policy stems from the fact that member states had to subordinate their economies to much more developed forms of institutional integration than in the case of CEFTA. The EU is not only a free trade zone, but also a customs union, a common market and a monetary union as well as an economic union. Ultimately, it will feature full supranational economic integration.[18]

This means that, after their accession to EU, the eight CEECs moved from a 'software' to a 'hardware' policy – albeit in a limited scope when it comes to the geographic range of globalization, which covers only 25 countries.

CEECs joined the free trade zone in 1991–8 under their respective Europe Agreements establishing their association with the EU. The agreements took effect only after approval by CEEC parliaments, the European Parliament and the national parliaments of the 15 EU member states.[19] In view of the protracted process of ratification, the EU decided that those of the Agreement's provisions that were within EU authority should take effect as soon as possible. To this end, Interim

---

17 P. Bożyk (ed.), *CEFTA a integracja ekonomiczna w Europie* (Oficyna Wydawnicza SGH, Warsaw, 1996).

18 See P. Bożyk, J. Misala, *Integracja*, op. cit., pp. 36–43.

19 Poland and Hungary were the first CEECs to sign a Europe Agreement (on 16 December 1991). The agreement took effect on 1 April 1994. Romania followed suit on 1 February 1993 (the agreement took effect on 1 February 1995), Bulgaria on 8 March 1993 (effective 1 February 1995), Slovakia and Czech Republic on 4 October 1993 (effective 1 February 1995), Lithuania, Latvia and Estonia on 12 June 1995 (effective 1997), and Slovenia on 10 June 1996 (effective 1998). See *Unia Europejska. Integracja Polski z Unią Europejską* (Foreign Trade Research Institute (IKiCHZ), Warsaw, 1996), pp. 149, 373.

Agreements were signed that regulated commodity trade between the EU and associated countries, especially the rules of competition and payments.

CEEC accession to the free trade zone established by the 15 EU member countries in Western Europe did not mean an immediate abolition of customs duties and other barriers in the EU's trade with associated countries (referred to as 'newcomers'). First and foremost, barriers were lifted with regard to value-added manufactured goods. On the other hand, the trading in food and some industrial raw materials continued to be subject to restrictions. An especially important role was attributed to quantitative limitations.

The Agreements stipulated that CEEC association with the EU would last no longer than 10 years, after which these countries would be allowed to apply for membership in further institutional forms of integration. CEECs quickly took advantage of that provision and immediately applied for EU membership.[20] Benefits from participation in the free trade zone, customs union, common market, monetary and economic union were to be divided disproportionately in favour of the newcomers. This approach was expressed by shorter deadlines for the old members – compared with the new ones – to lift customs duties within the free trade zone. This was regulated by a principle of asymmetry whereby old members, as economically stronger partners, agreed to liberalize their trade with the new members first. This applied to not only goods, but also services and factors of production (capital, labour and technology). Moreover, old members agreed not to resort to internal fiscal measures or practices that could either indirectly or directly discriminate against new members.

Furthermore, new members, as economically weaker partners, were granted clauses that unilaterally protected their production and domestic markets from potentially destructive competition from products exported by old members. These included a protective clause applying to agricultural trade, an anti-dumping clause, a clause on the prevention of domestic market shortages, a clause aimed against 'market disruptions' and a clause on countering disruptions in the balance of payments. They all enabled new zone members to increase their customs duties above the level stipulated in their respective Association Agreements, should imports by old members threaten newly emerging industries or sectors in the process of restructuring, especially those important for social reasons.

Despite these protective measures, the new zone members proved defenceless in the face of old members' exports. The share of imported goods on CEEC consumer and investment markets increased. Many national producers faced bankruptcy, and the gap in trade with old zone members widened. The new EU member states varied considerably in their level of development. In terms of per capita GDP, Slovenia and the Czech Republic were the closest to the EU-15 average, aiming for about 70%

---

20 The applications were submitted in the following order: Hungary applied on 1 April 1994, Poland on 8 April 1994, Romania on 22 June 1995, Slovakia on 27 June 1995, Latvia on 13 October 1995, Estonia on 28 November 1995, Lithuania on 11 December 1995, Bulgaria on 16 December 1995, the Czech Republic on 23 January 1996, and Slovenia on 10 June 1996.

of that level. Hungary and Slovakia each reached about 50%, Poland and Estonia represented 40%, and the remaining countries about 25%.[21] This means that per capita GDP in the two most developed CEECs was similar to that of Greece and Portugal, the countries with the lowest per capita GDP among the 15 old EU members.

The admission of the 10 new member states, clearly diverging from the old EU members in terms of economic growth, was based on an assumption that less developed economies would be able to grow faster than their highly developed counterparts.[22] That assumption seemed historically justified by the development of the US economy, Japan and Europe.[23] On the basis of long-term statistics, the convergence rate for these countries was set at about 2%, which means that economically backward regions should grow at a rate about 2% faster than their wealthier counterparts. However, if the new EU member states tried to bridge their gap in relation to old members with such a rate of convergence, they would take decades to do so. The most developed of the new member states (Slovenia and the Czech Republic) could at best shorten this time to 25 or so years. The remaining countries would remain far behind the old EU member states permanently unless they doubled or even tripled their convergence rate. This means that Hungary and Slovakia, as well as Poland and Estonia, would have to grow at a rate of 6% annually for 25 years, while the remaining countries would have to register 8% annually. Given the experience to date (1990–2005), such a scenario seems completely unrealistic, the EU-15 and the 10 new member states having demonstrated much smaller differences in GDP growth so far.

Some economists propose two solutions. The first is that new EU member states should receive economic assistance from the old member states. The second calls for the application of endogenous models of economic growth in the new member states, especially those with the lowest level of development.[24]

In literature on the subject, the first solution is called exogenous growth. It refers to the achievements of the neo-classical theory based on an uneven distribution of factors of production among individual countries. Some regions are 'well endowed' with capital, and consequently its price is relatively low, while others display a relatively low price of labour, which is plentiful. According to Heckscher and Ohlin, countries in the first group, specializing in the production of capital goods, should export them to the second group.[25] On the other hand, countries in the second group,

---

21 *Transition Countries in 1998/99: Widespread Economic Slowdown with Escalating Structural Problems* (WIIW, Vienna, 1999).

22 See R. Barro, X. Sala, I. Martin, *Economic Growth* (McGraw-Hill, New York, 1995).

23 See M.W. Orłowski, 'Możliwość osiągnięcia poziomu ekonomicznego krajów Unii Europejskiej przez kraje CEFTA', in *Korzyści i zagrożenia związane z przewidywanym członkostwem krajów CEFTA w UE* (SGH, Warsaw, 2000), p. 92.

24 See R. Solow, 'A Contribution to the Theory of Economic Growth', *Quarterly Journal of Economics*, vol. 70, no. 1, 1956.

25 See E. Heckscher, 'The Effect of Foreign Trade on the Distribution of Income', in *Readings in Theory of International Trade* (Philadelphia, 1950); B. Ohlin, *Interregional and International Trade* (Cambridge, 1935); K. O'Rourke, J. Williamson, *The Heckscher-Ohlin*

which specialize in the production of labour-intensive goods, should export them to the first group. Unfortunately, embracing this neo-classicist rule did not guarantee equal chances for development in the past. Countries abundant in capital grew faster than countries lavishly equipped with labour.

The transfer of capital from the first group countries creates chances for an accelerated growth of the second group. Contemporary economics, which rejects the assumptions of the classicists and neo-classicists about the non-transferability of factors of production among countries, provides for such a possibility in two forms: commercial and in the form of assistance. The commercial flow of capital to regions poorly equipped with this factor of production is encouraged by the relatively high benefits involved. At the same time, highly developed EU countries rich in capital can provide less developed regions with this factor of production in the form of assistance. In both cases, economic growth accelerates, making it possible for countries with a lower level of development to bridge the gap separating them from highly developed countries.

Alongside exogenous growth, endogenous growth models also occupy a prominent place in economic literature. In endogenous models, growth depends on economic policy.[26] In keeping with these models, under an adequate economic policy, a number of growth factors – which in exogenous models depend on foreign sources (transfer of capital, technology, organizational and management methods) – can become endogenous in character, which means that they are dependent on a specific country. However, that country must meet a number of conditions. First, it must guarantee stable institutional foundations for the economy, including inviolability of private ownership. Second, it must launch investment factors behind economic growth in the form of not only physical capital, but also human capital. To this end, expenditure on scientific research and education should feature prominently in investment spending. Thanks to this, factors of production can be used in the most effective way, guaranteeing speedy economic growth. Third, a macroeconomic policy designed to prevent inefficient growth is needed. This policy should be aimed, in particular, against inflation.

This means that a less developed economy can grow faster in the long term than a highly developed one if it follows an adequate economic policy and makes effective use of its own factors of production. This condition is more important than foreign assistance, which would easily be wasted were the economic policy to prove inadequate.

The philosophy of endogenous growth lay at the core of the 'Washington consensus', which defined the 'adequate' economic policy needed for such growth. According to its proponents, such a policy increases the propensity to save and

---

Model Between 1400 and 2000: When it Explained Factor Price Convergence, When it Did Not, and Why, NBER Working Paper, No. 7411 (National Bureau of Economic Research, Cambridge, Mass., November 1999).

26 R. Lucas, 'On the Mechanisms of Development Planning', *Journal of Monetary Economics*, vol. 22, no. 1, 1989.

consequently boosts investment. At the same time, it leads to the development of competitive sectors and goods on a global scale, thus promoting export growth.

Unfortunately, the years of CEEC transformation have not confirmed these expectations. It turned out that savings and consequently endogenous investment in less developed countries were lower than in highly industrialized countries. The highest figures were noted in the Czech Republic and Slovakia, while the lowest were in Bulgaria and Romania.[27] As a result, domestic savings in the least and medium-industrialized CEECs were insufficient to finance investments. Furthermore, FDI tended to be the smallest in the least developed countries of Central and Eastern Europe.

Consequently, CEECs have found themselves hard pressed to increase internal savings. In keeping with the 'Washington consensus', this should be done by reforming public finances to limit unproductive state expenditure on public administration, social welfare and the health service. At the same time, taxes have to be reduced for both individuals and companies. Another method to increase internal savings is to increase the profitability of the corporate sector through privatization and restructuring. No less important is an increase in household savings resulting from a stable macroeconomic policy, particularly low inflation and a strong domestic currency.

The relatively low standards of living and a high share of low-income earners are serious obstacles to efforts to increase internal savings, especially in the least developed CEECs. On the one hand, they limit the effectiveness of public finance reforms, especially when it comes to state expenditure on the social sector and health care. On the other hand, these factors discourage households from saving.

Fully fledged EU members among CEECs now expect financial assistance from old member states. Strangely enough, this approach is not only perfectly in line with the 'Washington consensus', but it actually legitimizes it in keeping with the motto that only a healthy economy can make good use of foreign assistance.

8.4. Prospects of Globalization of Economic Policy in Central and East European Countries Policy

Literature on the subject features two basic approaches to the prospects of system transformation in Central and Eastern Europe from the perspective of economic policy globalization. One approach is radical and the other is evolutionary; they are also referred to as fundamental and pragmatic respectively.[28] Neither questions

---

27 See W.A. Orłowski, 'Możliwości osiągnięcia poziomu ekonomicznego krajów UE przez kraje CEFTA', op. cit., p. 67.

28 S. Fischer, Sahay R.C.A. Vegh, 'From Transition to Market: Evidence and Growth Prospects', in S. Zachimi (ed.), *Lessons from the Economic Transition: Central and Eastern Europe in the 1990s* (Kluwer Academic, Dordrecht); M. Lavigne, *The Economics of Transition: From Socialist Economy to Market Economy* (Macmillan and St Martin's Press, London and New York, 1999); J. Williamson, 'The Washington Consensus Revisited', in L. Emmerij (ed.),

the need to introduce a market economy, though both call for different methods and foreign economic policy options.

The first approach recognizes the liberal-monetarist market economy option as a standard model for the analysed region. Those advocating this approach argue that the future of system transformation in Central and Eastern Europe requires unilateral adjustment of the region's political and socioeconomic systems to the model specified in the 'Washington consensus'. This should mean the fastest possible elimination of all the holdovers of the previous system in the form of public ownership, an active role of the state, egalitarian tendencies and social indifference, sometimes defined as the 'Homo Sovieticus' syndrome.

The second approach also ties the future of transformations in Central and Eastern Europe to a market economy, yet it makes the scope and methods of transition dependent on the condition of countries undergoing transformation.[29] So in this approach, the dose of liberalism that needs to be applied depends on the level of economic development, available market infrastructure, economic balance, the standard of living and the scope of poverty. This means that an evolutionary road to a free market is possible. It may be longer, but it protects the countries involved from the usual problems connected with shock therapy, which is fast but radical.

8.4.1. 'Hardware' Globalization Scenario

Under this scenario, CEECs have no other option than to adopt a radical method of system transformation and globalization and globalize their economic policies with the 'hardware' method.[30] There is no other, better method to guarantee economic growth and social advancement than that urged in the 'Washington consensus', which is based on many years of experience in highly industrialized countries.

However, the success of this method of transformation depends on consistent adaptation to the requirements of a liberal-monetarist economy. In particular, this requires fast elimination of the legacy of the previous system on both the macro and micro scale. In macro terms, this primarily involves limiting public ownership to the minimum and reducing the state's influence on the economy. Market infrastructure should be built quickly as well, including an independent central bank, a network of modern commercial banks, an efficient financial and fiscal system and the stock exchange.

Economic and Social Development into the 21st Century (Inter-American Development Bank, Washington, DC, 1997); P. Bożyk, 'Perspektywy transformacji systemowej w krajach Europy Środkowej i Wschodniej', in P. Bożyk, *24 kraje Europy Środkowej i Wschodniej*, op. cit., pp. 109–15.

29 See J. E. Stiglitz, *Globalization and its Discontents*, op. cit.

30 See L. Balcerowicz, *Wolność i rozwój. Ekonomia wolnego rynku*, (Krakow, 1998); D. K. Rosati, *Polska droga do rynku*, (Warsaw, 1998), M. Belka, W. Trzeciakowski (eds), *Dynamika transformacji gospodarki polskiej*, vols 1 and 2 (Institute of Economic Sciences, Polish Academy of Sciences (PAN), Warsaw, 1992).

The proper functioning of a liberal-monetarist economy is conditional on an adequate macroeconomic policy aimed at bringing down inflation, balancing the budget, promoting a stringent money policy and a full convertibility of the domestic currency. Other priorities include small tax burdens, high propensity to save and invest, especially in the development of human capital, and full openness of the economy to the movement of goods, services, capital, technology and other factors. Accelerated endogenous growth will then be possible, creating opportunities for less developed countries to grow faster and bridge the gap separating them from highly industrialized countries.

A successful macroeconomic policy aimed at promoting higher (physical and human) capital resources, along with technological and organizational advancement, will lead to faster convergence and a higher rate at which less developed countries will be bridging their GDP gaps. On the other hand, an inadequate macroeconomic policy will fail to stimulate growth and may even lead to a recession and the lagging behind of less developed countries.

An adequate economic policy is expressed by increased accumulation and a high rate of investment, while a rapid increase of consumption could hamper growth and retard economic development. That is why countries transforming their economies should in all possible ways promote savings and investment, while limiting consumption. Especially important from this point of view is the need to narrow the budget deficit and combat inflation. Budget deficit simply means that government outlays are greater than receipts. Likewise, inflation means that the demand for goods and services is greater than the supply. So both these situations are indicative of living above one's means. They also stimulate tendencies to increase interest rates, which collides with the propensity to invest.

System transformation must be conducive to high investment efficiency, which is impossible without a well-developed financial market that determines effective capital allocation. Such allocation is guaranteed by private sector investments, with public sector investments limited to the bare minimum as less effective by nature. Supporters of this approach call for changes on the micro scale, which means at the corporate sector level. In their opinion, profit must be the principal criterion that determines enterprise behaviour. The state should not centrally – with the use of either macro- or microeconomic policies – make enterprises co-responsible for the plight of economically underprivileged social groups.[31] Such policies feature high and progressive taxes designed to finance expenditure on social welfare, pensions and the health service. All these services should be commercialized, and state assistance should exclusively cover the disabled and underprivileged. The state should help the poor and unemployed by offering them opportunities for professional training and retraining, for example instead of dispensing benefits and offering other forms of economic assistance. Free medical treatment should be granted exclusively to the homeless, those unable to support themselves and the poorest citizens.

---

31 See P. Kozłowski, *Szukanie sensu, czyli o naszej wielkiej zmianie* (PWN, Warsaw 1998), p. 20.

Advocates of this point of view argue that highly developed countries have worked out ways to shape properly the role of the corporate sector. By maximizing profit, enterprises should accumulate funds to finance growth, technological advancement and job creation, and through taxes they should co-finance public priorities such as the police and armed forces and the justice administration system. Enterprises often feel co-responsible for the shortcomings of the free market system.[32] This means that, apart from being guided by the criterion of profit and personal gain, a growing number of enterprises voluntarily take into account general humanistic values, acting against the imperfections of the 'invisible hand of the market'. These include strict observance of the law and preventing the spread of poverty, for example, by creating new jobs, increasing employee pay cheques and social security benefits, and honestly paying taxes. Proponents of this point of view tend to cite subjective factors such as charity, human solidarity and care for the common good. In their opinion, an enterprise solves these problems in a different way when it is guided by the idea of social solidarity. It is usually more efficient when it acts on an independent basis than when it must do the same under government pressure – for example, when it is forced to pay high taxes. In the latter case, companies are tempted to resort to tax evasion, hold back some of their incomes or use various financial tricks.

Advocates of the liberal-monetarist version of a market economy argue that only strict adherence to the 'Washington consensus' will produce the expected results. According to this approach, the different effects of transformation in Central and Eastern Europe are due to an uneven implementation of the consensus. Countries that have implemented its recommendations comprehensively have generally recorded better results that those which adopted a fragmentary approach. The latter have reported worse results and many problems. The increased determination of governments and societies in introducing reforms will be accompanied by faster development, fewer problems and greater social satisfaction.

The conclusion is simple: CEECs have no other option than to get rid completely of the legacy of the previous system, both material and nonmaterial. The sooner the better. It is worth paying this price because the new liberal-monetarist system guarantees socio-economic progress. However, those supporting this approach do not say how high this price will be and how long it take to wait for the results of the new order. In some countries, including former Soviet republics, the costs incurred so far have been dramatically high, reaching two-thirds or more of their pre-transformation GDPs.

8.4.2. 'Software' Globalization Scenario

Under this scenario, 'hardware' globalization is bound to breed problems in a vast majority of CEECs. Most of these problems are the legacy of not only communism, but also the systems that existed in these countries prior to the introduction of the

---

32 See A. Noga, 'Cele przedsiębiorstw. Kontrowersje teoretyczne', *Ekonomista*, no. 6, 1996.

socialist economy. Many of these trends are structural, or long term, in nature. They cannot be eliminated in either the short or medium term using institutional instruments.

This primarily involves the absence of democratic traditions, which should be the main element of system transformation. Western Europe and the United States took decades – by trial and error approach – to reach their current mature parliamentary democracy models. These models take into account the specific features of individual countries. French democracy is different from that in Great Britain, and also different from the US system.

Most CEECs were never democratic in the past. This especially applies to former Soviet republics, among them Russia, Ukraine and Belarus. There were no parliamentary democracy institutions in these countries, so the patterns of democratic behaviour for politicians and voters are unknown. In some of these countries, democracy is actually contrary to the mentality of the people, who are accustomed to autocracy; they respect authoritarian rulers and have no respect for politicians elected by democratic vote. It is no accident that in many of these countries, politicians from the era of authoritarianism and their descendants are elevated to power. In some countries, former kings, dukes and counts enjoy special popularity.

In many of the analysed countries, a market economy in the American sense of the term never existed. Prior to the introduction of socialism, a feudal system that had nothing to do with a free market operated there. Seventy years of communism in the former Soviet Union led to a complete atrophy of whatever trace traditions of the imperfect 19th-century market were still available. People and businesses are familiar with no other patterns of behaviour than those developed under communism.

Most CEECs, especially post-Soviet states, had completely different economic infrastructures from those normally developed under capitalism. They could not be transformed to meet free market requirements. As a result, the economic systems of many of these countries responded with a drastic drop in production after the introduction of free-market mechanisms.

In most CEECs, free market rules caused many problems, such as a decline of industrial and agricultural production and a dramatic decrease in investment and consumption. Despite almost 15 years of transformation, some countries have not recovered their pre-transformation GDP levels.

In this context, supporters of fundamental ('hardware') transformation have a few questions to answer. The first is whether these countries will at all be able to build functioning market economies in the foreseeable future. Second, will these nations be able to bear the sacrifices involved, especially since most experienced similar sacrifices under communism? After all, they have to build industry and agriculture from scratch, using a major part of their national income for this purpose and seriously limiting consumption. This is required by the endogenous growth model strictly tied to the 'Washington consensus', which determines the rules of system transformation.

According to those supporting 'software' globalization and the related system transformation model, the same liberal-monetarist solutions applied in different

CEECs will never produce identical results. This is because individual countries implement these solutions in different ways and face different problems in the process, much as in the case of developed and backward countries. Would CEEC populations ever approve an approach under which some countries enjoy sustainable economic growth, while others are doomed to permanent backwardness? It seems that this question must be answered in the negative. The obvious conclusion, according to 'software' globalization policy supporters, is that the first scenario, based on a fundamental approach to transformation, should be discounted as unworkable. Quite simply, it is detached from the reality in the analysed region.

This explains why the 'software' globalization scenario calls for different rules for introducing a market economy. It permits the existence of diverse forms of ownership, depending on management conditions and production efficiency. In sectors where private ownership is capable of guaranteeing high production efficiency, this form of ownership should dominate, and vice versa, in those sectors where public ownership ensures high efficiency, privatization is unnecessary. Public and private ownership co-exist everywhere, including the United States, though the share of the public sector varies considerably.

The 'software' globalization scenario also provides for a greater role of the state in economic policy. In the 'hardware' scenario, the state only performed three basic functions – making law, making sure the law is respected and countering disruptions of the free market and free trade – while focusing on a macroeconomic policy. In the 'software' scenario, the state can additionally pursue a microeconomic policy, including industrial, agricultural, developmental, scientific/technological, educational and ecological. Before liberal concepts were reinstated, developed market economies followed the principles of Keynesianism for years, with various forms of state activity. These methods protected the economy from major crises and ensured robust growth. From the current perspective, it cannot be argued that Keynesianism was a mistake and that a liberal-monetarist doctrine would have been a better solution had it been available at the time. At that stage of development, Keynesianism was a better solution, permitting the attainment of goals that would not have been attained under liberal monetarism.

Overall, contemporary CEEC economies display many similarities to the Western European economies of the late 1930s and the first 25 years after the Second World War. This especially applies to their economic imbalance, demonstrated by unemployment, foreign debt, budget deficit and the need for structural changes in industry and agriculture. At the time, the most important issue was to ensure an economic balance as a condition for improving management efficiency. This could only be done under Keynesianism. In today's developed market economies, where ensuring a macroeconomic balance has been replaced by the need to improve microeconomic efficiency, liberal monetarism has become a better solution than Keynesianism. However, this does not mean that liberal monetarism is an optimal solution in CEECs which find themselves in a completely different economic situation.

Macroeconomic policy in CEECs should be oriented toward different economic goals from those in developed market economies. In economically advanced countries with balanced economies, the basic goal is to maximize profit on a micro scale – in enterprises. In most CEECs, which feature unbalanced economies (marked by high unemployment, a current-account deficit and a budget deficit), the most important thing is to guarantee a macroeconomic balance. Without such a balance, profit cannot be maximized on a micro scale.

CEEC macroeconomic policy should thus be oriented toward sustainable economic growth (instead of recognizing a specific macroeconomic policy as the main condition of economic growth on an *ex ante* basis). Due to the specific features of CEECs, it seems more rational to follow a neo-Keynesian model of growth (that is Keynesianism adapted to current conditions), while focusing on an optimal use of real factors of growth in individual countries. Such a model seems to be a better option than the liberal-monetarist model specified in the 'Washington consensus'.

The need to diversify CEEC system transformation methods is confirmed by the economic results obtained by these countries under a uniform approach compatible with the 'Washington consensus'. While the best developed countries in the region (those in Central Europe) have recorded some positive results thanks to this approach, countries less advanced in the process (Bulgaria, Romania and Croatia) have shown moderate success, and post-Soviet states have had completely negative experiences.

This diversification of system transformation effects stems from the application of an endogenous model of economic growth, which assumes that an identical macroeconomic policy is capable of stimulating growth under different conditions if the basic requirements of this policy are met. In reality, many CEECs, even those which implemented the most restrictive version of this policy (calling for a budgetary balance, stable exchange rates and low taxes) have ended up with a slump in the economy, high inflation, unemployment, plummeting consumption and decreased investment.

There can only be one conclusion from the CEEC experiences to date: the slump in many of these countries was not brought about by an inconsistent macroeconomic policy characteristic of endogenous growth, but resulted from an inadequate version of this policy. A macroeconomic policy geared toward exogenous growth should have been applied – a diversified policy taking into account the conditions existing in individual countries.

According to this point of view, the best bet for CEECs is a 'software' globalization policy. Despite pressure from the IMF and the World Bank, these countries are unprepared for a 'hardware' policy.

Chapter 9

Chinese Foreign Economic Policy

9.1. Three Stages of China's Foreign Economic Policy

The foreign economic policy of China is primarily determined by endogenous factors resulting from the country's substantial human and economic potential. Only to a lesser extent does this policy rely on exogenous factors, though their role has increased significantly over the past two decades. As a result, the trends in China's foreign economic policy only marginally reflect the global changes, which determine the economic policies of highly developed and newly industrialized countries as well as less developed countries and CEECs. The Chinese trends are primarily a reflection of the social and economic policy transformations taking place within China itself.

As most less developed countries, China used to be a colonial country with a poorly developed industry and backward agriculture, devoid of economic infrastructure and developed economic links with foreign countries. What made the country different from other less developed countries was its huge population and extensive resources of practically all raw materials, including coal, oil, natural gas, iron ore, nonferrous ores, uranium and plutonium.

Broadly speaking, two stages in China's foreign economic policy may be distinguished: a stage of autonomous development with a tendency toward far-reaching autarky and a stage of gradual opening of the economy.

9.1.1. The Stage of Autonomic Foreign Economic Policy (1949–72)

This stage consisted of two periods: 1949–57 and 1958–72. The first period witnessed reconstruction of the economy from wartime destruction (1949–52) and the introduction of the Soviet economic policy model, including foreign economic policy (1953–7). In the second period (1958–72), China embarked on its own path of political and economic transformation, isolating itself from both economically developed countries and Central and Eastern Europe.

The introduction of the Soviet model of systemic transformation meant that emphasis was put on industrialization and, consequently, on the development of the extraction, heavy and machine industries with an orientation toward armaments. The economy was centralized and nationalized. It functioned in accordance with the mechanism followed in CEECs at that time.

Foreign economic policy was reduced to a trade policy in its typical autarkic form, with importers supplying products necessary for the implementation of key development plans in industry and exporters selling goods necessary to finance imports. The Soviet Union was China's main trading partner in 1953–7, accounting for 60% of China's total trade, followed by CEECs with 20%. Other countries accounted for the remainder. The Soviet Union supplied machinery, equipment, technology and whatever locally unavailable raw materials were needed as the model of China's economic development was similar to that in Central and Eastern Europe. Foreign trade as a whole generated a paltry 4–6% of national income, which means its role was marginal.

Internal accumulation, generated mainly in agriculture, constituted the primary source of investment financing. Agriculture was also a major reservoir of labour for industry, population growth being the main factor behind increasing industrial production and national income.

After industrialization got under way, agriculture generated three-quarters of the national income, while industry provided only 18%. In 1949–57, total industrial output increased at a rate of almost 18% annually, agricultural production grew by 4.5%, while national income increased by 9% annually. In 1957, the structure of national income generation in China changed markedly in comparison with 1952. The share of industry almost doubled, while the share of agriculture declined by a few percent. The rapid growth of industrial output was, to a large extent, the result of a low starting point, since in 1952 China belonged to the group of less developed countries with an extremely low level of industrial development.

In 1958–72, China drastically limited its economic relations with Central and Eastern Europe, while developing ties with highly industrialized countries. During that period China pressed ahead with autonomous development in accordance with the guidelines of the 'Big Leap' policy (1958–61) and the 'Cultural Revolution' (1966–9).[1] The economic policy pursued by China in those days was oriented at the country's isolation from the international community, which particularly implied strong emphasis on the development of import-substituting production. First of all, the country sought to accelerate the development of its heavy and machine industries subordinated to the central state administration and based on five-year plans. The production of consumer goods and the development of small industry, services and agriculture were the responsibility of local administration, which was obligated to finance these projects on its own.

In practice, this meant that the development of both heavy and small industry had to be financed by agriculture. What followed was complete decapitalization of this fundamental sector of China's economy. The lack of investment in agriculture led to a halt in its development and deterioration of standards of living in rural areas. The possibilities of increasing accumulation and investment outside agriculture were limited.

After 10 years of experimenting, the Chinese economy witnessed a regression that manifested itself in a drop of industrial output, 'bottlenecks' in the development

---

1   Tien-wei Wu, *Lin Biao and the Gang of Four: Contra-Confucianism in Historical and Intellectual Perspective* (Southern Illinois University Press, Carbondale, 1983).

of industry and enormous procurement difficulties. Foreign trade dropped almost by half. All that combined led to deep political and economic shakeups.

9.1.2. The Stage of Departure from Autarkic Tendencies (1973–7)

Despite obvious mistakes committed during the 'Big Leap' period and the 'Cultural Revolution', departure from the extreme autarkic policy was gradual. This was due to discussions proceeding in the political management of China between proponents of different economic solutions.

The most spectacular changes took place in foreign trade. In 1973 China's trade doubled over the previous year as industry needed raw materials and technologies and the market was starved for consumer goods. In the following years, foreign trade continued to grow at a fast rate.

Developed countries, especially Japan and EU member states, moved to the top of the list of China's trading partners. Trade with these countries accounted for more than half of China's total turnover in that period, with Japan accounting for about one-quarter. The share of CEECs did not exceed 20%. Newly industrialized countries, Hong Kong, Malaysia and Singapore, became another important trading partner for China.

China's trade with economically developed countries was characterized by a surplus of imports over exports. This resulted in the growth of China's foreign debt until 1977. However, in absolute terms, the country's indebtedness was insubstantial, ranging from $1.5 billion to $3 billion annually. Machinery and equipment prevailed in China's imports, including turnkey industrial plants (for steel, petrochemicals, fertilizers and similar industries). In China's exports, foodstuffs and beverages as well as raw materials and fuels accounted for one-third, the remainder being industrial goods, in particular textiles.

In 1973–7, foreign trade played a balancing role since China did not give up its strategy of autonomous development, only departing from its extreme autarkic version. Imports continued to supplement domestic production and consumption, while exports offset imports with foreign exchange. The fast growth of China's foreign trade after 1972 showed that the country's import needs were considerable and kept growing.

9.1.3. The Stage of the Opening of the Chinese Economy (1978–2005)

After 1978, China's economy saw more significant changes related to economic reforms[2] which were to make the Chinese economy resemble those of developed countries, yet without undermining the canons of central planning. This led to an increased share of private ownership (in 1978, the state sector accounted for 77.6%

---

2   See F. Stachowiak, *Gospodarka narodowa Chińskiej Republiki Ludowej 1949–1982* (PWE, Warsaw, 1984); E.A. Winkler (ed.), *Transition from Communism in China: Institutional and Comparative Analysis* (Lynne Rienner, Boulder and London, 1999).

of industrial output), accompanied by the continued domination of state ownership in the key sectors of production. The government decided to limit the scope of central planning, though the state did not give up controlling the economy by other methods.

Reforms in agriculture were deeper and farther-reaching. In the first place, all communes were dissolved and replaced with family farms guided by market criteria in production.

The opening of the Chinese economy was reflected not only by a substantially higher growth rate in foreign trade, but also by the admission of foreign capital to the Chinese market, initially in the form of joint ventures and later also in other forms. However, full-fledged liberalization of foreign economic relations (by Chinese standards) did not occur until 1992.

To some extent, China modelled its reforms on the experience of Taiwan when that country was initiating deep economic reforms as a first-generation newly industrialized country. The opening of the Chinese economy proceeded through importation of advanced technology and development of export-oriented production.

One sign of opening imports was the removal or reduction of customs duties as well as para- and non-tariff restrictions. In this way China prepared to adopt the provisions of the GATT Tokyo Round and subsequently the Uruguay Round. After 1995, the aim of China's foreign economic policy was to join the WTO.

Following these changes, China's foreign trade increased more than 15-fold over 20 years (from $20 billion in 1978 to more than $300 billion in 1998). Initially, the balance of trade was negative, though in the 1990s China was recording a surplus.

The 1978–2005 period marked a tangible decline in the share of foreign loans and a rising share of foreign direct investments in the overall foreign capital involvement in China. Whereas in 1978 loans accounted for almost 90% of the total figure, by the end of the 1990s their share decreased to 20%. Japan remained the main lender throughout the period, followed by the United States and Germany. China's indebtedness at the end of the 1990s exceeded $100 billion, which accounted for three-quarters of the total value of exports and 20% of the gross domestic product. Thus, the limits of 'safe' indebtedness were not exceeded, as confirmed by the 10% share of debt service in the value of exports. At the end of the 1990s, the value of instalments and interest was lower than the surplus of exports over imports.[3]

In this area, China has pursued an extremely cautious, risk-averse policy, reflected by the country's foreign reserves, one of the world's highest (more than $100 billion at the end of the 1990s). They symbolize China's political independence.

---

3   See R. Pawlik, 'Kapitał zagraniczny w rozwoju gospodarczym Chińskiej Republiki Ludowej' (SGH, World Economy Faculty, Warsaw, 1999), typescript, p. 64.

9.2. Methods of Globalization of the Chinese Economy

Globalization of the Chinese economic policy is a process that combines 'software' and 'hardware' elements. The process began in 1978 when Deng Xiaoping announced his economic reforms,[4] which were facilitated by dramatic changes in Chinese policy initiated at a meeting of the Central Committee of the Chinese Communist Party on 18–22 December 1978. The 'Big Leap' and the 'Cultural Revolution' ideology were condemned and a new economic system was proposed. The system was based on four basic elements:

* construction of a democratic legal system from scratch;
* gradual introduction of a market economy on an increasingly wider scale;
* restoration of respect for Chinese traditions and culture;
* political, economic and cultural opening of China to the world.

The new directions of political and socio-economic reform enabled transformation of administrative, legal and economic systems in both urban and rural areas. First of all, the role of ideology in social and economic life was limited in favour of the pragmatic approach promoted by Deng Xiaoping. In practice, this meant the Chinese Communist Party lost its previous role as the guardian of the ideology, which determined the behaviour of the Chinese people. In this context, the basic tenets of the Maoist ideology were condemned, including egalitarianism and collectivism. The socialist credo of 'equal poverty' and the principle of 'revolutionary modesty' were scrapped and replaced with a new ideology that permitted private initiative as a method of increasing individual and household incomes. This was accompanied by a return to national traditions and culture and abandonment of measures aimed against the nation's heritage. Confucianism regained its role as a source of morality for the Chinese people. At the same time, authorities permitted free religious practices. Congregations recovered their shrines, and monks returned from exile.

In the state administration system, the 'dictatorship of the proletariat' was abandoned in favour of democracy and the rule of law. However, China's democracy was not supposed to be pluralistic in the sense of the multiparty system typical of Western democracies. The single-party system was maintained, and candidates elected to rural, commune and municipal councils had to be endorsed by the party and state authorities. As in the case of 'democracy', so the notion of 'the rule of law' had an unfamiliar ring for the Chinese. In the Maoist era, legal codes were laid down by party secretaries instead of the justice administration system. So the rule of law had to be built from scratch, which necessitated the construction of a legal

---

4 Deng Xiaoping, 'Neither Democracy nor the Legal System Should Be Weakened' (28 July 1979), in *Selected Works of Deng Xiaoping*, vol. 2, 1975–1982 (Foreign Languages Press, Beijing, 1995), p. 196.

K. Gawlikowski, 'Procesy demontażu komunizmu w Chinach i w Polsce. Mity i realia', in M. Tomala (ed.), *Chiny. Przemiany państwa i społeczeństwa w okresie reform, 1978–2000* (ISP PAN, Trio, Warsaw, 2001).

infrastructure to begin with. In 1959, the Ministry of Justice had been dissolved, as had the prosecutors' offices and courts. University law departments were also shut down. In addition to legal infrastructure, new legal norms had to be created, because those available under Maoism were useless.

Especially radical changes took place in rural areas, with a return to family farms and the abolition of what were called people's communes. On the basis of long-term contracts, land was allotted to farmer families working on their own. In this way, 80% of China's (rural) population found itself in a different economic reality. People were no longer dependent on the work of 'collectives' headed by party secretaries. They could rely on their own labour and the work of their families.

A characteristic feature of Deng Xiaoping's reform was its pragmatism and the absence of a target model. In essence, the reform was composed of many experiments conducted in various areas of economic and cooperative endeavour. Despite efforts by party and state authorities, programmes aimed against anarchy and progressive decentralization of the state and the economy were unsuccessful. Anarchy was reflected by growing disproportions among individual provinces and social groups.

Still, an undoubted advantage of the reform was its consistency in making the Chinese economy function according to a model similar to those followed across the modern world, especially in economically developed countries. From the outset, the transformations were aimed at increasing the effectiveness of the economy and accelerating its growth. This goal was expected to be attained by combining free market mechanisms with central planning. Market mechanisms were supposed to determine day-to-day and short-term development, while central planning was intended to determine medium- and long-term growth. According to Deng Xiaoping, any method was good as long as it contributed to the attainment of the intended goal. In other words, it did not matter if the cat was white or black as long as it caught mice.

9.2.1. Methods of 'Software' Globalization Methods

The opening of the Chinese economy to external cooperation was an important instrument for implementing the reform. Initially, this applied exclusively to goods and services, but later factors of production, including technology and capital, were covered. In the 1980s, the Chinese economy opened to industrial equipment bought on credit. Later the country opened to companies with foreign capital involvement – formed by state-owned enterprises on the basis of spun-off assets, together with foreign private investors. Finally, wholly foreign-owned enterprises held by private owners were admitted.

Until 1978 only state enterprises could import foreign goods. Imports played a balancing role and were used for autonomous development, but any opening of the economy to foreign competition was out of the question. Deng Xiaoping's reforms initiated a process of diversification in terms of ownership.

The strategic sector, also known as 'the first sector', was the pillar and successor of the autonomous development system. At first, it dominated in the economy, but with time it began to shrink in favour of other sectors. The strategic sector included several thousand large enterprises formed in 1948–77, in part according to the Soviet industrialization model, in part in line with China's own models of development. These enterprises represented strategic sectors of the economy, including infrastructure (roads, rail, sea ports, airports and subways), energy (construction of conventional and unconventional power plants and power transmission lines), mining and drilling (construction of coal mines, oil rigs and mines for other raw materials), metallurgy (construction of large steel mills), heavy machinery, shipbuilding, defence and the aerospace industry. The basic methods for managing these enterprises were central management and long-term planning. Deng Xiaoping's reforms did not foresee the use of market mechanisms to replace these methods. The reforms were based on Japan's postwar experiences and of first-generation newly industrialized countries (from the late 1960s and early 1970s) where economic growth in strategic sectors was based on large – chiefly state-run – enterprises, taking advantage of central planning and management methods. The development of large strategic enterprises in China was financed by the state, so it was ineffective by nature. Enterprise management boards were committed to carrying out the political preferences of the ruling party, while economic goals played a secondary role.

Deng Xiaoping's reforms launched a process whereby some state enterprises financed from the state budget moved to the second sector, which grouped enterprises that financed their operations from their own business activities. Predominately, these were medium-sized and small businesses, but the sector also included large enterprises. Supervision over these enterprises was transferred from the central administration to individual provinces. To begin with, authority was delegated to two provinces, Guangdong and Fujian.[5] At the same time, second-sector enterprises were granted much greater freedom than those in the first sector. This primarily applied to the possibility of signing contracts with foreign companies. Moreover, enterprises could retain a part of their hard-currency profit from exports. They could also co-determine the prices of their goods, wages and employee social security benefits. However, the state stopped financing this sector from the national budget, which meant these enterprises could go bankrupt.

The state continued to influence these enterprises using both macro- and microeconomic policy instruments. The most active macroeconomic policy instruments included exchange rates, interest rates, financial policy, tax policy and budgetary policy. Initially, China's macroeconomic policy stance was Keynesian rather than liberal/monetarist. The objective was to ensure real equilibrium rather than just a financial-and-monetary balance.

The balances of trade and of payments were in special focus, with exchange rate policy used as the key instrument. After the introduction of a uniform exchange rate nationwide, efforts were made gradually to make the yuan externally convertible. This was expressed by increased possibilities for repatriation of profit by foreign

---

5 See T. Kowalik, *Systemy gospodarcze. Efekty i defekty reform i zmian ustrojowych* (Innowacja Foundation, Warsaw, 2005), p. 227.

enterprises investing in China. At the same time, the value of the yuan was reduced substantially vis-à-vis the dollar (four-fold, according to American estimates). The depreciation of the yuan became an important factor adding to the profitability of exports and accelerating their growth. At the same time, the undervalued yuan led to a major increase in the prices of imported goods on the Chinese market; it restricted the demand for these goods and slowed the growth of imports. Overall, the undervalued yuan was conducive to the trade balance.

The interest rate, or the price of capital, was another macroeconomic policy instrument controlled by the state from the outset of China's reform. The country was always poorly equipped with capital. During the 'Big Leap' and the 'Cultural Revolution', it attempted to orient economic development toward labour-intensive and capital-saving technology. However, these efforts ended in a complete fiasco, which explains why, in Deng Xiaoping's reform, the growth of capital-intensive investments became an important factor for economic growth. At the same time, the emphasis was placed on financing these investments – primarily on the basis of internal accumulation. China drew from the experiences of other Asian countries, especially Japan and newly industrialized countries characterized by a high propensity to save and low standards of living. As a result, internal accumulation in China approached 40%, making it possible for the country to finance more than 95% of all investment projects.

Financial – and in particular fiscal – policy became an important element of China's macroeconomic policy. This is reflected by the low level of corporate income tax and that company revenue is free from any encumbrance posed by pension, health or social insurance. All this is designed to encourage enterprises to invest in economic growth, favoured by low wages linked with cheap labour.

In its macroeconomic policy, China attributed an important role to a balanced state budget, with the deficit not exceeding 3%. The basic factor ensuring this balance is the lack of social expenditure by the state. Health services in China must be paid for, and pension insurance is optional.

All these macroeconomic policy instruments were oriented at ensuring a real equilibrium, meaning full employment, a balance between the country's investment needs and the possibilities of their financing, along with a balance of trade and a balance of payments. No less important were measures to bring down inflation. That goal was attained in China – much as in other newly industrialized countries in Asia – with little difficulty, chiefly thanks to the population's high propensity to save, coupled with low wages, considerable health service and social welfare expenditure burdening household budgets as well as the relatively high prices of consumer goods.

Alongside macroeconomic policy instruments, industrial, agricultural, foreign trade and other forms of microeconomic policy were other important channels of influence on the second sector. An especially important role was played by industrial policy in the form of influencing enterprises through tax breaks, various types of subsidies and grants and concessions in access to loans.

No less significant changes took place in agricultural policy, which had been especially neglected and subject to dogmatic treatment in the past. First of all, the official policy of financially draining agriculture in favour of rural development was discarded. Until 1978, the agriculture sector was perceived mainly as a reservoir of cheap labour and a source of accumulation to finance industry. In 1978–2005 rural areas were allowed to retain a major part of their earnings to finance development and upgrade consumption. That first goal was actually attained with a surplus: agricultural production began to grow at a rate 2.5 times faster than previously. The rural population markedly increased its interest in and possibilities of developing agricultural processing, especially in the form of small food industry. The simultaneous growth of rural incomes, from 134 yuans in 1978 to 2.713 yuans in 2002, boosted the demand among farmers not only for food, but also for industrial goods and various services, including education.

Foreign trade policy featured a move away from influencing exports and imports by directives – which were an almost exclusive form of policy in the previous stage of China's development – in favour of indirect influence by using tariff, para-tariff and non-tariff instruments of foreign trade policy. In the initial period of implementing Deng Xiaoping's reforms, tariff barriers were at a high level, and the range of para- and non-tariff limitations was expanded. However, with time, all these barriers decreased substantially. In 1992, the average level of customs duties in China's foreign trade ran at a level of 40%; 10 years later it was around 15%, down to 11% in 2003. Moreover, when joining the WTO, China undertook to remove quotas on the importation of manufactured goods. At the same time, when signing the agreement with the WTO, China agreed to embark on a campaign against computer piracy and enforce measures further to respect intellectual property rights.[6]

The importance of the first and second sectors – which means the sector grouping strategic enterprises and that covering other state enterprises (chiefly small and medium-sized) – decreased with the progress of economic reforms, while the role of the third private sector increased. Until 1978, that sector, practically speaking, did not exist. Private industrial enterprises accounted for only 0.2% of total industrial production, and the share of private industrial production in overall retail sales was about 2.1%.

The third sector developed along two paths. The first involved establishing originally private businesses, since Deng Xiaoping did not foresee privatization of state enterprises to avoid corruption. The second path was initially based on the formation of joint-venture companies together with foreign enterprises on the basis of capital spun off from state enterprises. As reforms progressed, SOE privatization was also permitted, along with the establishment of enterprises wholly held by foreign capital.

In the first period after the start of reforms, China's private sector developed slowly. Ten years after the reforms were launched, a constitutional provision was

6 See J. Niemiecki, 'Prognozy rozwoju gospodarki Chin do 2005 roku', in *Biuletyn No. 2/2004*, (Polish Academy of Sciences Committee Polska 2000 plus), p. 58.

introduced on protection of private property, and laws were passed to guarantee private ownership and free trade of private property.

9.2.2. Methods of 'Hardware' Globalization

In 1977, the 15th Congress of the Chinese Communist Party endorsed a package of reforms which marked the second stage of globalization of economic policy. The package provided for political, administrative and economic changes.

The most important political changes included the adoption of the rule of law as a universal and obligatory principle for all levels of state administration. Even though work to introduce the rule of law began in the early 1980s, the project ran into a number of stumbling blocks. In 1997, Chinese government administration found itself hard pressed to accelerate reforms, introduce a new legal order and recognize citizens' rights. Of special note among administrative changes was a reduction in the number of ministries and central offices by one-third and a 50% reduction in the number of civil servants. American models were used to create the country's new administrative structure.

In the economy, the authorities decided to privatize state enterprises through commercialization and bankruptcy proceedings. Thus a process of mass privatization of the state sector was initiated, primarily covering the second sector while excluding the first – strategic – sector. Mass privatization was initiated in the mid-1990s. Prior to that the number of private enterprises was small, and their share in global production limited. State enterprises continued to dominate, their number estimated at roughly 300,000 in the mid-1990s.[7] After SOE privatization was permitted, the private sector's share in market supply and overall industrial production increased radically. In 2000, the share of private enterprises in China's total industrial production increased to more than one-third, and their share in retail sales grew to more than 50%. The state sector displayed the reverse trend. In 1978, its production accounted for 77.6% of China's total industrial production, falling to around 25% in 2000. The share of state industry in retail sales also dropped by more than half, from 54.5% to 24%.

Mass privatization of SOEs (except for the first – strategic – sector) covered chiefly small and medium-sized enterprises, most of them generating losses for the state. Primarily domestic capital was admitted to buy them. However, in some (poorer) provinces, such capital was unavailable, and foreign investors were uninterested in buying unprofitable state enterprises in these regions. Foreign entrepreneurs were discouraged by the absence of a well-developed infrastructure (such as roads and hotels) and educated personnel. In the poorer part of China, just over 50% of the state enterprises were privatized. By contrast, in southern China almost all small and medium-sized production, commercial, transportation and service enterprises were transferred to private owners.

---

7   T. Kowalik, *Systemy gospodarcze. Efekty i defekty reform i zmian ustrojowych*, op. cit., pp. 224–5.

Privatization of the Chinese economy in the second half of the 1990s is sometimes referred to as the second radical transformation, as opposed to the first one, conducted by Mao Zedong at the start of the 1950s in the form of nationalization.[8] The second radical transformation featured a departure from the approach adopted by Deng Xiaoping, who did not foresee a transfer of state enterprises to private owners. On the one hand, he was afraid of a massive sale of state assets in the context of the abusive practices and corruption which had plagued China in the past. On the other hand, he evidently believed that competition between newly established private enterprises and existing SOEs would help the latter improve their profitability. However, this did not come about because the number of newly established private enterprises was limited, and the efficiency of state enterprises administered by inflexible methods showed no signs of improvement.

In this area, China followed the trail blazed by Japan and, particularly, newly industrialized Asian countries (chiefly South Korea and Taiwan), which at one moment of their development sold most of their state enterprises to private owners. However, while the newly inducstrialized countries privatized their state enterprises after making them competitive – to generate the greatest possible revenue for the national budget – China mostly sold unprofitable enterprises. The massive scope of SOE privatization in China was in part due to the loss of state control over this process soon after it got under way. Some politicians and economists adhered to the 'Washington consensus' dogma about the prevalence of private ownership over state ownership in the area of management efficiency.

The massive privatization of China's SOEs was promoted by misguided loans provided by state banks. Even though most of these loans were used, they did not produce the expected results in the form of improvement in the competitiveness of state enterprises. This chiefly applied to large and medium-sized businesses. Some were transformed into commercial companies wholly owned by the Treasury and then partially privatized, with the state retaining a controlling stake.

Despite these transformations, state enterprises still generate roughly 75% of the state budget income. Consequently, their further privatization is bound to lead to a reduction in government revenue, what with private enterprises often enjoying tax concessions, and many trying to report low profitability to pay lower taxes. This is shown by the results of system transformation in China to date. Even though the share of private companies in total industrial production increased from around 25% to 75%, their participation in state budget revenue does not exceed 30%.

Mass SOE privatization in China has suffered problems similar to those plaguing CEECs. This primarily applies to preemptive rights enjoyed by the party and government *nomenklatura* for the purchase of state enterprises, accompanied by an artificial reduction of the value of companies sold, affecting the amount of taxes

---

8   See K. Willhelm, 'Trimming the State Sector: Big Bang Chinese Style', *Transition*, February 1999.

paid.[9] This has had an effect on the creation of monopolist structures and attempts to limit competition.

As a result of system transformation in the Chinese economy, a specific division of labour has developed among the three sectors in question. The first – strategic – sector implements programmes concerned with long-term development, most of them unprofitable but indispensable for the country's economic and social development. Profitability criteria have been unimportant in this sector for many years. The second sector, composed of small and medium-sized state enterprises, and to some extent also large ones, concentrates on the development of labour-intensive production. Finally the third – private – sector predominately develops capital-intensive production.

Another form of 'hardware' globalization policy in China, alongside mass SOE privatization, is the opening of the economy to foreign direct investment.[10]

At the end of the 1990s, China absorbed more than 12% of global foreign direct investment. By comparison, in the same period Central and Eastern Europe benefited from only 3.5% of global FDI.

China admitted different forms of foreign direct capital investments to its territory, ranging from enterprises established with a share of Chinese capital to wholly foreign-owned enterprises. The principal condition to be met by foreign enterprises was the pro-export character of their production, most of their output being destined for foreign markets.

In the 1980s, China had 25,220 enterprises with foreign capital participation. In the 1990s, the number of such enterprises grew almost 10-fold to more than 300,000. Hong Kong, Japan, Taiwan and the United States became major investors in China. The majority of foreign enterprises were capital-intensive and labour-efficient, with a total employment of only 3 million, or 3% of the country's entire labour force.

The instruments of China's foreign economic policy included liberalization of customs regulations, exemplified by the 1994 introduction of a uniform exchange rate and recognition of China as a single-currency area subordinated exclusively to the internal Chinese currency. In addition, the country also increased the possibilities of repatriation of profit from enterprises belonging to foreign capital. Simultaneously, China broadened its system of tax breaks for foreign enterprises with the view of directing capital investments to specific sectors and regions.

Another key instrument was the creation of 'privileged zones' oriented at attracting foreign capital in the form of direct investments to stimulate technology transfer and the development of exports and imports. The privileged character of these zones, in relation to other areas, was based on greater freedom of operation

---

9   C. Fullin, 'Streamlining Corporate Governance in China's State Enterprises', *Transition*, February 1999.

10   K. Starzyk, 'Elementy zagranicznej polityki ekonomicznej Chińskiej Republiki Ludowej. Implikacje dla Polski', *Azja-Pacyfic*, no. 1, Toruń, 1998.

enjoyed by foreign capital, a wider range of tax breaks, better infrastructure and reduced bureaucracy.[11]

The privileged zones chiefly included economic zones. These enjoyed more liberal market mechanisms than other areas, introduced primarily as an experiment to test their effectiveness. When it turned out that those mechanisms worked, they were expanded to cover the whole of China.

Formally, Chinese economic zones acquired legal status in 1980, and have, ever become everyday practice in China. The first zones were established around Shanghai in 1981–5, further ones were created in the Pearl River delta, covering Canton. In 1988, the entire eastern costal region of China became an economic zone. In 1997, after the annexation of Hong Kong, a Special Administrative Region of Hong Kong was established, and in 1999 the Special Economic Region of Macao was converted into a special economic zone.

The economic zones, in fact market-economy enclaves within Chinese territory, began to promote the policy of opening the nation's economy to the world.

The opening of the economic zones was manifested primarily in the importation of advanced technologies. The technologies had to be advanced since the special economic zones were supposed to test their usefulness for the Chinese economy. If the evaluation was positive, the technologies spread throughout the country.

In another manifestation of economic opening, privileged zones were used to familiarize the Chinese with modern imported equipment so that this knowledge could subsequently be passed on to other regions of the country.

A third symptom of the opening of Chinese privileged zones was their use to introduce modern organization and management systems to test their practical value under Chinese conditions. When the test was positive, the systems were disseminated.

Finally, the fourth symptom of the opening was the testing of market mechanisms. Their practical usefulness meant they could be implemented throughout the Chinese economy. The issue was to check whether co-existence of market solutions and central planning is possible.

The location of the special economic zones in the coastal area was designed to facilitate the influx of foreigners, especially affluent Chinese businesspeople living in Hong Kong, Japan and the United States. At the same time, the considerable distance separating the zones from the state's main decision-making centres was expected to neutralize the adverse effect of a possible ideological nonconformity of the reforms with the official doctrine and the overall political situation in the country.

Today China is the world's largest FDI recipient. The total value of foreign direct investment in 1978–2002 reached an impressive $446.4 billion.[12] At the same time, investments financed by foreign loans totalled $177.2 billion. Total foreign capital involvement in the development of the Chinese economy consequently reached

---

11 R. Pawlik, *Kapitał zagraniczny w rozwoju*, op. cit., p. 155.

12 See J. Yukua, *Foreign Direct Investment in China: Its Evolution and General Trends* (SGH, Warsaw, 2004).

$623.4 billion in the analysed period. In terms of FDI inflow, China was first in the world, ahead of the United States.

In all, in 1979–2003, China attracted almost half a million foreign investment projects with a combined value of half a trillion dollars. Sixty per cent of the direct investments are wholly owned by foreign capital; 34% are owned by joint ventures, that is foreign companies with Chinese capital involvement. The share of foreign capital in the total value of investments in China is small, at around 4%. Industry accounts for 63.3% of the FDI, and real estate for 22%. The rest is in trade (3.2%), construction (2.7%) and transportation (2.3%).

As far as industry is concerned, foreign capital is especially interested in the production of high value-added goods. As a result, the manufacturing sector has become the main factor behind the growth of China's GDP. The share of manufacturing in the country's GDP increased from about 30% to 50% in 1993–2003, applying to not only the textile industry, but also electrical engineering, telecommunications, household appliances and the automotive sector.[13]

Investments from Asian countries are concentrated in labour-intensive sectors and are decidedly pro-export in character. Investments from highly industrialized countries – including the United States, EU and Japan – on the other hand, focus on capital-intensive sectors, with production oriented toward both exports and the domestic market. In all, FDI played a key role in the modernization of the commodity structure of China's exports in the analysed period. In 1980, low value-added goods accounted for half of the country's exports. In 2003, high value-added industrial goods accounted for more than 90% of total exports. Foreign capital has played an enormous role in modernizing production technology and upgrading quality and reliability. As a result, the competitiveness of Chinese industrial exports on foreign markets has increased.

The massive privatization of China's SOEs, combined with allowing a large number of foreign direct investments, initiated a new phase of reforms in the second half of the 1990s. It involved the preparation of the economy for the introduction of a liberal-monetarist economy.

The first phase of reform in China coincided with Keynesism in US and Western European economic policy. Under this policy, the state played principal functions in these countries, conducting business activity in select sectors and at the same time pursuing an economic policy vis-à-vis private enterprises. In their reforms, the Chinese proceeded from the assumption that the superior role of the state must not be questioned, and that state-managed sectors (such as heavy industry, raw materials, defence and infrastructure) should develop according to plan. This principle was expected to remain permanently inviolable. Some state enterprises not classified as strategic were at the start of reforms subordinated to a state-regulated market mechanism using macro- and microeconomic policy instruments. Finally, the third

---

13 J.W. Bossak, W. Bieńkowski, *Międzynarodowa zdolność konkurencyjna kraju i przedsiębiorstw. Wyzwania dla Polski u progu XXI wieku* (SGH, Warsaw, 2004), p. 350.

sector, comprising private enterprises established from scratch at the start of reforms, was exclusively subordinated to free market mechanisms.

With time, however, it turned out that the first two state sectors were inefficient and the third remained marginal since the financial resources of the Chinese population were limited. Consequently, far more drastic system transformations than those envisaged by Deng Xiaoping had to be undertaken.

SOE privatization and the admission of FDI to China considerably reduced the state's influence on the economy through microeconomic policy instruments. The state was left with the exclusive possibility of employing macroeconomic policy instruments. The only exception was the strategic sector, which was still financed from the state budget.

The rapid development of private enterprises not subsidized by the state and financing their own operations relieved the state budget. As a result, the role of the state budget in the Chinese economy decreased considerably. In 2004, China's GDP share of the budget did not exceed 25% and was lower than in the United States, not to mention Western Europe.[14] Tax revenue accounts for no more than 15% of the budget. There are no personal income taxes in China, and corporate income tax stands at 33%, a level similar to that in the United States. Government expenditure on social welfare in China is also low – lower than in the United States. Social needs are wholly financed by the people from their own incomes, not burdened with taxes and social insurance contributions.

This means that the role of fiscal instruments is unusually limited in China, and the state is not involved in the redistribution of national income. In this area, China has actually surpassed a number of countries pursuing economic policies based on liberal monetarism, including the United States. In China, the state budget is predominately used to finance economic growth and investment.

This is favoured by a high level of savings, similar to that in Japan. In 2002, the savings rate was 39% and was among the highest in the world. In connection with this, many investments are financed from internal accumulation. In 2000–2004, such investment accounted for 38–38.7% of the GDP. Considering that FDI and investments financed from foreign loans represent 4.3% of the GDP, the overall investment rate in China has reached 43%. This gives China a clear advantage over other countries, both the well developed and poorly developed. At the same time, investments in the first sector are financed almost exclusively from internal accumulation. In the second sector, both internal and external sources are used, while in the third sector, external sources prevail. Similar classification applies to the physical structure of investment: foreign capital focuses on financing technological advancement and capital-intensive sectors of the economy, while domestic capital concentrates on financing labour-intensive production.

The Chinese economy has grown rapidly under an economic equilibrium. The state budget deficit does not exceed 3% of the GDP, a level unthinkable for many countries. At the same time, inflation is practically nonexistent at less than

14 Ibid., p. 350.

1%. Unemployment is a moderate 4.5%, a rate lower than in the United States and Western Europe. However, the noninvolvement of the state in social affairs, coupled with the rapid expansion of the private sector, has deepened income disparities and aggravated the poverty zone. One of the causes is the absence of a social minimum set by the state. The Chinese work hard, about 2,000 hours annually, more than most other nations. However, employee incomes remain low, despite a multifold increase over the past 25 years.

This means that, in practice, the Chinese reform is evolving in a direction different from that stipulated by its architect, Deng Xiaoping. Instead of a socialist economy based on the domination of state ownership and insubstantial income disparities, China is ending up with a system based on domination of private ownership and income differences greater than in Japan, South Korea or Taiwan. The role of free market mechanisms in the Chinese economy has not exceeded the NIC level. This means that the scope of processes beyond anyone's control is assuming considerable proportions, given the size of the country. This also applies to differences between development of the richer and poorer parts of China. In 1992, per capita GDP in the poorest province, Guizhou, was one-eighth of that in the two most economically developed provinces, Shanghai and Beijing.[15] In 2004, these disparities increased substantially.

Since educational services at both secondary and university levels must be paid for, the possibilities of obtaining an education in the rich and poor provinces vary. The same applies to health care and social services.

9.3. Specificity of the Chinese Road to the Global Economy

The transformation of the Chinese economy bears some resemblance to the transformations in the development of newly industrialized countries, especially those of the first generation. In both cases, the principal orientation of economic policy was to open a given economy to the world. In newly industrialized countries, that opening was primarily pro-export in character, while in China it was import-oriented. The main goal of foreign economic policy in newly industrialized countries was to increase the GDP by winning foreign markets. Imports were mainly designed to supply industry with modern technology and raw materials. By contrast, in China imports and know-how were of primary importance because the country needed advanced technology. The goal was not only to increase export possibilities (although export growth was indispensable to balance imports) but, first of all, to modernize the economy. Internal demand in China is virtually unlimited so foreign expansion for the sole purpose of increasing sales opportunities is not a priority.

The transformation of the Chinese economy differed from those in newly industrialized countries. It was 'insular' in nature, with some sectors of the economy and regions excluded from transformation, especially in the initial stages of reform.

---

15 A. Jagiełło, 'Specjalne strefy ekonomiczne i inne obszary uprzywilejowane w Chińskiej Republice Ludowej', in *Azja-Pacyfik*, vol. 3 (Toruń, Korea, 2000).

This was especially true of key state-owned industries, which were modernized mainly on the basis of foreign technology imports financed with loans. The same was true of the key political and economic regions, which were transformed on the basis of experience gained in special economic zones.

Third, the transformation of the economic mechanism in China in principle featured division into two sectors: socialized industry, where the scope of central planning was significant, and agriculture, services and small enterprises, where the rules in force were determined on a free market basis. In newly industrialized countries, free market mechanisms were introduced throughout the economy together with the transition to subsequent generations.

The success of the Chinese economic transformation can also be attributed to evident government steering of foreign direct investments, especially from the point of view of their export orientation. By contrast, newly industrialized countries tended to be oriented toward steering exports.

Internal accumulation is a key factor behind the development of the Chinese economy. Its share in national income reaches 40%. In this respect, China resembles newly industrialized Asian countries of the first generation. In the process of opening its economy, China began to resemble newly industrialized countries also in terms of the use of FDI in the economy – although the share of foreign investment in China's total capital outlays is lower in percentage terms.

In general, the Chinese economy is far more autonomous than newly industrialized countries and the share of foreign trade in China's national income is many times lower. In this respect China still lags far behind the United States, where the share of foreign trade in national income is almost twice as high. It also differs significantly from newly industrialized countries, where wages, for instance, are seven to eight times higher than in China.

In 1978–95, the Chinese economic growth model reflected various trends in global economic policy, being a mixture of numerous solutions applied in newly industrialized countries, economically developed countries and less developed countries as well as in Central and Eastern Europe. It was characterized by pragmatism; any foreign solution that was likely to produce positive effects under Chinese conditions was adopted, while those that were unlikely to bring such results were rejected. As a result, the transformation of the Chinese economy did not have a pre-set long-term programme of changes. Its sole long-term goal was to maintain fast economic growth and develop a modern economic structure.

At the time, China's economic policy, including foreign economic policy, resembled the post-Keynesian pro-supply policy rather than the liberal and monetarist pro-demand policy. This means that, in this area, China tended to stay away from globalization trends worldwide.

That changed in the second half of the 1990s and at the start of the 21st century, when China, as a result of a major acceleration in privatization and the introduction of concessions for foreign direct investors, substantially increased the share of the third sector at the expense of the second sector. This reduced the scope of the state's influence on the economy with the use of microeconomic policy instruments. Only macroeconomic policy has been left in state hands. The only exception is the first – strategic – sector, influenced directly by the state financing it from the budget. Considering that instruments of macroeconomic policy – especially exchange rate and interest rate policies as well as fiscal and lending policies – are inactive, the question is how the state plans to influence the private sector to make it carry out goals indispensable from the perspective of the entire country. These include bringing down inflation and improving the trade balance and the balance of payments.

There is no clear answer to this question. The discussion among economists in China features two approaches: conservative and reform-minded.[16] The first approach refers to the roots of the 1978 reform, which means the Deng Xiaoping programme, focusing on the need to maintain a superior role of the state under the co-existence of central planning and market mechanisms. The superior role of the state should be expressed by the direct subordination of the first – strategic – sector, in keeping with Deng Xiaoping's assumptions. The state should influence the remaining sectors (second and third) using economic policy instruments. However, banks should remain in state hands, and monetary policy, in particular lending, should further implementation of the state's strategic goals – instead of being exclusively oriented toward maximizing business profits. This economic system is referred to as Chinese-style socialism, which means that the reforms introduced by the authorities should not be interpreted as moving away from socialism, but rather as an attempt to upgrade it.

The second approach highlights the discrepancy between the Chinese economic concept formulated by Deng Xiaoping and the actual situation. Instead of a rapidly growing second, state-owned sector covering SOEs, a powerful third sector has emerged. This is a private sector which the state cannot influence in any other way than by macroeconomic policy instruments. The first sector is also ceasing to be exclusively state-owned due to the need to increase the effectiveness of production and investment. Consequently, the state cannot influence the development of this sector solely by administrative instruments. An active macroeconomic policy is necessary.

Proponents of this approach wonder what will happen when private ownership begins to dominate in the Chinese economy; what methods will the state then use to influence the private sector? Should direct administrative instruments apply exclusively to the first sector, while macroeconomic policy in China is inactive? State-run banks, which provide almost 100% financing for Chinese enterprises, are particularly inefficient. Attempts to influence their financial and lending policies with the use of directives have not produced the expected results. So the Chinese economy

---

16 Discussion at an international seminar on Economic Security: Precaution and Risk Dissolution, Chongging, China, 16–20 October 2004. The seminar examined the following issues: the performance of government and system risk dissolution; public finance and state-owned capital budget; international capital flow and risk management; the risk and dissolution of local finance; state-owned economy in modern market economy; harmonious development in regional economy and economic security.

may eventually drift in a direction contrary to the government's preferences. In fact, such is already the case in the social sector, where, contrary to the declarations of the communist party, instead of a socialist economy with insubstantial income disparities, a capitalist economy – typical of the period of original accumulation of capital – is being built. This spells enormous diversification of incomes and a rapidly expanding poverty sector. Bank lending policies are also outside state control. As a result of informal pressure, banks provide loans not to those sectors whose development is indispensable for the state, but to those whose economic activities actually threaten to bring about a crisis (for example, real estate trade).

In this context, Chinese economists, especially those working abroad (in Hong Kong, the USA, Canada, Singapore and Taiwan), urge global solutions compatible with the 'Washington consensus'. This applies in particular to privatizing the Chinese banking system, allowing foreign banks to open subsidiaries in China, granting active functions to the stock exchange and permitting private foreign capital to invest freely and finance the development of all sectors of the economy. In other words, this involves measures to ensure free movement of capital between China and the rest of the world.

At the same time, the issue is to grant active functions to macroeconomic policy instruments such as exchange rate, interest rate, fiscal policy, budgetary policy and pricing policy. Until now these instruments were quasi-market in nature. Used chiefly as parameters for making economic decisions, they were not determined by the market. As a result, they tended to misinform businesses about the actual development of the economy. In this context, macroeconomic policy instruments should be excluded from state control.

Appeals for a full opening of the Chinese economy to guarantee free movement of goods, services and factors of production are infrequently voiced by economists. Furthermore, there is no indication that these appeals could gain the support of the government, which holds a major argument in the form of the country's economic successes to date. According to the government, the Chinese economy will not spin out of control because adequate instruments and mechanisms exist to prevent such a scenario. This is shown by the efficient management of the economy so far. The government, depending on need, can resort to sufficient tools either to accelerate or slow the rate of economic growth. For example, in 2000–2004, growth had to be decelerated to avoid overheating the economy. The government attained that goal by limiting state bank lending to unprofitable enterprises. To this end, it used central directives that were binding for banks.

The high competitiveness of the Chinese economy makes the country an increasingly active participant of globalization in the world economy. Meeting all the requirements of such participation, China is opening its economy to imported goods, services and factors of production. At the same time, China is a leading world exporter due to its high competitiveness in terms of both prices and quality. Globalization offers a chance for the development of the Chinese economy through opening of international markets to Chinese goods.

9.4. China's Role in the Process of Globalization of the World Economy

The system changes that took place in China in 1978–2005 were much deeper and more radical than those in Central and Eastern Europe.[17] They marked a transition from an orthodox communist system to a market economy based on private ownership. This was accomplished without the economic crises typical of Russia and other CEECs. As a result, China has transformed from a poor agricultural state to a medium-developed nation with a well-developed modern industry and vibrant research and development centres – a nation that today rivals Western Europe and other countries in space research. The achievements of the Chinese economy are exemplified by the development of mobile telephone and computer production as well as Internet access. In many of these areas, China ranks second in the world after the United States. This has been made possible by the country's speedy economic growth, the fastest in the world.

From a country that banned international contacts, China has transformed into a nation which boasts the world's highest FDI and is global runner-up in terms of the volume of foreign trade. China is among the world's 40 most competitive economies, ahead of many European countries, including Poland.

From a completely egalitarian state that forced its citizens to wear identical uniforms, China has transformed into a country with more than 100 million affluent citizens holding assets of more than $1 million value. The top 10% of China's wealthiest citizens account for about 30% of the GDP, while the poorest 10% provide just over 2%.[18] China is however effectively combating poverty. In the 1990s, more than 150 million Chinese citizens advanced from the poverty zone to the highest income group.

Finally, China is actively joining global processes in the development of a civil society. At the end of the 1990s, about 1,800 national and 200,000 local associations of all types were registered in China.[19] Moreover, there are more than 700,000 non-business organizations in the country. These include various types of foundations, centres, research institutes, business associations, scientific, educational and religious organizations as well as organizations focusing on sports, health and hobbies.

China's civil society shows no contradictions between state and individual; it is a state-led civil society. Many social organizations are inspired or even formed by the state to obtain assistance from citizens in administering the country. China is an East Asian communitarian state. As in other Asian nations, Chinese citizens do not defend their rights and liberties in opposition to the state nor do they seek to ensure participation in public life for themselves in this way. China's civil society

---

17 See L.T. White, *Unstately Power*, op. cit.; M. Pei, *From Reform to Revolution: The Demise of Communism in China and the Soviet Union* (Harvard University Press, Cambridge, Mass., 1998), E.A. Winckler, (ed.), *Transition from Communism in China*, op. cit.

18 See *Human Development Report 2003*, (UNDP, Oxford University Press, Oxford, 2003).

19 Chong Hor Lau, Geng Xiao (eds), *China Review – 1999* (The Chinese University Press, Hong Kong 1999).

is based on a readiness of collective participation and citizens assuming various state functions – not against the state, but in agreement with it.[20] Instead of seeking confrontation with the state, Chinese society is looking for ways and means of cooperating with it.

All this combined explains why China, alongside the United States, has eventually become the most important component of the global economy. In over a quarter of a century, it has travelled a long road from autarky to an open economy.[21] From a passive and marginal state, it has transformed into an active participant of the global economy.

20 B.M. Frolic, 'State-Led Civil Society', in T. Brook, B.M. Frolic (eds), *Civil Society in China* (M.E. Sharpe, New York, 1997).

21 See *Azja Wschodnia*, vol. 1, *Przemiany polityczne i społeczne w krajach regionu.*

Chapter 10

Conclusion – from Autonomic to Global Policy

The analysis of changes which took place in foreign economic policy in the second half of the 20th century makes it possible to trace some long-term development trends in the goals, means and instruments of this policy. Against this background, some theoretical generalizations can be made.

First of all, the period marked a significant object-related broadening of the scope of foreign economic policy. From a policy that exclusively covered commodity turnover (foreign trade policy) it gradually developed into a policy covering foreign economic relations in general (including the movement of services, capital, labour and natural resources, alongside exports and imports of goods). This resulted in a change of foreign economic policy goals and the development of new means of attaining these goals and new economic mechanisms used by the state to pursue foreign economic policy.

The main reason for these transformations was a change of the strategy of economic development during that time, involving a transition from a strategy of autonomous development to one of open development. This resulted from the action of numerous exogenous and endogenous factors which included fast technical and technological progress followed by deep structural changes in production and demand. The most important exogenous factors included the normalization of the international situation and the receding threat of war.

10.1. The Autonomic Policy

Under autonomous development, the needs and possibilities of individual countries moved to the forefront. They began to determine the structure of production, while foreign trade was given a passive role based on supplying goods indispensable to satisfy these needs and creating sales possibilities abroad for surplus goods in the form of exports to finance imports. Autonomous development was accompanied by a lack of possibilities to move production factors among countries.

As shown in Figure 10.1, the foreign economic policy pursued at stage C was, in this strategy, an expression of the autonomy at stages A and B. Each country not only shaped its own direction of development of its production and consumption, and subsequently exports and imports, but also tried to exert an autonomous influence on its foreign partners by applying a wide range of instruments to make them import or export specific goods.

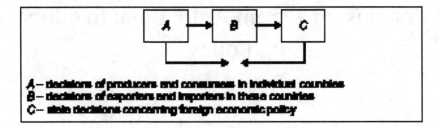

A – decisions of producers and consumers in individual countries.
B – decisions of exporters and importers in these countries.
C – state decisions concerning foreign economic policy

Figure 10.1. Strategy of Autonomous Development

Source: Author's own elaboration.

This policy was accompanied by the emergence of contradictions in preferences between individual countries, particularly concerning the size of exports and imports and the commodity structure of mutual trade. Attempts were made to solve these contradictions with the help of bilateral trade agreements, including barter and compensation, as well as the clearing of settlements of liabilities in virtue of mutual trade.

10.2. The Agreement Policy

An *agreement policy* is an attempt to reduce the autonomy of individual countries in shaping the size and structure of trade, as a rule conducted bilaterally, finding its expression in either partial or complete liberalization of commodity trade. On the other hand, the movement of factors of production remains outside the scope of liberalization.

An agreement policy is a symptom of the opening of the economy. It is pursued under conditions of transformation from the strategy of autonomous development to one of open development. This is shown in Figure 10.2.

As presented in Figure 10.2, the strategy of open development is a reversal of the process of making export/import decisions typical of autonomous development. In this case, the principal goal of the economic policy is not to seek opportunities for the most profitable sale of exported goods and the purchase of imported goods but to encourage domestic manufacturers to deliver goods that will be in long-term demand in the global economy and to give up manufacturing goods that do not offer prospects for successful competition with foreign suppliers. If producers meet these requirements, there is no need for the foreign economic policy to support artificially exports and limit imports, and trade can be liberalized. In the open development strategy, the foreign economic policy is a guideline not only for exporters and importers (stage B) but also for domestic producers and consumers (stage A).

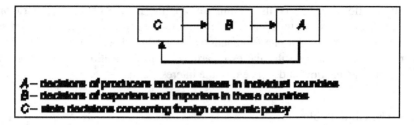

Figure 10.2. Strategy of Open Development

Source: Author's own elaboration.

The agreement policy, comprising a large number of countries, is referred to as an *international policy*. The growth of its importance is accompanied by liberalization of international trade in a both limited and unlimited geographical scope.

Geographically limited liberalization takes place within economic groups. The scope of international policy depends on the institutional form of the group, ranging from the establishment of a free trade area (and thus abolition of customs tariffs) to the establishment of an economic union (and thus the removal of all and any limitations to the movement of goods, services and – frequently – factors of production).

International organizations (such as GATT, WTO, IMF, OEEC, OECD and the World Bank) provide a wider geographical platform for the introduction of international policy and liberalization of world trade. Each organization develops uniform goals, means and instruments of international policy obligating its member countries to adapt their foreign economic policies.

Unlike international policy pursued under agreements signed by interested countries and coordinated by international organizations and institutions, a *supranational policy* is conducted directly by economic institutions or organizations set up especially for this purpose. Hence, in this case, countries give up their competence in favor of a supranational body. The significance of the supranational policy grows under a free movement of goods, services and factors of production.

Transition from an international to supranational policy was clearly visible, first, in the activities of the GATT (during the Uruguay Round) and, subsequently, in the activities of the WTO. It involves obligating member countries to adjust their national regulations and rules of procedure to the standards developed by the WTO. This means the autonomy of foreign economic policy should be completely done away with. Simultaneously, the WTO obligates its member states to respect all the rules of their modification or selective treatment being possible. Countries may obtain permission for an extended period of adjustment to specific WTO rules. However, this almost exclusively applies to the less developed countries and, in isolated cases, to countries transforming their economies.

The transition to a supranational policy also takes place within integration groups. This primarily applies to the EU, where an increasing number of decisions are passed from the state to the supra-state level.

Supranational policy is also commonly applied in transnational corporations, which use it to influence their subsidiaries in different countries. Their characteristic feature is the existence of one supranational centre that directs the production and/ or trade activities of its subsidiaries regardless of their location. Corporations are sovereign organizations independent of the interests of any state.

10.3. The Global Policy

Under globalization in the world economy – implying the development of a uniform market of goods, services and factors of production embracing all countries and geographical regions where both national and supranational markets merge to form a single whole – supranational economic policy becomes a *global policy*.[1] It can be conducted by either a superpower (the United States, for example) or a special institution set up for this purpose.

The principal goal of a supranational policy pursued under globalization should be to codify the rules of liberalization, to oversee the observance of these rules by everyone and to shape the parameters of a supranational policy (including prices, exchange rates and interest rates).[2] When a supranational policy is conducted by a dominant country, it tends to focus on the parameters of that country's macroeconomic policy. On the other hand, when it is shaped by an institution set up especially for this purpose, special macroeconomic policy parameters need to be developed to be pursued globally (for instance, a supranational currency).

In the case of globalization of foreign economic policy, a fourth link is added: global decisions (D).

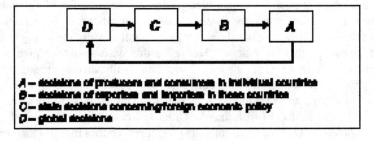

Figure 10.3. Strategy of Global Development

Source: Author's own elaboration.

Global decisions are made by individual businesses participating in the process of globalization on the basis of parameters which can be determined either on the

---

1   See P. Bożyk, J. Misala, M. Puławski, *Międzynarodowe stosunki ekonomiczne*, op. cit., p. 395.

2   See A. Giddens, *The Third Way: The Renewal of Social Democracy* (London, 1998).

free market or by international (supranational) institutions. Economists are not unanimous on this count. Some believe that parameters such as prices, international currency and exchange rates should be determined on the free market, while others urge the establishment of global institutions to be responsible for these parameters. These institutions would include a World Central Bank.[3]

In practice, to date, the United States has pursued a global policy, using the IMF and the 'Washington consensus' for this purpose. Countries that do not benefit from IMF assistance participate in the process of globalization of the world economy on a voluntary basis and are motivated exclusively by the potential benefits of the process.

---

3   See D. Held, 'Czy można regulować globalizację?', *Krytyka Polityczna*, no. 2, 2002; A. Giddens, *The Third Way and its Critics* (London, 2000).

Bibliography

Acocella N., *Zasady polityki gospodarczej*, PWN, Warsaw, 2002.

Azja Wschodnia na przełomie XX i XXI wieku. Studia i szkice. Pod redakcją Krzysztofa Gawlikowskiego we współpracy z Małgorzatą Ławacz, Instytut Studiów Politycznych PAN, wyd. Trio, Warsaw, 2004.

Balassa B., 'Przyczynek do integracji gospodarczej', in *Z problemów integracji gospodarczej*, PWE, Warsaw, 1968.

Balcerowicz L., *Wolność i rozwój. Ekonomia wolnego rynku*, Krakow, 1998.

Barro R., Sala X., Martin I., *Economic Growth*, McGraw-Hill, New York, 1995.

Begg D., Fischer S., Dornbusch R., *Ekonomia. Makroekonomia*, 3rd edition, revised, PWE, Warsaw, 2003.

Belka M., Trzeciakowski W. (eds), *Dynamika transformacji polskiej gospodarki*, Instytut Nauk Ekonomicznych PAN, Warsaw, 1997.

Bieńkowski W., *Oddziaływanie rządu USA na rozwój zdolności konkurencyjnej gospodarki amerykańskiej 1981-1988*, SGH, Warsaw, 1993.

——, *Reaganomika i jej wpływ na konkurencyjność gospodarki amerykańskiej*, PWN, Warsaw, 1995.

Bossak J., *Japonia. Strategia rozwoju w punkcie zwrotnym*, PWN, Warsaw, 1990.

Bossak J., Bieńkowski W., *Międzynarodowa zdolność konkurencyjna kraju i przedsiębiorstw. Wyzwania dla Polski u progu XXI wieku*, SGH, Warsaw, 2004.

Bossak J., Kawecka-Wyrzykowska E., Tomala M., *Stany Zjednoczone – EWG – Japonia. Współpraca i rywalizacja*, PWE, Warsaw, 1988.

Bożyk P., *Wymiana zagraniczna a dochód narodowy*, PWE, Warsaw, 1968.

——, *Korzyści z międzynarodowej specjalizacji*, PWE, Warsaw, 1972.

——, *Droga donikąd? Polska i jej sąsiedzi na rozdrożu*, Polska Oficyna Wydawnicza BGW, Warsaw 1991.

——, *Polityka gospodarcza Polski 1985-2000*, Wydawnicza Wyższej Szkoły Handlowej, Warsaw, 1995.

——, *Współpraca gospodarcza krajów RWPG*, 2nd edition, PWE, Warsaw, 1997.

——, *24 kraje Europy Środkowej i Wschodniej. Transformacja*, Oficyna Wydawnicza SGH, Warsaw, 2002.

—— (ed.), *Gospodarka światowa*, PWE, Warsaw, 1991.

—— (ed.), *CEFTA a integracja ekonomiczna w Europie*, Oficyna Wydawnicza SGH, Warsaw, 1996.

—— (ed.), *Korzyści i zagrożenia związane z przewidywanym członkostwem krajów CEFTA w UE*, Oficyna Wydawnicza SGH, Warsaw, 2000.

Bożyk P., Guzek M., *Teoria integracji socjalistycznej*, 2nd edition, PWE, Warsaw, 1980.

Bożyk P., Misala J., *Integracja ekonomiczna*, PWE, Warsaw, 2003.

Bożyk P., Misala J., Puławski M., *Międzynarodowe stosunki ekonomiczne*, 2nd edition, PWE, Warsaw, 2002.

Budnikowski A., *Zadłużenie jako problem globalny*, PWE, Warsaw, 1991.

——, *Międzynarodowe stosunki gospodarcze*, PWE, Warsaw, 2001.

Budnikowski A., Kawecka-Wyrzykowska E. (eds), *Międzynarodowe stosunki gospodarcze*, PWE, Warsaw 2000.

Chomsky N., *Zysk ponad ludzi. Neoliberalizm i ład globalny*, Wydawnictwo Dolnośląskie, Wrocław, 2000.

Ciamaga L., *Światowa gospodarka rynkowa*, PWN, Warsaw, 1990.

Corden W.M., *Trade Policy and Economic Welfare*, Oxford University Press, Oxford, 1974.

——, *International Trade Theory and Policy. Selected Essays of W.M. Corden*, Edward Elgar, London, 1992.

Deng Xiaoping, 'Neither Democracy Nor the Legal System Should be Weakened', 28 July 1978, in *Selected Works of Deng Xiaoping*, vol. 2, *1975–1982,* Foreign Languages Press, Beijing, 1995.

Directions of Trade and Statistics, International Monetary Fund, Annual Papers 1968–1974, 1991, 2000, Washington, 2001.

Economic and Social Development into XXI Century, Inter-American Development Bank, Washington, DC, 1997.

Economic Survey for Europe in 1996–1997, Economic Commission for Europe, UN, Geneva, 1997.

Economic Survey of Europe in 1989–1990, UN, New York, 1990.

Fischer S., Sahay R., Vegh C.A., 'From Transition to Market: Evidence and Growth Prospects', in S. Zechinni (ed.), *Lessons from the Economic Transition. Central and Eastern Europe in the 1990*, Kluwer Academic Publishers, Dordrecht.

Friedman M., *A Program for Monetary Stability*, Fordham University Press, New York, 1960.

——, *Capitalism and Freedom*, University of Chicago Press, Chicago, 1962.

Frolic B.M., 'State-Led Civil Society', in W. Brook, B.M. Frolic (eds), *Civil Society in China*, M.E. Sharpe, New York, 1990.

Fullin C., 'Streamling Corporate Governance in China's State Enterprises', *Transition*, February 1999.

Giddens A., *The Third Way and its Critics*, London, 2000.

Gorywoda-Michałowska K., Morawiecki W., Mulewicz J., *Międzynarodowe organizacje gospodarcze. Główne organizacje powszechne i grupowe*, PWN, Warsaw, 1987.

Grosse T.G., 'Dylematy państwa w obliczu globalizacji', *Wokół współczesności*, vol. 2, no. 4, 2002.

Guzek M., *Międzynarodowe stosunki gospodarcze. Zarys teorii i polityki handlowej*, Wydawnictwo Wyższej Szkoły Bankowej, Poznań, 2001.

Haberler G., *The Theory of International Trade with Its Applications to Commercial Policy*, London, 1968.

Heckscher E., 'The Effect of Foreign Trade on the Distribution on Income', in *Readings in the Theory of International Trade*, Philadelphia, 1950.

Held D., 'Czy można regulować globalizację?', *Krytyka Polityczna*, no. 2, 2002.

Human Development Report 2003, UNDP, Oxford University Press, Oxford, 2003.

Industry and Development – Global Report 1985 and *1991/1992*, UNIDO, Vienna and New York.

International Financial Statistics, International Monetary Fund, Washington, DC, 2000.

Iskra W. (ed.), *Międzynarodowe stosunki gospodarcze*, Fundacja Innowacja, Warsaw, 2001.

Jagiełło A., 'Specjalne strefy ekonomiczne i inne obszary uprzywilejowane w Chińskiej Republice Ludowej', *Azja-Pacyfik*, vol. 3, 2003.

Kaczurba J., Kawecka-Wyrzykowska E. (eds), *Od GATT do WTO. Skutki Rundy Urugwajskiej dla Polski*, Instytut Koniunktur i Cen Handlu Zagranicznego, Warsaw, 1995.

———, ——— (eds), *Polska w WTO*, Instytut Koniunktur i Cen Handlu Zagranicznego, Warsaw, 1998.

Kaja J., *Polityka gospodarcza. Wstęp do teorii*, SGH, Warsaw, 2001.

Keynes J.M., *Ogólna teoria zatrudnienia, procentu i pieniądza*, PWN, Warsaw, 1956.

Kisiel-Łowczyc A.B. (ed.), *Współczesna gospodarka światowa*, Wydawnictwo Uniwersytetu Gdańskiego, Gdansk, 1997.

Kisiel-Łowczyc B., 'Protekcjonizm w handlu zagranicznym w teorii i historii myśli ekonomicznej. Przyczynek do analizy polityki handlowej w rozwiniętych krajach kapitalistycznych', PhD thesis, University of Gdansk, Gdansk, 1974.

Klawe J., Makać A., *Zarys międzynarodowych stosunków ekonomicznych*, PWN, Warsaw, 1981.

Klepacki-Doliwa Z.M., *Encyklopedia organizacji międzynarodowych*, Wydawnictwo 69, Warsaw, 1997.

Kowalik T., *Współczesne systemy ekonomiczne; powstawanie, ewolucja, kryzys*, Wydawnictwo Wyższej Szkoły Przedsiębiorczości i Zarządzania, Warsaw, 2002.

———, *Systemy gospodarcze. Efekty i defekty reform i zmian ustrojowych*, Fundacja Innowacja, Warsaw, 2005.

Kozłowski P., *Szukanie sensu czyli o naszej wielkiej zmianie*, PWN, Warsaw, 1998.

Krugman P.R., Obstfeld M., *Międzynarodowe stosunki gospodarcze*, trans. and adapted by S. Ładyka, PWN, Warsaw, 1973.

Kucharski M., Rączkowski S., Wierzbicki J., *Pieniądz i kredyt w kapitalizmie*, 2nd edition, PWN, Warsaw, 1973.

Kulig J., *Dylematy polityki dostosowawczej w Trzecim Świecie. Wyzwanie dla Polski*, Polski Instytut Spraw Międzynarodowych, Warsaw, 1990.

———, *Strukturalne i systemowe dostosowania krajów silnie zadłużonych*, Wydawnictwo Poltext, Warsaw, 1994.

———, 'Strategia proeksportowa a restrukturyzacja gospodarki', *Ekonomista*, no. 1, 1996.

——, *Gospodarka Azji Wschodniej i Południowo-Wschodniej; konkurent czy partner dla Polski?*, Instytut Rozwoju i Studiów Strategicznych, Warsaw, 1997.

——, 'Znaczenie wzorca uprzemysłowienia krajów Azji Wschodniej dla krajów postsocjalistycznych', *Ekonomista*, no. 1, 1997.

Ładyka S., *Z teorii integracji gospodarczej*, Oficyna Wydawnicza SGH, Warsaw, 2000.

Latoszek E., Proczek M., *Organizacje międzynarodowe. Założenia, cele, działalność*, Wyższa Szkoła Handlu i Finansów Międzynarodowych, Warsaw, 2001.

Lavigne M., *The Economics of Transition. From Socialist Economy to Market Economy*, Macmillan and St Martin's Press, London and New York, 1999.

The Least Developed Countries, 1995 Report, United Nations, New York, Geneva, Annex.

Lerner A., *Economics of Control*, New York, 1947.

Lindbeck A., *Economic Dependence and Interdependence in the Industrialized World*, Seminar Paper No. 83, Institute for International Economic Studies, University of Stockholm, Stockholm, 1977.

Lipowski A., Kulig J., *Państwo czy rynek? Wokół źródeł 'cudu gospodarczego' w Korei Południowej*, Monografia no. 2, Wydawnictwo Poltext, Warsaw, 1992.

Lucas R., 'On the Mechanisms of Development Planning', *Journal of Monetary Economics*, vol. 22, no. 1, 1988.

Łychowski T., *Międzypaństwowe umowy gospodarcze*, PWE, Warsaw, 1968.

Marshall A., *Money, Credit and Commerce*, Macmillan and Co., London, 1929.

Marszałek A., *Gospodarka światowa*, Wyd. Uniwersytetu Łódzkiego, Łódź, 1993.

——, *Z historii europejskiej idei integracji międzynarodowej*, Uniwersytet Łódzki, Łódź, 1996.

Michałek J., *Polityka handlowa. Mechanizmy ekonomiczne i regulacje międzynarodowe*, PWN, Warsaw, 2002.

Międzynarodowe organizacje gospodarcze i ich rola w Unii Europejskiej, Biblioteka Przedsiębiorcy, Centrum Informacji Europejskiej, Warsaw, 1998.

Monkiewicz G., Monkiewicz J., Ruszkiewicz J., *Zagraniczna polityka naukowo-techniczna Polski; diagnoza, uwarunkowania, kierunki*, Wyd. Ossolineum, Warsaw, 1989.

Morawiecki W., *Międzynarodowe organizacje gospodarcze. System organizacji międzynarodowych*, PWN, Warsaw, 1987.

Nasiłowski M., *System rynkowy. Podstawy mikro- i makroekonomii*, Wydawnictwo Key Text, Warsaw, 1996.

Niemiecki J., 'Prognozy rozwoju gospodarki Chin do 2005 roku', *Biuletyn*, Wyd. Komitet Polskiej Akademii Nauk *Polska 2000 plus*, no. 2, 2004.

Niesiołowski M., *Japonia; źródła i kierunki rozwoju gospodarczego*, PWE, Warsaw, 1974.

Noga A., 'Cel przedsiębiorstwa. Kontrowersje teoretyczne', *Ekonomista*, no. 6, 1996.

Ohlin B., *Interregional and International Trade*, Cambridge, 1935.

O'Rourke K., Williamson J., *The Heckscher-Ohlin Model Between 1900 and 2000. When it Explained Factor Price Convergence, When it Did Not, and Why*, NBER Working Paper no. 7411, National Bureau of Economic Research, Cambridge, Mass., 1999.

Pei M., *From Reform to Revolution. The Demise of Communism in China and the Soviet Union*, Harvard University Press, Cambridge, Mass., 1988.

Pelkmans J., *European Integration. Methods and Economic Analysis*, Longman, New York, 1997.

Piklikiewicz M. (ed.), *Międzynarodowe stosunki gospodarcze na przełomie wieków*, Difin, Warsaw, 2000.

Prebish R., 'International Monetary Discipline and the Debt Problem', *Journal of Development Planning*, no. 16, 1985.

Review and Outlook for the Former Soviet Republic, PlanEcon, Washington, DC, September 1997.

Ricardo D., *Zasady ekonomii politycznej i opodatkowania*, PWN, Warsaw, 1957.

Rosati D.K., *Polska droga do rynku*, Warsaw, 1998.

Smith A., *Bogactwo narodów*, PWN, Warsaw, 1954.

Sołdaczuk J., *Współczesna gospodarka światowa. Struktury, mechanizmy, tendencje*, PWE, Warsaw, 1987.

Sołdaczuk J., Kamecki Z., Bożyk P., *Międzynarodowe stosunki ekonomiczne. Teoria i polityka*, PWE, Warsaw, 1987.

Sołdaczuk J., Misala J., *Historia handlu międzynarodowego*, PWE, Warsaw, 2001.

Solow R., 'A Contribution to the Theory of Economic Growth', *Quarterly Journal of Economics*, vol. 70, no. 1, 1956.

Starzyk K., 'Elementy zagranicznej polityki ekonomicznej Chińskiej Republiki Ludowej. Implikacje dla Polski', *Azja-Pacyfik*, no. 1, 1998.

Stiglitz J.E., *Economics of the Public Sector*, 3rd edition, Polish edition, Wydawnictwo Naukowe PWN, Warsaw, 2004.

——, *Globalization and its Discontents*, Polish edition, Wydawnictwo Naukowe PWN, Warsaw, 2004.

The Study on Japanese Cooperation in Industrial Policy for Developing Economies. Poland, Institute of Developing Economies, Tokyo, 1995.

Szentes T., *Ekonomia polityczna zacofania gospodarczego*, PWE, Warsaw, 1974.

Szpunar P., *Polityka pieniężna. Cele i warunki skuteczności*, PWE, Warsaw, 2000.

Szymański W., *Interesy i sprzeczności globalizacji*, Difin, Warsaw, 2004.

Teurissen J.J., Akkerman A. (eds), *Diversity in Development. Reconsidering the Washington Consensus*, December 2004.

Tien-wei Wu, *Lin Biao and the Gang of Four: Contra-Confucianism in Historical and Intellectual Perspective*, Southern Illinois University Press, Carbondale, 1983.

Tomala M. (ed.), *Chiny: przemiany państwa i społeczeństwa w okresie reform 1978–2000*, ISP PAN, Trio, Warsaw, 2001.

Transition Countries in 1998/9, Widespread Economic Slowdown with Escalating Structural Problems, WIIW, Vienna, 1999.

Unia Europejska. Integracja Polski z Unią Europejską, Instytut Koniunktur i Cen Handlu Zagranicznego, Warsaw, 1996.

Walther T., *The World Economy,* John Wiley and Sons, New York, 1997.

Wieczorek J., 'Znaczenie środków i barier pozataryfowych dla polskiego eksportu na rynkach rozwiniętych krajów kapitalistycznych', *Monografie i opracowania,* no. 273, 1989.

Wilhelm K., 'Trimming the State Sector: Big Bang Chinese Style?', *Transition,* February 1999.

Winckler E.A. (ed.), *Transition from Communism in China: Institutional and Comparative Analyses,* Lynne Rienner, Boulder, 1999.

Wojtyna A., *Ewolucja keynesizmu a główny nurt ekonomii,* PWN, Warsaw, 2000.

World Investment Report. Transnational Corporations and Competitiveness, United Nations, New York and Geneva, 1995.

Yukua J., *Foreign Direct Investment In China. Its Evolution and General Trends,* SGH, December 2004.

Zabielski K., *Finanse międzynarodowe,* PWN, Warsaw, 1998.

Zorska A., *Ku globalizacji. Przemiany w korporacjach transnarodowych i w gospodarce światowej,* PWN, Warsaw, 1998.

Printed in the United States
by Baker & Taylor Publisher Services